Here for Good

Here for Good

Community Foundations
and the Challenges of the 21st Century

Terry Mazany and **David C. Perry,** Editors

M.E.Sharpe
Armonk, New York
London, England

Library of Congress Cataloging-in-Publication Data

Here for good : community foundations and the challenges of the 21st century / edited by
Terry Mazany and, David C. Perry.
    pages cm
Includes index.
ISBN 978-0-7656-4255-4 (hardcover : alk. paper)—ISBN 978-0-7656-4256-1 (pbk. : alk. paper)
1. Community development. I. Mazany, Terry, 1956–

  HN49.C6H4657 2013
  307.1′4—dc23   2013014678

Printed in the United States of America

The paper used in this publication meets the minimum requirements of
American National Standard for Information Sciences
Permanence of Paper for Printed Library Materials,
ANSI Z 39.48-1984.

IBT (c) 10   9   8   7   6   5   4   3   2   1
IBT (p) 10   9   8   7   6   5   4   3   2

Contents

Preface

In one sense, community foundations are in no danger of vanishing. With endowments of some $50 billion, they are, quite literally, here for good. But how much good can they accomplish? Will it be enough to help lead American communities to prosperity in this new century? Those are the questions *Here for Good: Community Foundations and the Challenges of the 21st Century* considers.

Why this book, and why now? Community foundation leaders issued their first serious self-study, *An Agile Servant,* a generation ago. A new century is here, and with it have come a staggering array of alterations to the status quo. Technology and social change have disrupted business, government, and all manner of community institutions. Though the core values of a good community foundation remain the same, the limitless possibilities of the next hundred years present serious challenges. We need a new way of looking at life in the trenches of profound and undeniable community change—one that mixes timeless values with timely application.

In New York, that means looking at how change happens over generations. In Silicon Valley, it means expanding community beyond local boundaries. In Cleveland, it means taking new risks; in St. Paul, Minnesota, increasing impact; in Atlanta, gaining hyperlocal knowledge; and on the Gulf Coast, being a community anchor.

This book is a crazy tossed salad of ideas, because the foundations telling their stories here are as diverse as the communities they serve. They can be big or small, urban or rural, employing time-tested methods or embracing risky innovation. Each has a distinct flavor, yet together, like the United States itself, they somehow make a whole. This volume testifies to that. Each foundation may be unique, yet all of them want to find and share the lessons of their field. All of them want to learn and improve.

Here for Good does not try to cover every aspect of community foundation work. Such a task would require several volumes. You will not find detailed explorations of board governance, mission investing, or the scores of other issues that fill agendas at foundation conferences. The authors have focused instead on the big issues: the role of foundations in communities and the types of leadership that solve local problems. The authors hope this work will inspire other foundations to tell their stories.

Although we begin by establishing a much-needed scholarly framework for community foundation efforts, much of *Here for Good* is not theoretical. These are the stories of individual foundation leaders, those who take on the "implausible idea" of cleaning up Boston Harbor, or those who obtain funding for early childhood education in Colorado, secure training for the 911 dispatchers of Florida, create green spaces in Detroit, or build the Indianapolis Cultural Trail. They are stories of the fight against poverty and drop-out rates, the fight for literacy and community health, and—almost everywhere—a drive to rebuild economically.

To help newcomers see both the promise and pitfalls of community foundation work, we begin with the basics: The community foundation is an institution that seeks to be a central, affirming element of its community—*foundational* to the place it seeks to serve. The origins of this book stem from conversations among the leadership of community foundations about the challenges they must overcome in their second century to make such *foundational* contributions possible.

What began as an idea for how to institutionalize community giving in Cleveland, Ohio, in 1914 has spread to more than 700 urban and rural communities. Community foundations can now be found in every one of the United States, but their impact has not stopped at the U.S. border. The 2010 Community Foundation Global Status Report lists 1,680 community foundations in 51 countries (Worldwide Initiatives for Grantmaker Support 2010). Some observers argue that the community foundation is one of the most important of all American "exports," benefiting millions of people around the globe.

These grantmaking organizations are place based: They help improve the lives of people in a specific geographic area. Community foundations pool the financial resources of individuals, families, and businesses to support effective local nonprofits. They are concerned with building both short-term and long-term resources for the benefit of residents (Community Foundations National Standards Board 2013). Over the years, community foundations have demonstrated the ability not just to make grants but to lead the areas they serve toward innovative approaches to problem solving. They have carried out research, surveys, and community studies. They have designed programs to build the capacity of others to do good work. They have been both active advocates and community conveners. They do this in small and large ways: One community foundation may have less than $100,000 under management; another might have more than $3 billion in assets.

In 2011, the 700-plus community foundations in the United States gave an estimated $4.2 billion to a variety of nonprofit activities. Their partners work in all fields: arts, education, health and human services, the environment, disaster relief, and more. This grantmaking represents more than 10 percent of all foundation philanthropy in the country.

Because community foundations are public charities with a 501(c)(3) nonprofit designation, donations made to them are tax deductible. Charitable funds are set up in community foundations by both individuals and institutions. They can be established with a wide variety of assets—including cash, real estate, stock, and even artwork. Gifts come from living donors and through wills. In the United States, community foundations hold approximately $49.5 billion in assets. In 2011, they received an estimated $4.5 billion in donations from individuals, corporations, government agencies, and other foundations (Council on Foundations 2013).

As a public charity, a community foundation is governed by a board of directors that guides the mission, strategic direction, and policies of the organization (Community Foundations National Standards Board 2013). The board is comprised of local leaders who know their communities and, in many cases, have been widely recognized for their involvement in civic affairs (Austin Community Foundation 2012). Members of the governing body play a key role in identifying and solving community problems; they also oversee the distribution of funds to ensure they are used for charitable purposes.

The Community Foundations National Standards Board oversees operational excellence in six key areas—mission, structure, and governance; resource development; stewardship and accountability; grantmaking and community leadership; donor relations; and communications. Foundations that comply with these standards can display the official National Standards Seal. Nearly 500 community foundations in the United States do so.

Community foundations have a track record of achievement and innovation. Because of their local nature, community foundations rarely generate stories that are widely recognized, understood, or appreciated—except, of course, in their own backyards. But the editors of this volume aim to do more than just exchange high fives. The changing conditions of community in recent years reflect the new digital-age realities of modern American life and challenge even the most solid of institutions. In response, we have sought to marry theory and practice as our contribution to charting a course for the second century of this place-based institution of community philanthropy.

While this book is the product of many hands, coeditors and essayists among them, it never could have been completed without the work of many more contributors. First and foremost are the research efforts and constant oversight of research assistant Antonia Lalagos. This book is the outgrowth of a larger undertaking titled the Second Century Project. The backbone of that project grew out of materials used in three two-day seminars—two sponsored by the Chicago Community Trust in Chicago, Illinois, and one hosted and sponsored by the Miami Foundation in Miami, Florida, under the aegis of seminar participant and foundation head Javier Soto. Our thanks and appreciation go out to staff members at both foundations, including Marcia Gettings, Michelle Hunter, Cheryl Hughes, and Bill Lowry in Chicago and Nancy Granja in Miami.

Our work was made possible by the support of both national and local funders. Nationally, the James S. and John L. Knight Foundation and the Charles Stewart Mott Foundation added greatly to the success of this project, just as their work in the past has contributed to the development of the community foundation movement as a whole. Specifically, we thank Paula Ellis and Nick Deychakiwsky for their encouragement and guidance, as well as Eric Newton for his editorial suggestions. The George Russell Foundation has also provided funding to complete this project. Locally, we benefited greatly from support from the Chicago Community Trust and from the University of Illinois at Chicago's Great Cities Institute and the Institute for Civic and Public Engagement, backed by another of our seminar participants, Dr. Joseph Hoereth.

The Second Century Project goes far beyond this book. As we have already indicated, it is comprised of three national seminars with participants extending further than the chapters that follow here. All of us have been enriched by the seminar contributions of Bahia Ramos, Brian Byrnes, Carrie Menendez, Cheryl Hughes, Christopher Goett, Cynthia Schulz, David Maurrasse, Javier Soto, Joseph Hoereth, Nick Deychakiwsky, Terri Lee Freeman, Tom Wilcox, and Will Ginsberg. We will present findings from the seminar and the book at the 2013 and 2014 meetings of the Council on Foundations and appreciate the support and participation of Christopher Goett and Vikki N. Spruill from the council. The seminar and subsequent essay writing has generated more papers than could fairly be included in this volume. Various website versions of these and other essays on the future of the community foundation can be found by contacting individual foundations or the Council on Foundations.

We owe a great debt of gratitude to everyone who has worked with us at M.E. Sharpe, our publishers. We are especially grateful to Harry Briggs, our editor at M.E. Sharpe for his consistent support and encouragement. Speaking of editors, M.E. Sharpe has a wonderful team of production editors, copyeditors and citation and bibliography specialists. The level of patience and technical advice provided by Stacey Victor, Elizabeth Parker, and Barbara C. Bigelow has been admirable.

The goal of this project was to generate conversations in many places on the *foundational* nature of community foundations—of how they are, indeed, here for good. We hope you will agree that this has been accomplished.

Finally, this project has taken many hours of our lives; at every step, we had the constant partnership, analytical assistance, and support of our spouses, Judith Kossy and Lottie Mazany. Our deepest thanks for all they have done to make this project work.

Terry Mazany and David C. Perry

Acknowledgment

While we make reference to the editorial contributions of Eric Newton in our introductory chapter, we want to make special note of the care and attention to detail that informs his editorial contributions to this section of the book.

Bibliography

Austin Community Foundation. 2012. "What Is a Community Foundation?" http://www.austincommunityfoundation.org/?nd=whatis.

Community Foundations National Standards Board. 2013. "List of Standards." http://www.cfstandards.org/standards.

Council on Foundations. 2013. "Community Foundations Fact Sheet." http://www.cof.org/templates/41.cfm?ItemNumber=16889&navItemNumber=15626.

Worldwide Initiatives for Grantmaker Support. 2010. *2010 GSR Executive Summary*. http://www.wings-community-foundation-report.com/gsr_2010/gsr_about/2010_summary.cfm.

Here for Good

The Second Century

Community Foundations as Foundations of Community

David C. Perry
University of Illinois at Chicago

Terry Mazany
The Chicago Community Trust

> *We are missing in action as a field. The structure of how*
> *we think about the work is increasingly at odds with how*
> *people live their lives and how they think about problems.*
> —Emmett D. Carson, CEO, Silicon Valley
> Community Foundation (quoted in Duxbury 2011)

At the 2011 Fall Conference for Community Foundations (Council on Foundations 2011), Silicon Valley Community Foundation CEO Emmett D. Carson summed up the burgeoning critical literature and community foundation leadership experience in one succinct critique of the community foundations. He spoke of the importance of the foundation to place or city and to the need for community foundations, like the cities they are a part of, to reinvent themselves. Short of such reinvention, he predicted a far more ominous future for community foundations. As the quote leading off this essay suggests, Carson argues that the financial-transactional model of foundations built over the last 100 years is "broken." Sounding somewhat like the tough professor who, on the first day of class, says to the assembled class that not everyone will be around by the conclusion of the course, he told the 1,100 leaders and staff of community foundations: "In five or 10 years, I fear that many of the institutions in this room won't be here. . . . Revenues aren't meeting expenses. Other people offer what we perceive as our core product at a cheaper price—zero. . . . In this environment, that doesn't work" (quoted in Duxbury 2011).

Carson first made this argument years earlier, helping to spark a grow-ing body of literature on the field of community foundations. Leadership has, for some time, been calling for this field to change in the face of fun-damental challenges. Most notably, Lucy Bernholz, Katherine Fulton, and Gabriel Kasper (2005) suggested in a landmark study that the community foundations of today face challenges in the form of "inescapable external forces—economic pressures, demographic changes, shifting expectations for regulation and accountability, the emergence of the commercial sector as an innovator, and changing relationships between the sectors." These forces, noted the authors, are "leading community philanthropy toward something new." In short, the community foundation has in some very real ways lost its footing as the "foundation" of the community—with both external forces buffeting the identity of community, and internal services, which for so long had been a staple of community philanthropy, shifting to commercial sites of transactional philanthropy.

Since Bernholz, Fulton, and Kasper (2005) published their book, in many ways it appears that they underestimated the rate and magnitude of change sweeping the country and the globe: the financial crisis and subsequent Great Recession, the election of our country's first African American presi-dent, the great wealth disparities and increased rate of poverty, the massive federal deficit and record state-level fiscal crises, government restructuring and downsizing with corresponding cuts to human services and education, widespread foreclosures and the depreciation of housing prices leading to a corresponding decline in personal wealth. In the face of these changes, a host of new studies of foundations are being churned out—much of it recounting past successes and forecasting future challenges.

Rather than simply add another book to the literature on the field, we want to offer essays of practice that examine and reassert the role of community foundations in their communities. In undertaking this broad resetting of the foundation in its place, we certainly do not pretend to tackle all issues. For example, while we are clearly interested in the contemporary impor-tance of community foundations in both rural and urban areas, we are not extending the reach of topics in this collection to international experiences; nor are we focusing directly on the importance of the devolutionary shift in place from government to governance or the vicissitudes of a key topic like impact investment.

We begin this reassessment of community foundations with a well-researched assertion: like universities (Perry and Wiewel 2005; Wiewel and Perry 2008) and hospitals (Harkavy and Zuckerman 1999; Webber and Karlström 2009), community foundations are place-based institutions. They are key to the geography of place and thereby "anchor" their communities in real and palpable ways. Webber and Karlström (2009, 4) describe such institutions in the following way: "Anchor institutions are those nonprofit or corporate entities that, by reason of mission, invested capital, or relationships to customers or employees, are geographically tied to a certain location." The goal of the leadership of such place-based institutions is to understand and develop their impact on the urban and the rural communities in which we live. The question for all local anchor institutions is, What do they do to advance community development? And when it comes to community foundations, in particular, Bernholz, Fulton, and Kasper (2005, 24) put it quite simply: "The measure that matters will be impact, not asset size." What we are talking about is the impact of the institution on the development of its home, of place. The first lesson or argument of leadership, therefore, is equally simple—to what extent do community foundations truly live up to the assertion that they are place-based—that is, do they truly anchor development in their communities, and if so, how? In an era of massive change, the stakes and consequences of failing to answer this question in the affirmative are high.

It is our contention that, in response to this challenge, the field of community philanthropy must develop a more sophisticated theory of community identity, impact, and leadership. We propose that an appropriate field of investigation is the well-developed body of research and theory regarding anchor institutions and community planning and development. Hence we anticipate that the work here will contribute to theory building for community philanthropy and community development.

We begin by revisiting a definition that continues to serve the institution and the community equally well: community foundations have at their root, at their very essence, the *community*. They have always defined themselves as institutions of communal good—when all is said and done, the community foundation is the one institution, among all others, that seeks to mobilize the resources of the community to meet the community's needs. This definition may have evolved over time as the identity of community has evolved and the technologies of philanthropy have changed. At present, it might even be beset, as some would suggest, by a host of other forms of philanthropy; but there is one key feature that makes the community foundation stand out from all others—it seeks to respond to and define the *community*. Its mission is the community, not restricted to the interests of an individual donor, not limited to the interests of any individual grant recipient, nor constrained by a particular instrument of philanthropy (be it a donor-advised fund, a giving circle, an endowment, or a host of other competing sites of giving), and not beholden to the interests of any one political party or the allure of any particular initiative.

What is this notion of *community?* Paul Ylvisaker, like many social scientists, suggests that even he is confounded by it. *Community,* he says, is "a word of elastic meaning; its capacity to stretch has been challenged over the last century and will be tested even more dramatically during the next" (Ylvisaker 1989, 51). While some may argue that this claim of community-as-mission demands a clear term and singularly representative definition, we want to suggest that the power and impact of community foundations is specially derived from their intimate ties to a mission of community in its flexible and transforming meanings. It is this capacity to constantly develop and evolve the many meanings of community that has endured for 100 years and stands the test of time. While the "elasticity" of the community foundation's mission may be stretching the singularity of community as place—it is the meaning of this feature of community that "anchors" the community foundation to its city, region, or rural home. When the foundation starts to take on an individualistic, donor-driven mission that is not embedded as well in the *place* of community, then the community foundation can come unmoored and lose its anchoring function in the place of its community mission. Hence the community foundation is first and foremost a place-based institution, anchored in place and embedded in the development of community—no matter how "elastic" or "stretched" the meanings of the place become.

As more and more of the world's population lives in cities, it is important that we understand how place-based, anchor institutions broadly—and community foundations specifically—can play vital and powerful roles in the development of cities that produce more equitable outcomes for their residents' quality of life, well-being, and prosperity. And, as rural populations thin, it is important to understand the nature, structure, and asset base of those community foundations that serve rural communities and preserve wealth for those communities. The essays in this collection extend much work already conducted on community foundations in particular (Bernholz, Fulton, and Kasper 2005; Lowe 2004; Magat 1989) and anchor institutions in cities more generally (Harkavy and Zuckerman 1999). It is meant to help us frame, if not fully answer, the following overall question:

> In different types of metropolitan areas (cities, their suburbs, and linked rural surroundings), how do community foundations work with donors, civic and community institutions (including institutions of higher education), the governmental sector, and the business sector to mutually define and shape (i.e., "anchor") individual and collective interests as they relate to planning, community development, and, most important, philanthropic initiative—all in an effort to achieve meaningful and sustained impact?

This overarching question gives rise to corollary questions, many of which are addressed by the individual contributions to this volume:

- How do community foundations define and measure impact?
- How do community foundations collaborate with donors, with other philanthropic institutions, and with the other sectors to pursue individual and collective interests? And what influences the success of these collaborative efforts?
- How involved is each place-based sector in identifying key issues, strategies, and projects for the region as they relate to planning and community development in its full meaning and context?
- What role does each sector play in developing and pursuing these issues, strategies, and projects?
- What are the effects and outcomes of the process?
- How do community foundations in particular enhance their own capacity and the capacity of other sectors to pursue these issues, strategies, and projects?
- How do the differences between regions in terms of their local, national, and global roles and functions affect the process?
- What are the implications for equity and distribution of resources?
- How do community foundations transform themselves into the forums or sites of discourse that meaningfully develop their places, turning themselves into the institutional foundations of community?

This work is meant to engage leaders in our field, test the Carson proposition of community foundation entropy, and explore the possibility that the role of place-based institutions such as universities or community foundations has never been more necessary. Furthermore, we consider whether this institutional necessity imposes on such institutions greater pressure to establish deeper roots and reinvent their purposive practices in localities. This essay and the chapters that follow in this book center on the premise that the future of cities, suburbs, and rural areas are dependent upon (1) the activities and success of place-based institutions in general, and (2) the anchoring role of community foundations in particular, as they seek to address the challenges facing the "elasticities" "stretching" the meaning(s) of community.

While we have certainly engaged this topic in the past from various experiential, case study, and quantitative perspectives (Perry and Wiewel 2005; Wiewel and Perry 2008; Gaffikin and Perry 2009; McEldowney, Gaffikin, and Perry 2009; Chicago Community Trust Strategic Plan 2010), the questions posed are best addressed through a new case-based study approach engaging foundations, small and large, that are geographically representative of the entire nation, including its range of cities and sub-urban and rural areas. The cases in this collection are grouped into five sections or parts. Part I is organized around the overarching theme of adaptation of the community foundation model to the challenges of the twenty-first century. Part II is concerned with the identity of community itself, with chapters organized around the topic of connecting community to prosperity. The five essays in Part III address the issues raised by community change, no matter how big or small the community might be. Part IV is also somewhat internally directed, meant to address the risks and rewards of different leadership practices. Part V offers a brief summary of the volume's key themes. Many of the essays that follow this introduction could just as easily have been placed in another section or part of the collection, but we have tried to organize them as responses to the overarching themes identified in Parts I through IV in ways that at once meet the demands of organized giving and the role of place-based anchor institutional practice.

Theory Building: The Realpolitik of Communities as Defined by the Agonistic Planning Approach to the Fluid (Glocalizing) City

A normative goal of this project is to enhance the collective capacity of leaders in the community foundation, higher education, civic and community sectors, and the business arena to mutually realize the planning and development of their communities. With that in mind, the discussion of theory building for community foundations and community leadership will be based on the formulation of two theoretical frameworks of understanding in the rural or urban community context. Put another way, our purpose here is *not* to offer a theory qua theory of community foundations but to offer a theory that grounds the practices—now and in the future—of the agents of place-based community foundations.

The first theoretical frame relates to the reality of rapid change, and indeed "fluidity," of the various societal sectors of our lives and our communities/regions (Bauman 2000). The second relates to the diverse, plural, conflictive, and often deeply contested goals of the competing interests vying for responsive community development, termed by many social theorists as *agonistic pluralism.*[1] While the case studies featured in this project are not precisely organized around the theoretical considerations of "fluidity" and deeply conflicted, competing interests of identity-based (or "agonistic") pluralism, we expect that these two features of the realpolitik of contemporary development will be borne out, if not precisely articulated, in the cases used in the chapter experiences.

Metropolitan Fluidity

Community development is a "fluid" goal, or, as Ylvisaker (1989) so clearly put it, an "elasticity" or "stretching" of the meaning of the term *community*. The goals and conditions of such development of community are in a constant state of change, serving an environment of the new, globalizing cities and rural regions that are themselves in a constant state of "global and local" (or *glocal*) change (Sassen 1996; Swyngedouw 1997). While each urban or rural regional sector (as described next) is foundational to the health and development of the community context, it is important to note that each is far from static. In fact, the contemporary condition of those institutions at the core of the development and planning of the metropolis, either urban or rural, is often one of heightened change, making them dynamic and flexible in the ways they define and "anchor" the modern community. For example:

1. The *market sector* of the modern city or rural region is in a state of major economic restructuring in the space of production (moving from centers to networks of production), the technology (the sectoral specifics) of production, and in global "places" of production (from the "developed north" to the "global south" and "south-south" relations as well) (Scott 1997; Roy 2005).

2. The *community sector* and its new levels of diversity are in a state of change. This sector's demography or membership is shifting due to (a) transnational trends in immigration, (b) market trends in real estate, and (c) gentrification, the requirements of an aging population, and corresponding demands on health systems and Social Security safety nets. The conditions of community development are being redefined spatially and in terms of the culture and identity of those who make up the "community."

3. The *government sector* is shifting at two levels—both at the level of the "de-centering" state (Sassen 2006) and at the level of regulatory purpose (from government to governance). National politics in the United States has shifted dramatically for most of the last half of the twentieth century. The historian Roger Biles (2011) in a recent book titled *The Fate of Cities* suggests that, since the administration of President Richard Nixon, the shift of the federal-local relationship has constituted a "new federalism." Put another way, this new federalism has meant a shift from central "government" to what Europeans call "localisms" (Gaffikin and Morrissey 2011) and what Americans call the "devolution" to "governance" (Judd and Pagano, forthcoming). Such a devolution to the local and a partnering of private and public has further "stretched" the meanings of community—politically, socially, and economically—repositioning place in the foundational nature of communities and the collaborative politics, the governance, of place-based institutions.

Consequently, the community foundation is increasingly asked to provide leadership to address matters of civic importance that have simply disappeared because government no longer has the resources to tend to them.

4. *Community foundations* and other "anchor" institutions of rural or urban place are rethinking their role in the local community arena in particular and in the larger national and global environment more generally. Universities, for example, are moving from enclave to rural/urban "anchor" institution (Perry and Wiewel 2005), serving as sites of empowerment (students and communities) and development (real estate, community, and economic development). Colleges and universities are increasingly de-localized global institutions competing for students worldwide and providing generative inputs into the (global) knowledge sector (research, entrepreneurship, and understanding, for instance). Just as the place of the academic institution has changed, so too the foundational nature of institutions of community giving is changing. The reality of community foundations as once a key, even somewhat singular, place of local philanthropy is no more. Just as the differing notions of sectoral "fluidity" or Ylvisaker's "elasticity" require different notions of place or community, the roles of community foundations as place-based anchors will be as different as they remain central. For example, early on in their study, Bernholz, Fulton, and Kasper (2005) describe what they call the "competitive environment for community foundations" (11), which seems to be squeezing the foundation from all sides—from technical and other forms of products and services to vendors of new products, commercial players, and nonprofits, to say nothing of the other social service programs inside the foundation (Bernholz, Fulton, and Kasper 2005, 11). Some would call this the new normal; others consider it the competitive death knell of community foundations. We would prefer to call this a particularly important aspect of the "globalizing and localizing" features (*glocalizing*) of community diversity and the services and resource environment of communities that foundations must engage.

"Agonistic" or Contested Planning and Policymaking

Planning, for example, in such a "global/local" state (Swyngedouw 1997) is an equally "mobile" (McCann and Ward 2011) phenomenon—one that leads to a collective practice that is not served well by the vertically realized goals of top-down, rational, comprehensive planning nor the horizontally structural nostrums of communicative planning and policymaking (Fainstein 2010). Rather, the processes of community development (notably planning and policy formation and execution in the "fluid," pluralistic environment of contemporary city/regions) require a mobile, "agonistic" politics (Mouffe 2009). Such politics neither ignore the cultural and institutional goals and differences of communities and sectors nor assume that "mutuality of interests" results in consensus (Amin and Thrift 2002; Gaffikin and Morrissey 2011; Gaffikin, Perry, and Kundu 2011). On the contrary, the differences between community interests, institutions, and sectors are real and inescapably part of the contemporary fabric of place, such that collective capacity comes not from the aforementioned top-down rationality nor from artificial consensus but from an evolving process of "agonistic" or contested pluralism (i.e., political and even conflictual), producing a planning and policy formation of multiple interests defined by multiple identities and the differences such identities fully represent. As such, planning and policy in the real world assumes mobile politics (Amin and Thrift 2002; McCann and Ward 2011) that seek neither to overcome nor ignore the full array of contested differences that define communities. Rather, such politics build plans and policies recognizing these differences, engaging them, and providing the resources and regulations to accommodate them (Gaffikin and Morrissey 2011; Gaffikin, Perry, and Kundu 2011).

Strategies for the Second Century

The irony, if not the "paradox" of community, as Mouffe (2009) infers, is the fact that in the United States, at least, our dependence on government to provide basic services is shifting. Government at the national and at the local level is devolving responsibilities down the federalist ladder (Biles 2011) and increasingly into a localism of public-private partnerships (Gaffikin and Morrissey 2011). In a panel discussion at the Harvard Business School, the former Indianapolis mayor Stephen Goldsmith commented, "The government is delivering fewer services, with the private sector delivering more public services" (quoted in Moore 2008). He further noted, "Since President Clinton's second term, the number of government employees has fallen as the number of contractors and vendors has risen. This trend will accelerate with the retirement of 40 percent of all public employees within the next six years. Expect more outsourcing to business of infrastructure, social services, and other traditional government activities" (quoted in Moore 2008).

What Goldsmith is identifying is a pattern in U.S. federalism going back to the post–Great Society era of President Richard Nixon—the production of a "new federalism"—a shift from central government to local governance (Biles 2011). The irony here, as we suggested earlier, is that as the networks of community have grown and become more complex, even leading to a less physical, technology-driven "space of flow" (Castells 2000), the role of the physical local (either urban or rural) has become all the more important, if for no other reason than the national and even local governments have drifted away in their historic institutional responsibilities. In short, place matters, and when the community needs service and either the state or the privatized market fails to deliver, the role of place-based entities such as community foundations becomes all the more necessary.

However, just as the role of the government has shifted to an increasingly privatized, partnership model suggesting a host of different forms of localized service delivery, so too has the landscape of place for community foundations shifted and evolved. Bernholz, Fulton, and Kasper (2005) go so far as to suggest that this changing landscape offers a "striking" increase in a diversity of competitive forces that challenges the very organization and purpose of community foundations. They suggest that "recent years have seen expansion and diversification in the range of other community philanthropy organizations including United Ways, giving federations, identity-based funds, giving circles, hometown associations, health care conversation foundations, commercial charitable gift funds, and other community-based public foundations—in large cities and rural areas in the U.S. and around the globe. Community philanthropy organizations now number in the thousands, manage billions of dollars, and regularly act in the public eye and on the public's behalf" (Bernholz, Fulton, and Kasper 2005, 2). As a result, assert the authors, the principles that once guided community foundations no longer apply simply to the foundations. This agonistic competition has shifted the purposive nature of collective giving to serve a set of far more distinct and somewhat incompatible functions—even tax evasion (Lowe 2004). The once secure nature of the community foundation as a somewhat singular site for philanthropy is now guided and regulated at multiple jurisdictional levels (Bernholz, Fulton, and Kasper 2005, 3).

In perhaps no area or jurisdiction has this shift in philanthropy been more apparent than in the move of donors into the commercial sector. The emergence in the 1990s of commercial charitable funds forever changed the philanthropic world. Financial service companies such as Fidelity Investments, the Vanguard Group, Schwab, Oppenheimer Funds, and J.P. Morgan Chase have all opened immensely popular charitable gift funds (Hussey 2010). *The Chronicle of Philanthropy* ranks the 400 largest charities in the United States each year; and from 2005 to 2008, Fidelity Gift advanced up the list from ninth, to sixth, to fourth, to third by 2008. Schwab ranked ninth and Vanguard ranked sixteenth. In 2008, only the United Way of America and the Salvation Army ranked higher on this list (Hussey 2010). As of June 30, 2011, Fidelity Gift held $5.6 billion in assets (Fidelity Charitable 2011).

Commercial charitable funds have been successful in part because they are flexible and accessible. Donor-advised funds (DAFs) give donors more control over their contributions by allowing them to select investment vehicles, recipients, and timing of distribution (Marsh 2002). And compared to other philanthropic options such as private foundations, commercial DAFs are usually cheaper and less restrictive. To engage more donors, Fidelity, for example, reduced the minimum grant amount to $50, reduced the minimum amount to open an account to $5,000, and increased the ease of use of their website so that donors can directly control their charity contributions much like an IRA account (Hussey 2010). The commercial sector is seeking to expand its customer base by providing services to the "mass affluent," those who are not considered super-rich but make comfortable six-digit incomes and can afford to make significant donations (Weber 2005).

Strategies and Modes of Action

At its competitive worst, the "landscape," as Bernholz (2005) and Lowe (2004), among others, call the potpourri of other types of products, vendors, nonprofits, commercial players, and service agencies, constitutes a growing plurality of agonistic or conflictual sites of governance. While much can be said against the devolutionary tendency of the state and the privatizing notions of the market, the strategic reality is that there will not soon be a consensus on new service levels of governance. To put this even more starkly, consider the range of opinions regarding the bundle of goods and services to fulfill the basic social contract between government and those with needs for survival, subsistence, or opportunity. If there is to be any notion of what the new localism will be, it will be grounded in a diverse local geography of collaboration. The community foundation of the future will "anchor" the "fluidity of community" through collaborative leadership embedded in the diverse ethnicities, races, nationalities, identities, donors, and tax regulations that make up community. The three theoretical touchstones most likely to emerge in the future are (1) *community* or place as a "fluid" and "elastic" site of plurality; (2) *anchors* of leadership and practice; (3) and an understanding and acceptance of the agonistic or the identity-based conflictual reality of the diversity, political plurality, and differences that make up the one and many.

Several ways such a theory of second-century leadership moves into the future of the community foundation are discussed next.

1. The Honest Convening and Brokering of Information

This is defined as accepting the reality of agonistic relationships proactively seeking and including diversity in forums that stretch and (re)define the meaning(s) of community.

Working in concert with other place-based, anchor institutions such as universities, museums, hospitals, and governments, the community foundation must seek to be an anchor of community diversity, ideas, discussion, and engagement. More than ever, the foundation will need to be a source of support for the rich array of diverse ideas and identities—stretching the communal sense of definition and difference to achieve the new meaning(s) that so confounded and directed Ylvisaker (1989). If you accept the premise of agonism or identity-based contestation as a defining reality of community, and grant that the mission of community foundations is in the service of community, then community foundations are the one institution with the standing, credibility, and capacity to convene the collaborations required to move beyond the paralysis of competing interests and forge agreements that lead to development.

2. Networks: Theory That Grounds Collaboration

Moving beyond Ylvisaker (1989), Morgan (2007) details the political network phenomenon in "new governance theory," in which coordination of public projects moves from hierarchical public agencies into cross-sectoral networks, where the authority is shared between the participants rather than in one central body. This particular version of the shift from government to governance becomes problematic when no coordinating entity is identified to facilitate communication, goal setting, and accountability. Community foundations can emerge as the most effective facilitators because they can incentivize participation in voluntary networks. They do this by providing local legitimacy, bridges to additional resources, and local knowledge; and they are welcoming institutions serving as honest brokers of conversations that will necessarily engage diverse interests.

When the community foundation is viewed as the one institution that seeks what is best for the community and does not promote a predetermined agenda, it is able to credibly convene and advance the conversation. Put simply, the community foundation has a stake in arriving at a solution or course of action contributing to the common good of the community, but not a stake in any *specific* solution or course of action. On the other hand, the increasing emphasis on community leadership by community foundations challenges community foundations to have a point of view and assert their position. Such examples are highlighted in several of the chapters in this volume, along with a discussion of risk, but it is still too early to know if this shift from the traditional role of *neutral convener* to *advocate* reduces the identity of a community foundation to yet one more self-interested stakeholder not distinguishable from any other deep-pocketed donor with a cause. After all, what gives the community foundations' position greater legitimacy or righteousness than any other?

3. Communities Need Their Community Foundations to Be Repositories of Understanding, Knowledge, and Expertise

Through staff and outreach, and in collaboration with other community sites of expertise and knowledge, the community foundation should seek to be a valued source of program innovation and responsiveness, based upon the very best knowledge, values, and projects.

4. The Donors as Roots That Anchor the Community Foundation in the Community

Here we ask that community foundations, in light of the diversity, fluidity, and political identities that together combine to create the meanings of community, rethink their relationship with their donors. This will require new rootedness or anchorage in place in this globalizing, devolving, new federal and localizing world. It means that the notion of donors—those local resources of the community—must be engaged in multiple, often agonistic ways that define the diversity, politics, and, yet, the identity of the city/regions or communities of our urban and rural world.

The Second Century

All of this, from the strategic and theoretical grounding and repositioning of community forward, will require different modes of action for community foundations in the next century if they are not to go, as Carson puts it, permanently "missing in action" (quoted in Duxbury 2011). Each community—urban, metropolitan, or rural—will need its own particular mix of these differing modes of action, definition(s) of diversity, collaboration, and discourse.

Two distinct lessons clearly emerge from the 18 chapters that follow. On the one hand, the authors of many of the chapters (indeed, in some ways, all of the chapters) supply either directly or through their active deeds a reaction to Carson's somewhat gloomy assessment of the future of the community foundation in the United States. In fact, even Carson himself, in his essay for this book titled "The Future of Community Foundations," supplies corrective actions to all in the community foundations movement with which to address what he has often called the "broken" nature of the community foundation model. This book does not shy away from the challenges confronting the future directions of community foundations, but it does not argue that anyone should "throw in the towel" either.

Second, returning for a moment to the observations of Paul Ylvisaker (1989), perhaps no greater heuristic obtains when discussing the many meanings of *community* than to join this scholar in describing each of the communities discussed in this book in a somewhat "elastic" relationship with their history and with each other. Hence, for us, this term of "elasticity" describes not only the different, "fluid," and transformative nature of each community, but also the internal ways in which each foundation is and will continue to adapt to changes in the nature of the place in which it is anchored. This "elasticity" or transforming nature of place—and all that it requires of the foundations—demands, in turn, good and realistic theories of practice. For us, the ongoing changes in the nature of community require societal theories of "fluidity"—or, to borrow from Zygmunt Bauman (2000), "liquid modernity." As each of the following chapters examines what activities, projects, and programs go into making up their futures, they combine to give us full and practical cases of such liquid modernity.

Equally realistic is the notion of agonistic or identity-based, contested pluralism—the theoretical expression of the real world challenges and practices described in each of the chapters in this volume. Such challenges and practices are characterized by a plurality of interests—the identities, interests, and goals which often place them in a contested relationship with each other. Rather than search for artificial consensus that could easily erase the legitimate, albeit conflicted, identities of the community, the community foundation serves as a site of diversity and plurality of interests. Therefore, it is in the modern community foundation where identity, and not artificial consensus, finds a home. As such, the foundation becomes an important element of place, anchored in the plural identities of community, not in their erasure. While this is much easier said than done, the realpolitik of a "fluid," pluralistic future of community may be the best lesson learned when the chapters of practice that follow are taken as a whole.

Returning to the prior discussion on page 8, the remainder of this book is divided into five parts, with essays written by the heads of some of the nation's leading community foundations. The last section is but a single chapter written by the editors; it offers a general assessment of the prior 19 essays and suggests what lessons can be drawn from the varied practices of leadership in community foundations.

The several parts of this collection are each headed by a particular overarching theme, and each of the chapter-length essays sets out in its own way to engage that theme, using the experience of the community foundation head who authored the chapter as evidence to bolster the essay's argument. Part I is a collection of five essays written by community foundation leaders who set out to respond to Silicon Valley Foundation head Emmett Carson's assertion that we enter the second century of the movement in need of a fundamentally new model of community foundation. The five essays comprising Part II work at the notion of connecting community and the prosperity of a place. Part III addresses a theme that each of the community foundation heads in this collection must successfully meet in their daily professional lives—namely, the ways in which the shape and size of a community affects its development. Part IV brings together five more authors to write four essays about the risks and rewards of leadership in the foundation world. The final section, Part V, is a brief essay that summarizes a response to the question, Are there lessons to be learned from the experiences and initiatives discussed here—lessons that can carry community foundations into their second century?

Part I. Facing a Limitless Future: Can Foundations Adapt?

While most of the chapters in this collection address the question framing this section, five are particularly well focused on the transforming model of the community foundation. From the beginning, the community foundation has served as a "civic agenda-setter and problem-solver" argues Ronald B. Richard in Chapter 2, on the first community foundation, the Cleveland Foundation. However, asserting such a role does not make it so, and recent examples of activity by the Cleveland Foundation introduce new practices of innovation and risk-taking to produce credible new ways for the foundation to bridge gaps in resources and advocate for change. Such actions of *bridging* and *advocacy* require changes in the foundation model—changes that challenge prior assumptions and allow for innovative experiments in community development.

It is within the twenty-first-century context of fast-moving social, economic, and political change that Silicon Valley Foundation head Emmett D. Carson contends in Chapter 3 that the traditional or founding form of the community foundation is "broken," and if community foundations fail to reevaluate their value proposition and adapt their business model, they will not survive. He goes on to suggest that there are several phenomena that pose challenges to the foundation, among them fluid geographies, rapid technological change, and new donor behavior. In response, community foundations must understand and define their new geographies in order to tailor their model to the community's needs and opportunities. Grant Oliphant of the Pittsburgh Foundation points out in Chapter 4 that the threat of obsolescence has helped community foundations focus on the issues at hand, reframe the possibilities, and act ambitiously to achieve those possibilities.

Chapter 5, "The Digital Age Foundation," by Mariam C. Noland of the Community Foundation for Southeast Michigan and Eric Newton of the Knight Foundation, takes a very different approach to resetting the role of the community foundation. Rather than assert that the community foundation model is "broken," it contends that foundations must master emerging technologies to facilitate information flows in the community and to build efficiency in their own operations. Most important, this perspective emphasizes that technology has not freed us from geography, as Carson is inclined to infer; rather, they suggest that community foundations are anchored in place, albeit differently than they have been in the past, operating with one foot in physical space and the other foot in cyberspace. As such, this new form of the community foundation, the "digital age" version, has a mission to "inform, engage, and lead." This mission, and the information-related technology it requires, demands new resource strategies such as establishing digital giving days and crowdsourcing. Accomplishing such a mission will also demand flexibility of leadership and acceptability of risk.

In Chapter 6, Lorie A. Slutsky and Ani F. Hurwitz of the New York Community Trust offer commentary on the longevity of community foundations and their particular institutional role in the giving function of a place. Coming from a large, urban foundation, Slutsky and Hurwitz argue that community foundations, now and in the future, serve as key sites of "patient capital," providing communities with the flexible ability to respond to either unforeseeable issues or those needs that require multigenerational efforts. Put another way, they are one of the few place-based institutions that build giving patterns and programs, that deal with the "totality" of community needs, and that engage the challenges of a place that stretch across times of economic and political instability.

Part II. Connecting Community and Prosperity

Several chapters offer versions of the ways foundations embed themselves in communities. These essays address the argument that our current models of institutional collaboration are not able to keep pace with the changes we see in our communities. In direct response to this assertion, Carleen Rhodes of the Saint Paul Foundation and Minnesota Community Foundation, contends in Chapter 7 that community foundations can keep pace with the changing nature of communities if they seek to be "impact multipliers." By this she means that community foundations in the second century of their existence will need to be special network nodes that are able to convene diverse constituents and pool resources more effectively across time and space. Various strategies will be required of community foundations seeking to multiply their impact, including sharing services by co-locating with other foundations and creating targeted print and digital media publications to influence more donors. In many cases, she writes, the role of the community foundation will be to serve as a "bridge"—arguing that the foundation must be an "intentional broker" in an increasingly pluralistic, contested, or dare we say "agonistic" society.

In the second century more than the first, the community foundation must become the community's "development office," argues Rochester Area Community Foundation head Jennifer Leonard in Chapter 8. For Leonard, the future of the community foundation will be found in the many types of funds that a community foundation can raise on behalf of the different notions of community. More like Slutsky and Hurwitz and less like Carson, she argues that the days of seeking traditional, unrestricted funds are not over; such types of giving remain both important and possible, and can be generated in tandem with the pursuit of donor-advised funds, federal funding, and annual campaigns. In fact, Leonard goes so far as to suggest that multifaceted fundraising expertise is what gives community foundations a competitive edge over the "one-size fits all" approach of commercial charitable funds. When armed with a diverse set of tools, community foundations can successfully build relationships with a wide range of donors, thus ensuring that the community has sufficient resources for present and future needs.

The definition of *community*, of which the foundation is a part, requires an understanding of the importance of transparency and fairness in collective decision making, and enhancing the role of community foundations as knowledge brokers. Community foundations are seen as credible institutional leaders because they have "granular" knowledge of the community. All of this is fully argued in Chapter 9, "Ensuring There Is 'Community' in the Community Foundation," by the Community Foundation for Greater Atlanta head Alicia Philipp and Tené Traylor (senior program officer). They suggest that community foundations obtain such ground-level "granular" knowledge through relationship-building in the community's neighborhoods, as evidenced by the Atlanta Foundation's work with Adamsville, Georgia. Their examples demonstrate the kinds of authentic, microlevel engagement efforts that community foundations facilitate as part of the equitable transfer of social capital across the scales and sectors of a community.

In Chapter 10, on the notion of community, G. Albert Ruesga, head of the Greater New Orleans Foundation, employs Michael Piore's notion of "borderlands" (1995) (a space in which contesting parties can communicate their respective needs and concerns to society at large) to enhance our understanding of the challenges facing modern community foundations. The most successful community foundations, argues Ruesga, rather than seeking "consensus" between conflict-ridden community interests, accept the conflictive nature of community and seek projects built upon a "more workable kind of pluralism," becoming "borderland" institutions themselves. Thus, community foundations, as borderland entities, are in a unique position to generate critical discourse about our differences, be they race, class, or gender. The challenge is how community foundations can tackle these difficult tasks and build "bridges of understanding" between the pluralities of social classes. Fundamentally, Ruesga concludes, we must explore the moral and practical challenges faced by community foundations in understanding their purpose and mission as advocates for social justice.

The role of national foundations in engaging this theme is addressed by Chris Rurik, Henry Izumizaki, and Nillofur Jasani of One Nation in Chapter 11, "Never Second-Guess the Locals." In this essay, the One Nation organization is used as a case example of how a national foundation can be employed as a fiscal and programmatic catalyst for the development of the field of community foundations. This is accomplished in a well-structured relationship between One Nation and several community foundations that combines the resources of a national funder with the local, "granular" knowledge that comes through building trusting personal relations in the community. Rurik, Izumizaki, and Jasani argue that if this relationship works and the community foundation succeeds in the community, the end result will be a productive sum of "social capital." They further note that that the supportive presence of such an active, collaborative national funding partner is often needed to stimulate the risk required to innovate outside of the traditional framework of local grantmaking.

Part III. Community (and Change) Comes in All Shapes and Sizes

When the essays in this collection turn to personal experience at a particular community foundation, the authors are responding to the challenges of leadership that comprise this section. Several take an even more direct approach to explicitly reflect on leadership at the community foundation. Throughout the seminar conversations among the authors that formed the basis of this volume and many of the essays, special emphasis was placed on the challenge to strengthen rural community philanthropy. One of the key chapters in this volume on this topic—Chapter 12—is by Nancy Van Milligen, head of the Community Foundation of Greater Dubuque, who argues that in rural places, especially, leadership of community foundations is often built around nonmonetary incentives, innovative communication tools, and strong personal relationships. Examples of leadership and network-based initiatives include community visioning, women's giving circles, and state tax credit incentives. Paul Major of the Telluride Foundation backs up the Van Milligen argument with his essay (see Chapter 15) on the idea that leadership can be found in human capital initiatives, especially in rural communities. For example, investment in human capital becomes an important leadership strategy in communities like Telluride, Colorado, where community foundations are becoming increasingly significant place-based anchors of change and development in a resource-starved, post-extraction economic age. The seed money for such leadership strategies focused on new human capital development will come from community foundations, suggests Major, making them key actors in rural initiatives in the new century.

It is also apparent that community foundations in the future will play even more central roles in filling what Brian Payne (see Chapter 13) of the Central Indiana Community Foundation calls the civic leadership vacuum created by the combined forces of a globalized business environment and cash-strapped local governments. Community foundations, he argues, have the capacity to lead in ways that other institutions cannot: They have the ability to build cross-sector, long-term, public-private initiatives because they can be equally legitimate to various constituencies, thereby connecting the dots and moving between changing and evolving sectors of the public, the government, and the market. Antonia Hernández, head of the California Community Foundation of Los Angeles County and author of Chapter 14, argues that leadership is difficult and requires an assumption of risk, a real stepping up to assume a role as advocate and public policy initiator within the conflictive communal context of agonistic pluralism.

Finally, in Chapter 16—about a community and its relatively new institution of philanthropy—Gulf Coast Community Foundation head Teri Hansen and Mark S. Pritchett suggest that community foundations can serve as "place-leaders" that root, or otherwise anchor, the somewhat transient populations of communities by fostering a "culture of philanthropy." Hansen and Pritchett argue that new community foundations can serve as "catalytic" institutions of civic leadership by building strong governance practices within the foundations and within other local nonprofits and by engaging in new innovative technologies that can help them ward off threats from for-profit philanthropic models and budgetary crises.

Part IV. The Risks and Rewards of Strong Leadership

Common to many of the essays in this volume are questions related to institutional identity and mission. Paul Grogan, the head of the Boston Foundation, suggests in Chapter 17 that community foundations will need to use research and resources to establish new functions for themselves. For example, he argues that community foundations may have previously taken a behind-the-scenes approach to philanthropy, but in the new century, they must be more visible and vocal if they are to facilitate positive change in communities. His experience at the Boston Foundation suggests that the foundation, through its research and convening roles, needs to become a *trusted* "knowledge broker" by creating new communications functions and partnering with area think tanks to research local and regional problems. Armed with the results of such research, the foundation is better equipped, Grogan suggests, to more visibly lead public policy discourse and public education campaigns, along with other local policy dialogues about housing and pension reform.

The challenges may be somewhat different for smaller community foundations, notes Josie Heath of the Community Foundation Serving Boulder County, Colorado. In Chapter 18, "The Courage to Lead: Worth the Risk?" Heath observes that the smaller foundations are constantly pushed to muster the resources to address the huge needs facing their communities. Heath sees small foundations stepping up to address those needs, leveraging extensive engagement by board members who perform important roles such as securing the tax levy for early childhood education. The chapter spans several key themes, including the risks associated with community leadership and political engagement; the bridging of individual and community needs; the production and execution of a non-neutral agenda; and the agonistic realities of leading change in a community where, for example, the lead agencies working for early childhood education did not support the property tax levy.

Innovation is the theme of Chapter 19 by Douglas F. Kridler, the president of the Columbus Foundation. Innovation has long been a community foundation tradition, and foundations entering the second century must find the best methods with which to share their new uses of innovation (that is, their "expertise") with others, argues Kridler. Increased engagement with community includes alignment of donor-advised funds to maximize impact by dovetailing donor interest with expert information about the community, which results in better targeting of philanthropic dollars.

In Chapter 20, Kelly Ryan and Judith L. Millesen of the Incourage Community Foundation argue that the production of the "mission" of the community foundation sector can be based on modes of learning and listening as well as vocal advocacy. Community foundations, especially those serving rural areas, often look to their peers elsewhere and to others in their region engaged in community development work in order to learn about new ways of building social and financial capital. Building on the initiatives of local residents, community foundations promote dialogue that identifies shared values, strengthens relationships, encourages risk-taking, and cultivates adaptive leadership in community members. This institutional identity, based as it is on local dialogue, often requires community foundation representatives to speak less and listen more.

Part V. Conclusion: Into the Second Century

With each of the essays in the volume, we hope to add more to the understanding of the place-based importance of community foundations in their shifting, "elastic" geography. Certain key elements of the foundation should emerge as ever more important not only to the foundation but also to the community and its future development. We ask the reader to join us in Chapter 21 as we step back from the details of each of the chapters and try to determine what lessons we can derive from the whole. This does not mean that we should take anything away from the "granularity" of each experience, but it should demand that we interrogate each of the essays to determine more about the overall place of community foundations, along with other place-based anchor institutions, in the new century of community formation.

Acknowledgment

This chapter benefits greatly from the research of Antonia Lalagos and the editorial contributions of Eric Newton. However, all mistakes of content are those of the authors.

Note

1. The term *agonistic pluralism* comes from the work of Chantal Mouffe, who in her seminal work *The Democratic Paradox* (2009) speaks not of some unattainable "theory" of consensus and negotiated settlement of the tension between the highly differentiated conditions of democracy and liberalism, of collective equality and individual freedom, but of their agonistic relationship with each other. Like everyone in the realpolitik world of contemporary community formation, she sees that "the dynamics of liberal-democratic politics as the space of a paradox whose effect is to impede both total closure and total dissemination, whose possibility is inscribed in the grammars of democracy and liberalism, opens many interesting possibilities. To be sure, by preventing the full development of their respective logics, this articulation represents an obstacle to their complete realization: both perfect liberty and perfect equality become impossible. But this is the very possibility for a pluralist form of human coexistence . . . in which freedom and equality can somehow manage to coexist" (10–11). This is, says Mouffe, an "ineradicable" tension, one that cannot be resolved through a deliberative negotiation leading to rational outcomes. Therefore, pluralism and diverse coexistence are the only real ways out. As a result, rather than rational communication (in the style of Habermas [1995]), we call for an "agonistic pluralism" (a realpolitik à la Mouffe [2009]) as the contextual starting point for community foundation practice.

Bibliography

Amin, A., and N. Thrift. 2002. *Cities: Reimagining the Urban.* Cambridge, UK: Polity Press.

Bauman, Z. 2000. *Liquid Modernity.* Cambridge, UK: Polity Press.

Bernholz, L., K. Fulton, and G. Kasper. 2005. *On the Brink of New Promise: The Future of U.S. Community Foundations.* New York: Monitor Group. http://www.monitorinstitute.com/downloads/what-we-think/new-promise/On_the_Brink_of_New_Promise.pdf.

Biles, R. 2011. *The Fate of Cities: Urban America and the Federal Government, 1945–2000.* Lawrence: University Press of Kansas.

Castells, M. 2000. *The Rise of the Network Society.* 2d ed. Malden, MA: Blackwell.

The Chicago Community Trust. 2012. http://www.cct.org.

———. 2010. "Guiding Principles of the Trust." http://www.cct.org/about/our-mission-our-vision-our-values.

The Chronicle of Philanthropy. 2012. http://www.philanthropy.com.

Council on Foundations. 2011. Fall Conference for Community Foundations. September 19–21. San Francisco, CA. http://www.cof.org/events/conferences/2011fall/index.cfm.

Duxbury, S. 2011. "Emmett Carson: Community Foundation Model 'Broken,' at Risk." *San Francisco Business Times,* September 20. http://www.bizjournals.com/sanfrancisco/blog/2011/09/community-foundation-model-at-risk.html?page=2.

Fainstein, S. 2010. *The Just City.* Ithaca, NY: Cornell University Press.

Fidelity Charitable. 2012. *Fidelity Charitable Policy Guidelines: Program Circular.* Cincinnati, OH: Fidelity Charitable. http://www.fidelitycharitable.org/docs/Giving-Account-Policy-Guidelines.pdf.

———. 2011. *2011 Annual Report.* Cincinnati, OH: Fidelity Charitable. http://www.fidelitycharitable.org/2011-annual-report/annual-letter.shtml.

Gaffikin, F., and M. Morrissey. 2011. *Planning in Divided Cities: Collaborative Shaping of Contested Space.* Chichester, UK: Blackwell.

Gaffikin, F., and D.C. Perry. 2009. "Discourses and Strategic Visions: The U.S. Research University as an Institutional Manifestation of Neo-liberalism in a Global Era." *American Educational Research Journal* 46, no. 1, 115–144.

Gaffikin, F., D.C. Perry, and R. Kundu. 2011. "The City and Its Politics: Informal and Contested." In *The City Revisited: Urban Theory from Chicago, Los Angeles and New York,* ed. D.R. Judd and D. Simpson, 260–285. Minneapolis: University of Minnesota Press.

Habermas, J. 1995. "Reconciliation Through the Public Use of Reason: Remarks on John Rawls's Political Liberalism." *Journal of Philosophy* 92, no. 3, 109–131.

Harkavy, I., and H. Zuckerman. 1999. *Eds and Meds: Hidden City Assets.* Report, September. Washington, DC: Brookings Institution.

Hussey, M.J. 2010. "Avoiding Misuse of Donor Advised Funds." *Cleveland State Law Review* 58, no. 1.

Judd, D.R., and M. Pagano, eds. Forthcoming. *Reinventing the Local State: State-Making and Governance in America's Urban Regions.* Urbana: University of Illinois Press.

Lowe, J. 2004. "Community Foundations: What Do They Offer Community Development?" *Journal of Urban Affairs* 26, no. 2, 221–240.

Magat, R., ed. 1989. *An Agile Servant: Community Leadership by Community Foundations.* New York: The Foundation Center.

Marsh, T.D. 2002. "A Dubious Distinction: Rethinking Tax Treatment of Private Foundations and Public Charities." *Virginia Tax Review,* 22.

McCann, E., and K. Ward, eds. 2011. *Mobile Urbanism: Cities and Policymaking in the Global Age*. Minneapolis: University of Minnesota Press.

McEldowney, M., F. Gaffikin, and D.C. Perry. 2009. "Discourses of the Contemporary Urban Campus in Europe: Intimations of Americanization or Globalization?" *Globalisation, Societies, and Education* 7, no. 2, 131–149.

Moore, M.H., moderator. 2008. *From Government to Governance: The Challenge of Managing Cross-Sectoral Partnerships*. Global Business Summit, Harvard Business School. http://www.hbs.edu/centennial/businesssummit/business-society/from-government-to-governance-the-challenge-of-managing-cross-sectoral-partnerships.pdf.

Morgan, D.L. 2007. *Community Foundations and New Governance Networks: Three Studies Exploring the Role of Regionally Networked Philanthropic Organizations in Local Problem Solving*. PhD diss., Department of Public Administration, University of Southern California.

Mouffe, C. 2009. *The Democratic Paradox*. New York: Verso.

Perry, D.C., and W. Wiewel, eds. 2005. *The University as Urban Developer: Case Studies and Analysis*. Armonk, NY: M.E. Sharpe.

Piore, M.J. 1995. *Beyond Individualism*. Cambridge, MA: Harvard University Press.

Roy, A. 2005. "Urban Informality: Toward an Epistemology of Planning." *Journal of the American Planning Association* 71, no. 2, 147–156.

Sassen, S. 2006. *Cities in the World Economy*. 3d ed. Thousand Oaks, CA: Pine Forge.

———. 2001. *The Global City: New York, London, Tokyo*. Princeton, NJ: Princeton University Press.

———. 1996. *Losing Control?* New York: Columbia University Press.

Scott, A., ed. 1997. *The Limits of Globalization*. New York: Routledge.

Swyngedouw, E. 1997. "Neither Global nor Local: 'Globalization' and the Politics of Scale." In *Spaces of Globalization: Reassessing the Power of the Local*, ed. K.R. Cox, 137–166. New York: Guilford Press.

University of Illinois at Chicago (2012). College of Urban Planning & Public Affairs website. http://www.uic.edu/cuppa/.

Webber, H.S., and M. Karlström. 2009. *Why Community Investment Is Good for Nonprofit Anchor Institutions: Understanding Costs, Benefits, and the Range of Strategic Options*. Report. Chicago, IL: Chapin Hall at the University of Chicago.

Weber, J. 2005. "Demolishing Shaky Tax Shelters." *Bloomberg Business Week*, July 11.

Wiewel, W., and D.C. Perry, eds. 2008. *Global Universities and Urban Development: Case Studies and Analysis*. Armonk, NY: M.E. Sharpe.

Ylvisaker, P. 1989. "Community and Community Foundations in the New Century." In *An Agile Servant: Community Leadership by Community Foundations*, ed. R. Magat. New York: The Foundation Center.

Part I

Facing a Limitless Future: Can Foundations Adapt?

2

A Mandate to Innovate

Ronald B. Richard
The Cleveland Foundation

In the nearly 100 years since our field was born, community foundations have enriched the lives of people in countless ways, channeling philanthropic resources to reform education, improve economies, strengthen neighborhoods, provide a safety net of social services, enhance the arts, and much more. Many of our efforts began as creative new approaches to help people deal with life's challenges. Driven by our missions to improve quality of life, community foundations often incubate high-risk ideas to overcome stubborn social and economic challenges. We can take pride in this legacy.

But we *must* expand on it. Like so many other fields and institutions, community foundations are at a tipping point in their history, facing technological, economic, and social challenges that are reshaping and/or putting at risk communities everywhere. To carry out our missions in today's environment of rapid-fire change, we must adopt new ways of thinking about critical civic issues and devise new approaches to accomplish our goals of improving life for our citizens. We also must help other community organizations develop a greater capacity to innovate, and work with them to increase our collective impact. And we must do it all with a sense of urgency. As a contributor to the *Chronicle of Philanthropy* points out, innovation is "a concept that has shaken up the business and technology worlds and now is buzzing around community foundations eager to extend their reach in a tough economy" (Sataline 2012).

At the Cleveland Foundation, the world's first community foundation, we believe a commitment to innovation can complement the place-based philanthropy that is our field's hallmark—especially in older cities like ours with populations that, though diminished, remain deeply rooted. Clevelanders, like residents of other midwestern cities that flourished early in the twentieth century, have a very strong sense of place. We are not a transient community like Silicon Valley or the DC metro area. Perhaps we are more akin to Starbucks, which succeeds in part because it is a convivial public space where people like to gather, connect, and feel "at home."

Against this backdrop, the Cleveland Foundation attempts to protect, preserve, restore, and enhance place. Many of our efforts have been successful; a few have fallen short of our expectations. Now, as we confront old, entrenched problems—along with contemporary issues undreamed of at our founding—we recognize that to revitalize our community, we need to innovate, take risks, form coalitions, and lead. There are no easy answers on the brink of our second century. But with the right focus and a bold approach, we can continue to improve our communities in meaningful ways.

One Hundred Years of Innovation

The community trust concept originated in Cleveland in 1914. Back then, Cleveland was a hotbed of invention, entrepreneurship, and vision. Inventors pioneered technologies in electricity, chemicals, metals, paints, and machining. Our founder, lawyer and banker Frederick Harris Goff, initiated a new philanthropic model: a permanently enduring organization flexible enough to address the needs and seize the opportunities of any era. Goff wanted to do away with what he dubbed the "dead hand" of philanthropy, and instead give people the ability to leave their money to an organization that would continue to use it for the good of the community long after the donors' designated purposes, such as the eradication of specific diseases, had been achieved. The brilliance of the concept can be seen in its replication around the world; today, more than 700 community foundations exist in the United States, and approximately 1,700 operate worldwide.

It is not surprising, then, that our early history was distinguished by big ideas and approaches. During our first decade, we initiated and funded comprehensive studies of major urban issues such as welfare, public education, recreation, justice, and lakefront development. Our goals were to stimulate public debate, recommend reforms, and guide eventual grantmaking. These studies informed and rallied the community, leading to a major reorganization of Cleveland's social service programs, including the creation of the forerunner of today's United Way of Greater Cleveland; substantial changes in a corrupt criminal justice system; a large-scale modernization of the Cleveland public schools; formation of the Cleveland Metroparks, the "Emerald Necklace" that encircles the city; and the merger of two academic institutions to create Case Western Reserve University (though that one took 50 years to come to fruition).

In *Rebuilding Cleveland*, which commemorates the Cleveland Foundation's 75th anniversary, author Diana Tittle (1992) observes, "The most enduring contribution of the survey years was to establish a precedent of a local philanthropy acting as a civic agenda-setter and a problem-solver"—roles we pursue to this day.

Throughout the ensuing decades, the Cleveland Foundation continued to innovate to address community problems. We helped establish the nation's first public housing, the Free Clinic of Greater Cleveland, Cuyahoga Community College, and the city's renowned arts institutions. In the belief that saving Cleveland's beloved theater district from the wrecking ball was critical to our community's future, we invested a portion of our assets in the performing arts center known as Playhouse Square, becoming the first community foundation to use a program-related investment (loan) as a tool to advance a philanthropic objective.

We have been inspired by similarly remarkable innovations by our counterparts over the past century. As Claire Gaudiani writes in *The Greater Good: How Philanthropy Drives the American Economy and Can Save Capitalism* (2003):

> The dynamic marketplace of ideas essential to successful capitalism is significantly enhanced by new ideas, many of which are initially tested and implemented because of philanthropy. This third way of funding—beyond the government and private, return-expecting investors—opens the door to ideas that are still too young to have gained the backing of a majority of voters or shareholders, and brings dynamism and prosperity to our economy.

The World Has Changed

Our field's next century will be radically different from its first. The disruptions we see all around us—in the job market, financial markets, education, communications—reflect systemic change driven by technology, globalization, and other unstoppable forces. Iconic community institutions such as daily newspapers atrophy, and corporations evolve into global players with little sense of attachment to their old hometowns. Likewise, people are more mobile, which weakens connection to community—and, arguably, to one another.

Meanwhile, the federal government of big twentieth-century ideas—the Marshall Plan, the New Deal, the interstate highway system, the Environmental Protection Agency, the openings to Russia and China—now lacks the ability to forge a national consensus on any issue, including industrial policy. Public confidence is just one casualty of this abdication of leadership. Careening toward a cataclysmic national debt crisis, the government comes up woefully short in its ability to fund basic social services and infrastructure. According to their trustees' latest projections, the Medicare and Social Security trust funds will be exhausted by 2024 and 2033, respectively.

As Michael Cooper points out in the *New York Times,* "budgetary pain flows downhill" (2011). States squeezed by a financially strapped federal government are in turn slashing aid to local governments, leaving them little choice but to reduce or eliminate services, lay off employees, and raise taxes to stay afloat.

This drama plays out in Ohio, where the biennial budget the General Assembly passed in 2011 cut funding to local governments by more than $550 million, for a 25 percent reduction the first year and a 50 percent decrease the following year. Compounding this loss, Ohio's estate tax was eliminated, effective in 2013.

This retrenchment is alarming in Cleveland and Cuyahoga County, where the need for social services can be gauged by a few salient statistics. Cleveland was ranked the nation's second-poorest city in the 2010 federal census. In the preceding decade, poverty rates increased in 80 percent of the core city's neighborhoods and in 75 percent of its suburbs (Piiparinen and Coulton 2012).

What does the combination of growing need and shrinking tax revenues portend for the nonprofit sector? Lacking sufficient resources to pay workers, deliver services, and address basic problems, local governments are ever more likely to appeal to foundations to bridge the gap. It is easy to imagine future requests for grants to supplement teacher salaries, police and fire services, and even public infrastructure.

We are at an inflection point—socially, politically, environmentally, fiscally, and perhaps even morally. With this shift of government responsibilities, it seems clear that leadership will have to come not just from stymied politicians, but from the community at large. Community foundations are trusted stewards of philanthropic resources, viewed as honest and objective brokers on issues of public concern. With money and credibility, foundations have the ability and influence to make a powerful impact.

As Douglas W. Nelson, former president and CEO of the Annie E. Casey Foundation, noted prior to his 2010 retirement, community foundations have unique advantages over public- and private-sector organizations in initiating and propelling change, including greater latitude to experiment with ideas and strategies involving a degree of risk that businesses and governments would deem unacceptable.

Reinforcing the point Gaudiani makes in her book *The Greater Good,* Nelson (2010) stated,

> Unlike the private sector or the political sector, we can afford to be very patient. We don't have to look for next year's election returns or next quarter's financial returns, and therefore can take risks—whether it's

through our grantmaking or through the use of our endowments as social investments—to explore and experiment with investments and interventions that try to increase the human capital of low-income families or increase the opportunities and investability of low-income neighborhoods.

While these advantages position us to be agents of change, we also possess attributes that hinder our ability to innovate. Our field is not pressured by the kind of competition that fuels a flurry of new ideas. Our organizations value intellect, study, and debate, often at the expense of working efficiently and seizing the right moment to put ideas into action. As a result, we appear less nimble, entrepreneurial, and assertive than we could be.

Can we step up the pace of change for the benefit of our communities? Absolutely. Awareness is the first step. To begin, we must rethink the premises that guide our operations and the approaches we have traditionally taken to help our citizens and our communities. In a 2012 position paper, Clara Miller, president of the private F.B. Heron Foundation, makes a compelling case for reexamining the logic models and theories of change on which Heron and many other philanthropic, for-profit, and government entities have long based their programs to serve disadvantaged families. Strategies based on helping these families purchase homes and acquire assets as reliable steps toward the mainstream have been "helpful but not adequate," says Miller (2012). She adds: "Despite the widespread structural change transforming the economy, the assumptions behind most antipoverty policy and programs, both in government and in civil society, remain fundamentally unaltered. . . . Only by rigorously questioning and transcending our own cherished assumptions will we progress." Miller's paper outlines how her foundation is changing the way it defines its resources and deploys capital, and it calls for being "intentionally experimental" in developing workable strategies (2012).

This is a big leap for many in the community foundation field. As a *Foundation Review* article entitled "Philanthropy's Civic Role in Community Change" observes, "Civic work sometimes requires foundations to take greater risks, to put their own name and credibility on the line publicly in order to advance a cause, and to support less powerful partners. This . . . is difficult for institutions like foundations that are often risk-averse" (Auspos et al. 2009).

At the Cleveland Foundation (2012), we are becoming more adept at embracing risk and being "intentionally experimental" in our programming because we believe this path can lead to greater rewards for our community. Our track record is bearing this out. While we do not claim to have all the answers, we hope some of our hard-earned insights will prove helpful to others and lead us to further progress.

Based on our experience, innovative programming demands fresh thinking—from viewing old problems in new ways to using our community's assets more effectively to adapting successful approaches from other communities, both within the United States and abroad. It obligates us to take a stand, voice a clear opinion on civic issues, and follow through with targeted action. It calls for a willingness to lead in bringing together parties that may never have come together on their own.

These qualities must permeate the culture of our organizations and characterize the way we approach community challenges. Ultimately, it comes down to assembling the right mix of people, empowering and motivating them effectively, and having the steadfast support of a strong, focused board of directors.

A closer look at a few of our recent initiatives illustrates how these elements of innovation can combine to make an impact on community problems traditionally viewed as "too big to fix."

Putting People to Work, Sharing the Wealth

The Evergreen Cooperatives are a network of for-profit, employee-owned "green" businesses that we catalyzed and are helping to launch in a comprehensive, collaborative effort to revitalize Greater University Circle. This Cleveland neighborhood comprises University Circle, the city's elite educational, medical, and cultural hub, and six adjacent struggling neighborhoods where median household income hovers around $18,500 a year and unemployment exceeds 25 percent.

More than a simple jobs strategy, the Evergreen companies enable wealth-building among their employees as they serve customers that include three of University Circle's powerhouse anchor institutions: Case Western Reserve University, Cleveland Clinic, and University Hospitals. The cooperatives are capturing a portion of the $3 billion these institutions spend annually for goods and services.

This "Cleveland model," as it has become known, builds upon the anchor-based economic inclusion work undertaken by the Johns Hopkins Hospital complex in East Baltimore, Maryland, and the urban revival that the University of Pennsylvania spearheaded in West Philadelphia. Our model, however, involves not one but multiple anchor partners that have worked together toward a shared vision; these partners are magnifying their economic might and driving it locally, with a willingness to invest in creative, collaborative projects that demand institutional trust among all partners and flexible deployment of resources.

To date, the Evergreen Cooperatives encompass a commercial laundry and an energy services firm. A third enterprise, Green City Growers, the nation's largest urban food production greenhouse, was constructed in one of Cleveland's most blighted neighborhoods and began operations in early 2013. When fully operational, these first three businesses will employ approximately 100 people, most of whom live in Greater University Circle.

The nonprofit Evergreen Cooperative Corporation (ECC) is a holding company that houses the businesses, provides strategic guidance, and retains veto power over any activities that could put the entire network at risk. The ECC also includes a revolving loan fund, a shared services company, and a real estate unit. The Cleveland Foundation invested $3.4 million in the $6.5 million Evergreen loan fund, and these funds have leveraged $22 million in additional capital to finance and build the first three businesses.

Embarking on this archetype of social-sector innovation in 2009, we had many unanswered questions and risk factors to consider: Would launching for-profit businesses present us with legal liabilities? Could these businesses succeed and, ultimately, become self-sustaining? If they failed, would our judgment and financial stewardship be questioned across the board? Would it be better to play it safe and give in the traditional way?

Ultimately, we felt we needed to demonstrate that these neighborhoods were worthy of the first new investment in several decades, and we wanted to stem the outflow of citizens from these once highly stable neighborhoods. As a team, we concluded that the risks, while significant, did not outweigh the potential benefits, and we moved forward.

Adapting Successful Approaches

The Cleveland Foundation has benefited from adopting proven models of innovation from other organizations, then adapting them in ways that leverage local strengths. The Evergreen Cooperatives were influenced greatly by our study of employee-owned cooperatives in Mondragon, Spain. Mondragon has built a network of more than 120 worker cooperatives that employ more than 100,000 worker-owners in the industrial Basque region. We learned valuable business lessons in Mondragon—from how to be responsible stewards of capital, preserving and enhancing it for the next generation, to how to establish an appropriate level of employee ownership.

Another example of replication tailored to local trends and needs is Cleveland's NewBridge Center for Arts and Technology, which is patterned after the highly successful Manchester Bidwell training center in Pittsburgh. Manchester Bidwell has validated founder Bill Strickland's vision: Treat people as world-class individuals and tap their human potential by giving them the skills to be successful.

NewBridge offers after-school, arts-based enrichment for high school students at risk of quitting school. Since the center's November 2010 launch, the arts program has attracted more than 350 students from over 40 high schools in Cleveland and nearby suburbs. A medical career training program for adults graduated its second class of phlebotomy technicians and its initial class of pharmacy technicians in July 2012. Among a total of 36 graduates, 18 had found jobs with local health care providers by August 2012; one trainee chose to pursue higher education. Pay and benefits for those hired average $32,000 a year.

NewBridge opened with a $6 million investment from various funders, including the Cleveland Foundation, and we remain a financial supporter. Just as important, we were among the nation's first foundations to step up as conveners in the site replication process, galvanizing the local groups and individuals who could make this dream a reality for many more people.

Innovative Leadership

The convener role is embedded in the DNA of many community foundations. According to the Council on Foundations, we play "a critical role in providing a safe space where diverse local groups can meet and have often-difficult conversations about their community's future" (2011). But if we are to lead innovatively in our next century, we must move beyond our own safe space.

Historically, community foundations have been reluctant to wade into controversial territory and advance a point of view. Fear of alienating donors and potential donors is an understandable concern. While we must always be thoughtful about how we engage, failure to speak forthrightly on issues that impact the community's well-being is an abandonment of our responsibility as a voice for positive change. Moreover, if we are silent, we bypass the opportunity to jump-start difficult but necessary conversations.

A good example is our work to reform public education. With the encouragement of the chair of the Cleveland Foundation's board of directors, I addressed two high-profile forums on the foundation's conviction of the need for bold change in education. In these appearances, I attacked the myth that low-income minority students cannot succeed academically, and I espoused contentious ideas such as abolishing teacher seniority and tenure and moving to a performance-based pay system.

These remarks coincided with and supported an ongoing drive in the Cleveland Metropolitan School District, which we had helped stimulate, to "establish a new school system alongside the old" by opening a portfolio of innovative schools that provide some site-level autonomy in exchange for increased accountability. The portfolio approach is based on an emerging national model: New York City, Chicago, Baltimore, and Denver are among big-city districts that have experimented with various iterations of the portfolio strategy, with promising results.

In Cleveland, the foundation teamed with a diverse array of community partners, including the private George Gund Foundation, to open 13 new district schools and seven new charter schools dedicated to educational excellence. In the first five years, the two foundations invested a total $17.6 million in this endeavor. These new schools have consistently outperformed their traditional peers on almost every measure.

A stellar example is the Cleveland School of Science and Medicine, which graduated its first class in 2010. All 78 seniors were accepted at colleges and universities across the country, and they were offered more than $6 million in scholarships. These trends continue, with all 89 of the school's 2012 graduates winning acceptance to four-year institutions and receiving scholarships collectively valued at more than $7 million. The schools they will attend rank among the nation's most prestigious, including Johns Hopkins, Stanford, Cornell, Wake Forest, and Case Western Reserve universities.

Seeing results like these, Cleveland mayor Frank Jackson introduced a sweeping plan in February 2012 to take the portfolio concept to scale across the district. The first hurdle in implementing this plan was to change state law to authorize no less than a reinvention of public education in Cleveland.

This territory was familiar to the Cleveland Foundation. Through the Ohio Grantmakers Forum (OGF), a regional association of grantmakers, we have worked since 2005 to mount a sustained, strategic effort to influence education public policy, reaching out to a broad range of stakeholders to develop a strong reform agenda. Since 2009, we have seen some payoff as state legislators have adopted numerous OGF recommendations to strengthen academic standards, impose some limits on teacher seniority as the sole criterion in layoffs and recalls, create innovation schools and zones, and move toward a new teacher evaluation system.

In 2012, the Cleveland and Gund foundations joined with a partnership that included Cleveland's business community to advocate for passage of a compromise—but still highly robust—version of the mayor's school transformation plan, which eventually garnered the support of the Cleveland Teachers Union. In June, this plan was approved and signed into law, with key provisions allowing the district (1) to make staffing decisions based primarily on performance, not seniority; (2) to toughen teacher evaluation procedures; (3) to share tax revenues with partnering high-quality charter schools; (4) to lengthen the school day and year; and (5) to intervene quickly in failing schools.

All these provisions are controversial, yet politicians from both major parties united to support them—symbolized by the concord on this issue between Cleveland's Democratic mayor and Ohio's Republican governor,

John Kasich. Many actors contributed to the positive outcome, including Ohio's foundations. This effort reflects current theories that foundations can achieve greater impact by focusing limited resources on influencing public policy. Providing leadership and working collaboratively to develop and advance a reform agenda, we succeeded in establishing philanthropy as a credible and knowledgeable voice for education reform in Ohio. This work continues.

Seeing Differently

The portfolio approach to innovative schools is an example of looking at an old problem in a new light: rather than continuing to pour money into low-performing schools, commit instead to building a parallel network of excellent schools within the district and then expand it, enrolling increasing numbers of children who may never have had access to a first-class education. To address our communities' most intractable problems in our next century, we will often need to adjust our view to see beyond the obvious.

Another example comes from Cleveland's world-renowned arts sector, which the Cleveland Foundation has long supported; but recurring grant requests to cover growing deficits at multiple arts organizations caused us to question the wisdom of repeated short-term fixes. The deeper issue for our arts community was the need to attract new, next-generation audiences.

Looking at the problem this way, we launched a three-year initiative dubbed "Engaging the Future" in 2011. We agreed to provide operating support to 11 local arts organizations if they, in turn, would participate in an intensive series of seminars, workshops, and individual consultations to think in new ways about how to develop younger, more diverse audiences that more closely reflect contemporary—and future—demographics. A team of expert arts consultants is guiding this program.

"Engaging the Future" illustrates how our field is adapting its own thinking to help people help themselves, rather than simply doling out money to them. In this respect, we and our partners are embracing the global model of our national peers. Foundations throughout the world have worked to empower impoverished people by showing them how to organize and proactively improve their own living conditions.

The Cleveland Foundation's aforementioned Greater University Circle Initiative presents another instance of bringing a new perspective to familiar problems. The word "Greater" frames an expanded view that joins University Circle with the surrounding neighborhoods to form an inclusive new identity—a "Greater" identity—that spans stubborn psychological and economic barriers. Instead of seven distinct neighborhoods, we see one.

Big and multifaceted, the Greater University Circle Initiative encompasses transportation-focused development projects and neighborhood revitalization programs designed to encourage individuals and businesses to live, buy, and hire locally. Our anchor partners are integral to the success of these programs.

Although they have been generous supporters, we know that Case Western Reserve University, Cleveland Clinic, and University Hospitals are not philanthropists; they will never replace the corporate foundations that donated millions of dollars to civic causes when Cleveland was a stronghold of Fortune 500 companies. But by seeing them differently—not just as service providers, but as potential customers that could meet some of their supply needs through local sources such as the Evergreen Cooperatives and the emerging biomedical cluster in Cleveland's nearby Health-Tech Corridor—we have helped structure a new economic model that is transforming a vital section of the city and improving lives as it brings disadvantaged individuals into the economy.

Residents of Greater University Circle are reformulating perceptions of their neighborhoods as well. Neighborhood Connections, the Cleveland Foundation's small-grants and grassroots community-building program, is encouraging residents to engage with one another and become involved in the life of the community: applying for grants to fund their ideas, hosting their neighbors in living room dialogues, working on the resident-produced newspaper, serving as greeters at local events, and much more. This path points toward active citizenship, bonds of trust between residents and institutional leaders, and a strengthened social fabric. Like our peers, we are invested in building a sense of community through inclusion fueled by innovation.

A Culture of Innovation

The ability to recast old problems, create potentially game-changing initiatives, and convene and gain consensus among disparate parties are all skills that spring from an innovation-oriented culture.

Over the years, we have reconstituted the Cleveland Foundation's board of directors with innovative thinkers, many of whom combine a passion for civic engagement with expertise in new business development. They are not risk-averse. They balance prudent decision making with a willingness to accept the possibility of failure. They understand it takes time for staff to assess a situation, get to know the players, gain credibility and trust, and then effect change. They know it takes patience and perseverance to allow an initiative to succeed, and there will be bumps along the way.

Complementing the board's perspective is an internal culture that values innovation and an organizational structure that supports it. We invest our grantmaking team with the responsibility not just to make recommendations for funding, but to lead, innovate, and advocate. We let them know they have the support of management and the board. As our grantmaking entrepreneurs, they are adept at initiating, implementing, and managing complex, high-stakes projects and programs that involve networks of nontraditional partners.

Our staff also understands that, as the F.B. Heron Foundation puts it, "the dominant context for our work is a range of mega-problems," citing the interplay of the environment, health, global security, civil society, and other factors that magnify and complicate our challenges (Miller 2012).

In recruiting this staff of thinkers and doers, we looked not to the usual suspects, but to people who were new to philanthropy yet had extensive track records in the public and private sectors. They include our program directors for education, economic development, human services, architecture and urban design, and neighborhoods and housing. The ability of these experts to move easily among sectors and to work with diverse partners has been critical to demonstrating proof of concept with our boldest initiatives.

We also invest in global learning opportunities for our staff. Our program director for education has traveled to Singapore to study that country's well-regarded education system, and two of our program directors have visited Spain to learn from the Mondragon Cooperatives. Our director of arts initiatives has worked with Turkish artists in Istanbul.

Augmenting the permanent staff, we pull in additional experts for specific long-term projects. For example, in 2010, we created a two-year fellowship for social justice. The appointee to this position has been instrumental in developing a comprehensive job creation and wealth-building strategy for the Evergreen Cooperatives—so much so that our board renewed his fellowship for another two years.

Alone among community foundations, we established an energy fellowship and, in 2006, we hired a national expert with 20 years' experience in the energy industry to serve as a regional thought leader and advocate for clean energy. With his guidance, the Cleveland Foundation became a prominent voice in this ongoing debate, urging Greater Clevelanders to view advanced energy as an economic development opportunity for the region. On his watch, Ohio legislators enacted a renewable energy portfolio standard, mandating that utilities in the state obtain 25 percent of their electricity supplies from advanced energy sources—half of them renewable—by 2025.

During his three-year tenure, our energy fellow was active in efforts to establish Northeast Ohio as the epicenter of the wind power industry. We and our partners have not yet achieved this goal, and we have yet to realize our vision of Lake Erie as the site of North America's first freshwater wind farm. The economics have proved daunting, but we remain committed to our long-term goal of positioning Cleveland as a leader in advanced energy, and we have made headway on many fronts.

Final Thoughts

Our field is inherently forward-looking, so naturally it is tempting to speculate on where we will be 100 years from now.

In 1920, only six years after the Cleveland Foundation was founded, Leonard P. Ayres, a nationally known educator, economist, and statistician, was asked to imagine himself speaking far in the future, reviewing the Cleveland Foundation's activities over its first 100 years. According to Ayres (1920), the Cleveland of 2014 will have the nation's most progressive school system, a great and harmonious institution of higher learning, an accessible art museum, and a government that encompasses its suburbs. It will be a faultlessly clean community, with little noise, smooth and durable streets, buildings of the highest architectural standards, and free access to its lakefront.

While a couple of Ayres's predictions have been realized, it is safe to say that few of our communities could measure up to this ideal. Predicting the future is never easy, yet we are compelled to try.

What is heartening is that the powerful driving force of community foundations remains unchanged. What Ayres said of our founder is true of all donors: "He worked for those whom he never saw and never could see in the hope that he might aid in making the lives of his fellow citizens better and brighter" (1920).

Today, our communities are being reshaped by formidable new forces, and we are dealing with increasingly complex issues. We are being asked to help solve municipal problems commonly viewed solely as the province of government. We are working to help our grantees change to remain relevant. We are seeking new revenue streams to supplement donations.

Like Ayres, I am optimistic. I believe that, through innovation, our field will rise to these and other challenges. Wherever our evolution takes us, I am confident that community foundations will endure as valued fixtures of the civic landscape in 2114, when our descendants will ponder how to make their fellow citizens' lives "better and brighter" for a third century.

Bibliography

Auspos, P., P. Brown, A.C. Kubisch, and S. Sutton. 2009. "Philanthropy's Civic Role in Community Change." *Foundation Review* 1, no. 1, 135–145. http://dx.doi.org/10.4087/FOUNDATIONREVIEW-D-09-00010.

Ayres, L. 1920. *The First Century of the Cleveland Foundation, 1914–2014.* Speech, September 29. Cleveland, OH: The Cleveland Foundation.

The Cleveland Foundation. 2012. http://www.clevelandfoundation.org.

Cooper, M. 2011. "States Pass Budget Pain to Cities." *New York Times,* March 23. http://www.nytimes.com/2011/03/24/us/24cities.html?_r=0.

Council on Foundations. 2011. "How Community Foundations Can Spur Regional Innovation Through Economic Development." Brief, Issue 3, November. http://www.cof.org/files/Bamboo/whoweserve/community/documents/Issue3_Economic%20Development.pdf.

Gaudiani, C. 2003. *The Greater Good: How Philanthropy Drives the American Economy and Can Save Capitalism.* New York: Henry Holt.

Miller, C. 2012. "The World Has Changed and So Must We." Frontline with Faculty Series, Graduate School of Design, Harvard University, February 26.

Nelson, D. 2010. *Casey Connects: Reflections on Doug Nelson's 20 Years of Leadership.* Report. Baltimore, MD: The Annie E. Casey Foundation. http://www.aecf.org/~/media/Pubs/Other/C/CaseyConnectsReflectionsonDougNelsons20Yearso/Connects_S2010.pdf.

Piiparinen, R., and C. Coulton. 2012. *The Changing Face of Poverty in Northeast Ohio.* Research summary, No. 12–01, January. Cleveland, OH: Case Western Reserve University. http://blog.case.edu/msass/2012/01/23/Briefly%20Stated%20%2012–01%20-%20Changing%20Face%20of%20Poverty%20Jan2012.pdf.

Sataline, S. 2012. "Community Foundations Seek Winning Ideas That Are Fresh and Bold." *Chronicle of Philanthropy*, February 19. http://philanthropy.com/article/Foundations-Support-Risky/130816/.

Tittle, D. 1992. *Rebuilding Cleveland.* Columbus: Ohio State University Press.

3

The Future of Community Foundations

Emmett D. Carson
Silicon Valley Community Foundation

As community foundations approach their hundredth year anniversary in 2014, they have much to celebrate. There are over 700 community foundations in the United States that collectively manage assets of nearly $50 billion and annually distribute over $4 billion in grants (The Foundation Center 2011). Community foundations have proven uniquely adept at bringing disparate social, political, and economic interests together to promote the common good within their communities and accumulating unrestricted gifts to support future unanticipated local community needs. In times of emergency, community foundations have provided rapid and locally led responses to both natural and human-caused disasters such as the Oklahoma City bombing, the 9/11 World Trade Center tragedy, the devastation caused by Hurricanes Katrina and Rita, the Minneapolis–Saint Paul bridge collapse, and the BP oil spill in the Gulf of Mexico, among others. U.S. community foundations also can take pride in having helped to inspire a vibrant and growing international movement that is estimated to include more than 910 community foundations in 45 countries, not including the United States (Worldwide Initiatives for Grantmaker Support 2010).

Notwithstanding their vital role and many successes, community foundations are confronting the most significant external threats to their continued growth and future existence that they have ever faced. These threats are driven by changing consumer expectations and behavior based on new cultural norms coupled with evolutionary advances in technology. How people think about their geographical community and relate to and engage with others within their defined community also is changing. As in other fields, technological advances are disrupting community foundations as faster, cheaper, and more efficient ways of learning about nonprofit organizations and making donations to charitable causes become available through the Internet (Bernholz 2010).

This essay is an urgent call to action for community foundations to reevaluate their core business and how they will finance that business. It is premised on three strong convictions. First, there is an immediate need for community foundations to reposition themselves for a future that will be vastly different from their past. How community foundations define and accomplish their core work will be fundamentally different in the next 10 years than it was in the last 100 years. Second, community foundations must accept a new reality that their unstated motto of all for one and one for all is no longer possible in a world where community and geography are no longer synonyms and community foundations no longer enjoy a monopoly on donor-advised funds (DAFs). Community foundations will likely serve overlapping geographies with varying missions. Third, community foundations must develop the comfort level to ask hard questions and experiment with new ideas and structures if they are to create new, distinct, and sustainable models to serve their communities. Community foundations that are unable to adapt to the cultural and technological changes that are under way will find it increasingly difficult if not impossible to survive. And, if community foundations fail to meet this challenge, their local communities will lose a valuable asset for addressing community problems.

Organized into seven sections, this chapter first describes the value proposition underlying community foundations, followed by discussions of the early and current financial business model of community foundations. The next several sections describe the challenges of changing definitions of community—namely, the disruption from the Internet and changing consumer behavior that is threatening the community foundation model. The last section offers ideas as to how some community foundations might adapt to meet these transformative challenges.

The Value Proposition of Community Foundations

Every institution, regardless of whether it is a for-profit or nonprofit organization, must identify its value proposition—its core business. In the case of a for-profit, the value proposition is the product or service that is sold in the marketplace at a price that people are willing to pay that meets or exceeds the product's cost of production. In the case of a nonprofit, the value proposition is determined by the cause to which people are willing to make a charitable contribution of money and/or time that meets or exceeds the cost of production for what is provided. Identifying what an organization offers that people want is essential for developing strategic plans and knowing what trends and changes in consumer behavior or technological advances will strengthen or undermine the success of the organization. By monitoring the right trends, an organization can determine when its value proposition needs to be modified or is no longer relevant.

History is filled with examples of industries that either did not correctly identify their value proposition or did not respond to fundamental cultural or technological changes that impacted their value proposition or both. The classic example of an industry that failed to understand how changing cultural and technological trends would affect their value proposition is the passenger railroad industry. In their heyday, railroad business owners saw themselves competing with, and benchmarking themselves against, other railroads. They failed to recognize the shift when passengers started thinking of railroads as part of a larger transportation system, including airlines and superhighways. The newspaper industry is today's equivalent of the passenger railroad industry.

For decades, hometown newspapers believed their value proposition was providing quality local daily news on a 24-hour cycle that was paid for largely by advertising revenue (the finance model). So resilient was this value proposition that newspapers survived the introduction of both radio and television. However, with the availability and acceptance of the Internet, people now have free access to unlimited news information delivered to their personal handheld device as it happens. Companies that once spent significant sums to advertise in newspapers have new, cheaper, and more effective ways of targeting customers. Individuals also have shifted to online tools to sell their personal goods and services. With the loss of this advertising revenue, newspapers can no longer produce the same quality of news because readers have been unwilling to pay more for the same news that they can get for free. Today, everything from mail delivery, books, entertainment, health care, education, and banking is being disrupted by advances in information technology, and community foundations will be no exception.

In such a world, how should community foundations answer Peter Drucker's (1993, 1) perennial question: What business are we in? This essay maintains that, for most community foundations in the United States and abroad, the answer is to build community consensus around critical community issues and then take leadership positions on those issues (Carson 2005). Importantly, this value proposition does not require ever increasing assets to successfully implement its goals, nor does it rely on assets under management as the measure of success. Ideally, community foundations should arrive at their leadership positions after engaging all segments of their community: wealthy and poor, government, for-profit and nonprofit interests, and those with different racial, ethnic, gender, and sexual orientation backgrounds. When engaging heterogeneous community groups, consensus means general agreement, not unanimity, on values, strategic directions, and objectives. Creating consensus and taking leadership positions are not easy; they require authentic relationships in which a significant number of people agree on an agenda and then act based on what they have learned.

The core business of most community foundations is not investing assets under management, although some community foundations excel at this service. The core business of most community foundations is not the acquisition of DAFs, although the fee revenue from these funds certainly helps to finance operations. And, while this may be heresy to some, the core business of most community foundations is no longer to develop unrestricted assets to address unforeseen community problems of future generations.

For decades, community foundations have extolled the importance of accumulating unrestricted assets and promoted this view with emerging community foundations abroad. However, poorer nations in Latin America, Africa, and Eastern Europe have largely rejected the idea of a core business model based on asset accumulation. Recognizing that individual wealth in their communities is limited and lacking national laws that provide tax benefits for charitable giving, the international community foundation movement has focused on community building and taking leadership positions. In some countries, the decision to take leadership positions can quite literally put the lives of the community foundation leaders and their partners in jeopardy (Carson 2008).

Undeniably, unrestricted endowment assets provide resources for community foundations to engage in community building, support important grant-making initiatives, and help pay for operations. However, when community foundations have had to react to disasters, they typically have not responded by spending down their unrestricted assets. Instead, they have relied on their reputations for integrity, broad community participation, and the ability to serve as trustworthy conduits for monies from givers at home, across the nation, and around the world to address the emergency. While, in theory, the unrestricted resources could be used during emergencies and/or economic dislocation, in practice, few community foundations have done so.

A further challenge to a primary focus on endowment building is the growing effort to encourage those with significant charitable resources to disperse those resources in their lifetimes or within a specified time period following their demise (Schmidt 2008; Meyerson 2012). The Buffett-Gates billionaires' giving pledge has contributed to this changing sentiment (although they do not advocate spending out over a perpetual endowment) by encouraging the ultra-wealthy to commit to donating a significant portion of their wealth. This has been widely interpreted that givers should donate their wealth in their lifetimes. Just as Andrew Carnegie and John D. Rockefeller, Sr., influenced thinking about philanthropy for their generation, Bill Gates, Warren Buffett, and more recently, Mark Zuckerberg (Casserly 2013), are doing the same for their generation. This cultural shift away from creating a permanent legacy in perpetuity that ultimately will be controlled and distributed by others to spending all of one's resources in the present to make communities better has profound implications.

For community foundations that believe their core work is to build unrestricted assets, this newly emerging sentiment to distribute resources in the present will make their work significantly more difficult. However, as will be discussed, the changing views about endowment hold the promise of allowing community foundations to focus on leadership issues by engaging the current generation of donors to meet the community's current needs and then trusting the next generation will do its part.

None of the foregoing is to suggest that community foundations cannot or should not try to accumulate unrestricted resources as a secondary priority. Rather, it is to assert that endowment building is not the core business of community foundations. It was not enough for the newspaper industry to focus on providing quality content to survive. It was not enough for the railroad industry to guarantee that trains would run on time. It is essential for each community foundation to accurately identify its value proposition in the face of rapidly changing consumer expectations, technological transformation, and their community's unique cultural norms and traditions. Understanding the value proposition of a community foundation is different from determining the financial model that will sustain the value proposition.

The Early Financial Model

When community foundations first began, virtually all of their business was from endowments that were given to them by the trust departments of local banks. A community foundation's volunteer board members focused on how to ensure that the charitable bequests of donors were faithfully executed in serving community needs, while the banks continued to invest the assets for a fee. Over time, community foundations also received a small fee for operations from the bank-invested funds.

Beginning in the 1970s, two developments changed this financial model. The 1969 Tax Reform Act allowed community foundations to establish donor-advised funds that had tax advantages over private foundations (Minter 1989, 148), and these provisions were further clarified in 1976. While a handful of community foundations had begun experimenting with DAFs decades earlier—for example, the New York Community Trust created the first such fund in 1931—these laws spurred widespread interest by community foundations to establish DAF programs.

What is less well known is that during the same time, several community foundations began to raise ethical questions about the poor investment returns of some charitable funds held by trustee banks. These community foundations believed that they had a moral, legal, and fiduciary responsibility to ensure that the charitable assets were invested prudently to maximize growth in order to provide more grants to the community. Not surprisingly, some banks responded by largely ending the practice of designating community foundations to direct the grantmaking of bank-controlled charitable funds. Separately, other banks came to realize that the management of charitable assets was a business that they wanted to retain, which had the same result of severing bank transfers of bequests to community foundations. Community foundations needed to find another way to expand grantmaking in the community and a way to charge fees to pay for their operations.

Community foundations adapted by utilizing the new tax laws to engage individuals and families in philanthropy during their lifetimes through DAFs. Because successor advisors were limited to one or two generations, the community foundation was likely to receive a future unrestricted gift. This practice later ended, due largely to competitive pressures from commercial gift funds that had no such restrictions. Community foundations charged fees for investing DAFs and for providing advice to donor families about worthwhile charitable projects. The fees helped offset expenses and subsidized the convening and leadership work. This is the financial model that most community foundations rely on today, and it is under significant stress from cultural and technological changes.

A Broken Financial Model

As community foundations flourished financially by creating DAFs, they drew the attention and admiration of private foundations that envisioned having local partners with whom they could collaborate on local community issues. In addition, private foundations embraced the idea of helping to grow philanthropy in local communities. The Ford, MacArthur, Mott, and Rockefeller foundations, as well as the Carnegie Corporation and Lilly Endowment, among others, are to be commended for investing millions of dollars in the growth and capacity of local community foundations. Their efforts, over years, provided the essential investment capital necessary for community foundations to further establish themselves as key community leaders and helped them build both unrestricted assets and attract new DAFs (Berresford 1989; Mayer 1994; Wittstock and Williams 1998; Reynolds 2008).

The growing fundraising success of community foundations also did not go unnoticed by national financial institutions. The creation of Fidelity Investment's Charitable Gift Fund in 1991 was tangible evidence that charitable giving had become big business. Community foundations would now have to compete for DAFs against national commercial institutions with significant marketing budgets, investment expertise, superior technology infrastructure, and no self-imposed geographical boundaries. While commercial gift funds certainly increased the public's understanding and appreciation of charitable gift funds, they also significantly increased customer expectations for online access to investment options and performance as well as online grantmaking. The creation of Fidelity's gift fund also encouraged other financial institutions such as Vanguard, Charles Schwab, and others to create their own charitable gift funds, which increased competition even further.

The introduction of commercial charitable gift funds allowed investment companies, at minimum cost, to continue to invest the assets of their clients using their existing investment expertise and technological infrastructure. In addition, investment companies were generally able to produce better investment returns on the charitable funds at lower costs and also had substantial revenue from their core investment business to continually upgrade their technology systems. With no promise of providing any philanthropic advisory services or providing leadership on any social issues, commercial gift funds developed an online product that has driven the national market price for DAFs below the price at which most community foundations can offer donor funds with advisory services.

Community foundations rightfully maintain that they engage in important community work and provide donors with unique, local advisory services that are not offered by most commercial gift funds. The problem for community foundations is that many donors appear unwilling to pay higher fees to receive the benefits of advisory services. Community foundations with large unrestricted assets—almost universally older institutions that benefited from the long past practice of bank-directed bequests—have the financial capacity to meet the lower market price by using investment income from their endowments to subsidize a lower fee on their DAFs. This is very different from lowering the price because of increased scale or volume. The justification for using unrestricted endowment funds in this way is that it represents a relatively short-term investment, when measured against perpetuity, that will enable the community foundation to attract future philanthropic capital that will benefit the community. Whether this is true is an unproven proposition.

The vast majority of community foundations have only limited unrestricted endowment funds, and so their ability to match the fee structure of commercial gift funds and still meet their expenses is virtually impossible. While some community foundations have been able to attract general support from individual donors and/or private foundations to help subsidize their operations, such support is seldom large enough or long enough to allow the community foundation to reach sufficient scale to match market rates for DAFs. It should be noted that this is the same consumer behavior that explains the rise of online retailers over traditional brick-and-mortar operations. Retailers of electronics devices (Best Buy, for example) believe that their value proposition is having knowledgeable staff and allowing consumers to physically handle products before buying them. What has happened is that customers are going to brick-and-mortar retailers to gain the free knowledge and handle the devices, only to order the product online from the lowest-cost seller.

In truth, most commercial gift funds have an artificially low price that is subsidized by their core business investment operations. This is not the case for community foundations. The use of unrestricted monies to subsidize the true costs of DAFs is not the same as excess profit. Unrestricted assets used for this purpose means that there is less available to support the community foundation's grantmaking and convening work. Before Merrill Lynch was acquired by Bank of America, Merrill Lynch attempted to differentiate itself from other commercial gift funds by offering advisory services through partnerships with local community foundations. Unfortunately, this bold experiment was hampered by disadvantages that it could never resolve: Specifically, the program needed to charge a higher fee to support Merrill Lynch and the participating community foundation; community foundations had different capabilities resulting in different experiences for consumers; and there were occasional concerns about which organization owned the donor relationship.

Adding to community foundations' dilemma of greater competition at lower fees is that other nonprofit organizations also are offering donor-advised funds (United Ways, universities, women's and ethnic funds). Collectively, these organizations, as well as Internet-driven solutions such as Foundation Source, further undermine the current financial model of community foundations in two significant ways. First, the idea that community foundations have unique access to local community knowledge and information is undercut by Google and other search engines that provide thousands of references on demand in an instant. In addition, charity rating services, such as GuideStar and Charity Navigator, which many community foundations rely upon themselves, offer increasingly detailed information on local nonprofits that will only get better with time. And, individuals are beginning to use their online social networks to get insight and advice about specific nonprofit organizations and community issues. The growing availability and reliability of these free online tools make it harder for community foundations to claim they have unique community knowledge that can only be accessed by having a donor-advisor relationship with the local community foundation and paying a higher fee.

The second way in which the Internet is disrupting the existing financial model of community foundations is that it is easier than ever before for people to give directly and respond instantaneously to specific charitable appeals. Through cell phones, laptops, tablets, or even while paying for groceries or buying cause-related products such as crafts or clothing, individuals can engage in giving without an intermediary. There also are a growing number of online-giving vehicles, among them DonorsChoose and Kiva. Together, these online-giving vehicles create the same types of disruption that are affecting every other brick-and-mortar industry. Community foundations must once again rethink how they finance their work if they are to survive the current cultural and technological transformations.

Changing Definitions of Community

Community foundations, as their names suggest, have historically been defined by their geography. They were built on the idea that people identify with and care about the long-term future of a specific place. This traditional notion of place is at odds with an emerging world where people are more mobile, issues cross geographic boundaries, the Internet connects people around the world, and individuals see themselves as global citizens connected to multiple communities defined by their local, national, and global interests. As Paul Ylvisaker notes:

> Community is a word of elastic meaning; its capacity to stretch has been challenged over the last century and will be tested even more dramatically during the next. The changing dimensions are not only geographical but include forces of diversity, social fragmentation, values, and shared interests. . . .
>
> The geographic stretching of community is actually a constant process, simultaneously moving in opposite directions: downward, to the individual neighborhood, and outward, to embrace the entire world and eventually (certainly with environmental concern) all of space. (1989, 51)

The reality of our modern global society, connected 24/7 through the Internet, is both strengthening and eroding the power of place. On the one hand, disasters such as the Haitian earthquake or Japanese tsunami galvanize worldwide collective action by allowing people to see and act on our mutual humanity. With the world quite literally a keystroke away, local interests must now actively compete for the time, talent, and resources of people against regional, national, and global interests. As people become more mobile, they are less likely to be born, work, and die in the same community. The result is that they are likely to have affinities and connections to multiple geographic communities over their lifetimes.

Our world is ever more focused on allowing people to individualize their personal preferences down to the ringtone and photos on their iPods, iPhones, and Facebook accounts—a trend that is crowding out interest in the common good. In such a world, community foundations can and must provide a crucial counterweight. The changing definition of community is an opportunity enabling community foundations to better position their local efforts in a global context. They also can make connections across geographies that can bring more people into their circle of influence and motivate them to act for the common good. Unlike private and family foundations, community foundations have the ability and credibility to engage all sectors and individuals within their communities as partners.

The Disruptive Power of the Internet

Information technology has long since evolved from being considered a "nice to have" to a business necessity. While most community foundations understand the importance of these technologies, most cannot afford the continuous technological upgrades or hire the required staff expertise. Too many community foundations are unable to provide their fundholders with what is now considered basic online account information. They also have been slow to utilize social media tools to advance their community convenings and grantmaking priorities due to budget constraints. If these trends are not reversed, it is difficult to imagine the next generation of tech-savvy donors perceiving community foundations as being capable or competent stewards of their charitable contributions. Community foundations that are unable to offer online and social media tools will be marked as relics of the past rather than leaders of the future.

The Internet has fundamentally changed how people give and how they become informed about what causes to support. For all but the most complicated gift transactions, donors can give directly through the Internet via a credit card transaction and increasingly through their cell phones. Similarly, *Googling* has become a new verb. Every donor can now conduct their own Internet research or engage their social networks to crowdsource ideas and experiences about nonprofit organizations locally, nationally, and around the world. Whether or not Internet research is a viable substitute for what an experienced donor engagement or program officer can provide is not the real question, which is: Do donors see enough value added to pay for expert advice over the information they can get online for free?

Changing Donor Behavior and Expectations

Donors are fast changing how they view engagement, legacy, and perpetuity. Over the last several decades, donor attitudes have changed with regard to giving. Rather than giving up control of their giving to others who decide how their contributions can best be used, both individuals and corporations desire more involvement and engagement. Corporations have shifted from directing employees to whom and how to give (the traditional United Way model) to engaging employee groups to establish their own grantmaking interests while providing corporate resources to match employee contributions of time and money (Stahnke 2011). As discussed earlier, some donors increasingly appear less interested in leaving a philanthropic legacy for future generations.

These developing consumer trends about legacy will have significant implications for community foundations, especially those that have focused on building unrestricted assets. If the majority of donors now hope to spend out their resources in their lifetime, then community foundations will need to shift their focus to providing unique experiences and learning opportunities that excite and engage donor interests. In this new world, community foundation success will not be determined by how much they resemble private foundations by building endowment assets but how they engage people and institutions within their communities to take leadership positions.

More specifically, donors increasingly want to co-create in the learning. They seek to shape the agenda and participate in the implementation. This represents an enormous potential to engage the time, talent, and treasure of community members and their networks in new ways of making their communities vibrant places to live, work, and play. It could usher in a new renaissance for philanthropy and citizen engagement that would benefit and play to the natural strengths of community foundations. Imagine having access to the ideas, networks, and wealth of donors today to address key community problems rather than a fraction of income over time from a payout from an endowment and only limited donor engagement. Rather than being the "experts," community foundations become the guides, coaches, and partners on a philanthropic journey as families discover their passions for making their communities, however defined, better places. This is a fundamentally different relationship than most community foundations have today with donor-advisors, which is either to encourage them to donate to the community foundation's preestablished priorities or to passively transact their charitable interests.

What has occurred is a cultural shift in which information has been democratized and experts no longer have a power advantage in relationships. Patients no longer blindly follow the instructions of their doctors. They Google the treatments, they read blogs about the efficacy of various treatments and medicines, and they actively participate with their doctor in determining their care. The best doctors now encourage patients to do their own online research, direct them to websites, and encourage them to call or email with questions. Similarly, educators have come to expect that students are constantly fact-checking, in real time, their every statement during class and have learned to appreciate that it can result in better class dialogue and learning.

The survival of community foundations will require a change in approach to shared learning and co-experimentation with donor partners rather than a continued belief that they are the experts, possessing singular, unique, and accurate community knowledge. One example of this changing relationship is donor circles. Donor circles bring together groups of donors to learn about a topic area, pool their resources, and select projects and nonprofits consistent with their strategies. Silicon Valley Community Foundation (SVCF) has had some early success with its Donor Circles for the Arts, Environment, and Africa. In addition, SVCF's grantmaking and corporate social responsibility advisory services with over 150 companies and their employee committees have further confirmed the growing expectations that people have to participate in all facets of the decision-making process.

By engaging with donors as partners, community foundations have the opportunity to make them lifelong supporters of community and the issues for which they have passion. In turn, the community will benefit from the billions of dollars in the coming wealth transfer that they are prepared to spend today to help make communities and our world a better place. While donors may be unwilling to pay for information, analysis, and grant recommendations that they can increasingly get elsewhere for free, they may be willing to pay for unique learning experiences. The lesson of Starbucks is that people are paying a higher fee for a unique experience when they have *their* coffee, and it's not just for the coffee.

If community foundations are able to successfully engage donors, there is at least the possibility, no matter how remote, that some donors might change their views about legacy and decide to leave the community foundation a bequest. Unfortunately, the cultural and technological changes that are under way represent the new normal and will continue to make the community foundation's current financial model unsustainable. Serving communities in the future will require rethinking the business and financial models of community foundations.

The Future

Community foundations in the next decade, and beyond, will look very different than community foundations of the last 100 years. Historically, community foundations have operated as though each was the same in their values, approach to community building, investment acumen, and organizational capacity. This is not really surprising. When community foundations began, they were a small, tightknit group sharing their start-up experiences and lessons learned. Struggling to survive and often modeling themselves on the behavior of private foundations, they relied almost exclusively on financial measures—assets under management and annual fundraising totals—to measure their success. Because of this, community foundations developed a view of their field that is now counterproductive to their ongoing growth and development.

As an industry, community foundations have, at times, acted as if they were owner-operated franchises of a single company. In the most successful franchises, the customer experience is the same regardless of the franchise. For example, the French fries taste the same at nearly every McDonald's restaurant around the world. But community foundations do not offer the same experiences, products, or pricing. As an industry, community foundations more closely resemble institutions of higher education. Among institutions of higher education, there are community and private colleges, state universities, private research universities, and a growing number of online universities. All of these institutions actively provide students with access to higher education but define their niche and finance their institutions very differently. These institutions actively partner with each other to advance the cause of education while competing for faculty, students, and donors. The small private colleges do not necessarily see themselves competing with community colleges and the Ivy League schools do not necessarily see themselves as competing with state universities. Different types of educational institutions have developed very different value propositions and finance models.

The community foundation field has now matured to the point where their future will require them to experiment with different approaches and varying finance models to fit each community's needs and opportunities. Asset size will no longer be the singular measurement of success, and more appropriate measures will be developed to determine success at community building and leadership. As Ylvisaker predicted, we are seeing the development of community foundations that serve different and overlapping geographies. There also will be a proliferation of "kinds" of community foundations in the foreseeable future. One can expect not only differing scales of operation, from neighborhood to region and state, but also differential adaptations in form and style to diversifying constituencies, needs, and cultures (Ylvisaker 1989, 57; Carson 2013).

Examples abound of how community foundations are redefining their geographical reach. Silicon Valley cannot be found on a map, and the Silicon Valley Community Foundation focuses on meeting the local, national, and global interests of donors stretching from San Francisco to San Jose and increasingly from across the country and around the world. The Saint Paul Foundation has created a new umbrella, Minnesota Philanthropy Partners, to better address both local and state interests. The Kansas City Community Foundation created Greater Horizons, which serves donors and smaller community foundations across the nation. The Boston Foundation acquired the Philanthropic Initiative (a national consulting group) to better serve the national and international interests of their donors. The Puerto Rico Community Foundation changed its bylaws to position its work as supporting Puerto Rico as part of the interests of the entire Caribbean. And the Chicago Community Trust has begun to look at how multiple, overlapping government agencies with different geographic responsibilities are constraining the economic development of the greater Chicago region.

In virtually every business, scale and volume matter to lower costs. Mergers and sharing back office operations will need to be considered by community foundations. The SVCF is itself the product of an unprecedented mega-merger in 2007 between Peninsula Community Foundation and Community Foundation Silicon Valley, and there is much that can be learned from their example (Rae-Dupree 2011).

In the future, hyperlocal, regional, national, and even global community foundations will no doubt exist, with each in some way contributing to the building of community to address critical community issues. Their definitions of the *community* that is served will be different, and they will likely rely on different financing models and have different measures of success. There also will be community foundations that do not promote a leadership agenda consistent with the values of their community. Like some universities (Lewin 2011), we may see once exclusively local community foundations open offices in other states and perhaps even other nations. Every community foundation will need to think through its individual strategy of how to respond to changing definitions of community and how that will affect their value proposition to build community and finance their operations.

New competitors offering donor-advised funds, various online giving options, changing consumer expectations, and evolving concepts of place and community will require community foundations to reimagine how they envision and carry out their work. The problems confronted by local communities are more complicated, in part, because they are increasingly influenced by global trends. Climate change is a good way to understand the interplay of local and global interests: Unless local communities around the world control their emissions, all will experience the adverse consequences. Poverty is a more nuanced but no less important example. The ability to sell goods and services around the world from one's home is fundamentally changing local industries and labor markets. Services are now bid online by providers around the world for legal, accounting, and other services. This global marketplace drives wages down for those in high-cost markets, while increasing the wages for those in low-cost markets. Local antipoverty efforts must, at a minimum, understand these new dynamics and may be able to use them to improve the quality of life in their communities.

Without question, community foundations have the ongoing potential to provide their local communities and our world with enormous benefits. However, the continued future of community foundations should not be taken for granted. For institutions that routinely refer to themselves as their community's best kept secret, who would lament their demise when average citizens in all but the smallest communities are unaware of their existence? As a field, community foundations must guard against believing that they are essential or indispensable to their community's future. Institutions of all kinds come and go based on whether they can remain relevant to the needs of their customers over time. If an organization does not remain relevant, then new structures and organizations arise to take their place.

The transformational cultural and technological shifts will require community foundations to rethink their value propositions and how they finance their work. Local will, of course, always matter; it is where people live their lives and where their daily quality of life is determined. However, how local is interpreted (neighborhood, census tract, city, state, or region) and framed against changing cultural and technological trends that make the world *glocal*—global and local—will require community foundations to experiment with different business and financing models (Carson 1997). Opportunities abound but require the courage and will to reassess old ideas and beliefs. In the future, there will likely be global, national, regional, and hyperlocal community foundations all behaving very differently from each other, but most—at their core—will likely promote community building and taking leadership roles as core value propositions. Embracing this future will ensure that community foundations will continue to ably serve their communities for the next century.

Bibliography

Bernholz, L., with E. Skloot and B. Varela. 2010. *Disrupting Philanthropy: Technology and the Future of the Social Sector.* Durham, NC: Center for Strategic Philanthropy and Civil Society, Sanford School of Public Policy, Duke University.

Berresford, S.V. 1989. "Collaboration: Models, Benefits, and Tensions." In *An Agile Servant: Community Leadership by Community Foundations,* ed. R. Magat, 137–146. New York: The Foundation Center.

Carson, E.D. 2013. "Redefining Community Foundations." *Stanford Social Innovation Review* (Winter): 21–22.

———. 2008. "The Myth of Community Foundation Neutrality and the Case for

Social Justice." In *Local Mission, Global Vision: Community Foundations in the 21st Century,* ed. P. deCourcy Hero and P. Walkenhorst, 65–76. New York: The Foundation Center.

———. 2005. "Standing at the Crossroads." *Foundation News & Commentary* 46, no. 1, 34–39.

———. 1997. *Grantmaking for the Global Village.* Washington, DC: Council on Foundations.

Casserly, M. 2013. "Mark Zuckerberg, Priscilla Chan, and the Most Generous Young Americans of 2012." *Forbes,* February 11. http://www.forbes.com/sites/meghancasserly/2013/02/11/mark-zuckerberg-priscilla-chan-and-the-most-generous-young-americans-of-2012/.

Drucker, P.F. 1993. *The Five Most Important Questions You Will Ever Ask About Your Nonprofit Organization.* San Francisco, CA: Jossey-Bass.

The Foundation Center. 2011. *Key Facts on Community Foundations.* Report, April. New York: The Foundation Center. http://foundationcenter.org/gainknowledge/research/pdf/keyfacts_comm2011.pdf.

Lewin, T. 2011. "Joining Trend, College Grows Beyond Name." *New York Times,* December 27. http://www.nytimes.com/2011/12/28/education/northeastern-university-expands-its-geographic-reach.html?pagewanted=all.

Mayer, S. 1994. *Building Community Capacity: The Potential of Community Foundations.* Minneapolis, MN: Rainbow Research.

Meyerson, A. 2012. "When Philanthropy Goes Wrong." *Wall Street Journal,* March 9. http://www.philanthropyroundtable.org/topic/donor_intent/when_philanthropy_goes_wrong.

Minter, S. 1989. "The Search for Standards: Why Community Foundations Are Different." In *An Agile Servant: Community Leadership by Community Foundations,* ed. R. Magat. New York: The Foundation Center.

Rae-Dupree, J. 2011. *Tying the Knot: The Founding of Silicon Valley Community Foundation.* Report, October. Mountain View, CA: Silicon Valley Community Foundation.

Reynolds, D. 2008. *The Balancing Act: II. The Role of a Community Foundation as a Vehicle for Philanthropy.* Report, September. Flint, MI: Charles Stewart Mott Foundation.

Schmidt, A. 2008. "Escaping the Perpetuity Mindset Trap." *Nonprofit Quarterly,* December 9. http://www.nonprofitquarterly.org/policysocial-context/748-escaping-the-perpetuity-mindset-trap.html.

Silicon Valley Community Foundation. 2012. http://www.siliconvalleycf.org.

Stahnke, K. 2011. "Employee Engagement and Corporate Social Responsibility for Generation Twitter." *Forbes,* November 1. http://www.forbes.com/sites/causeintegration/2011/11/01/employee-engagement-and-corporate-social-responsibility-for-generation-twitter/.

Wittstock, L., and T. Williams. 1998. *Changing Communities, Changing Foundations: The Story of the Diversity Efforts of Twenty Community Foundations.* Minneapolis: Rainbow Research.

Worldwide Initiatives for Grantmaker Support. 2010. Facts & Figures. In *Global Status Report on Community Foundations.* http://www.wings-community-foundation-report.com/gsr_2010/gsr_theme_facts/facts.cfm.

Ylvisaker, P.N. 1989. "Community and Community Foundations in the Next Century." In *An Agile Servant: Community Leadership by Community Foundations,* ed. R. Magat. New York: The Foundation Center.

4

Designing for What's Next

Grant Oliphant
The Pittsburgh Foundation

Nothing focuses the mind like being told you're doomed.

Emmett Carson clearly had that axiom in mind when he delivered a bombshell of an address to a gathering of the nation's community foundations at their annual conference in 2011. Emmett, who is CEO of the Silicon Valley Community Foundation and one of our field's leading lights and most provocative thinkers, wanted to shake the field out of what he saw as a dangerous complacency. To do that, he served up a short speech centered on a single bold assertion: The community foundation model is broken.

As in, busted, kaput, crushed, cracked, no longer working. Full stop.

It was a powerful statement delivered in just the right context. Most of the community foundations represented in the room were still reeling from the deepening impacts of the Great Recession. Many attendees had been forced to cut back on their grantmaking programs, curtail community initiatives, slash budgets, lay off staff, or some combination of the above. Featured at that conference was a panel of wealthy philanthropists who spoke of community foundations as essentially irrelevant to their charitable work, and a separate panel of competitors who did their best not to appear gleeful as they touted their success in stealing away the prospective donors that community foundations once considered theirs by right and tradition. Emmett's pronouncement fit neatly into this depressing cavalcade of gloom like the silvery hearse sliding into place at the head of a long gray line of dour-faced mourners.

For the assembled community foundation executives, the takeaway that year was inescapable: We are all going to die.

In fairness, that was not actually what Emmett said, nor, I suspect, what the organizers of that year's conference intended to convey. Also in fairness, the end-is-nigh warning served its purpose: In the months afterward, community foundation leaders finally began a long-overdue discussion about the relevance of their model in a rapidly changing world. It was an important message and should be regarded as a crucial moment for a field that was desperately in need of a wake-up call.

But it was also wrong—and wrong not just in a trivial way but in the insidiously subversive way that always makes partial truths more dangerous than outright falsehoods. The idea that the community foundation model is broken contains the germ of a truth that is absolutely essential to the field's collective success in an uncertain future: that we must keep evolving to remain relevant and effective.

Unfortunately, the language of brokenness may actually get in the way of doing that as creatively as we otherwise might. It can launch us into an unproductive debate over whether it's true. (Almost invariably, most of the colleagues I have spoken with discount it in terms of their own foundations.) Or, just as bad, it can push us into a fruitless search for an easy cure or a quick fix. Neither response is adequate to meet the challenges we face.

To be clear, those challenges are profound. I am in violent agreement with Emmett and other like-minded colleagues on this point: We have problems, and they are not for the faint of heart. Our traditional fee-based model is ill-equipped to deal with sustained periods of market volatility and decline such as we experienced in the Great Recession. We are up against massive commercial competitors who already own their client relationships, can beat us like a drum on fees and technology, and are gobbling up a growing share of the philanthropic pie. The wealth advisors, lawyers, and accountants who are our primary bridge to prospective donors often have a financial incentive to steer clients into private foundations and trusts. Changing definitions of community in a more global, mobile America threaten to erode the value of our competitive identity. And shifts in giving patterns, donor interests, and online technology are reducing the need for philanthropic intermediaries.

That these dynamics are putting unprecedented stress on the community foundation model should be obvious. How could they not? It is important, though, for us to be clear on what we mean by that. Which model are we talking about?

The tendency is to think immediately in terms of our revenue model. A revenue model describes how an organization or industry monetizes its goods or services. It answers the sustainability question, How do we afford to stay in business? Even though this question applies uncertainly and unevenly to a field where many organizations have large endowments to sustain them, we can easily see how economic volatility, stiffer competition, and changing donor patterns would affect growth and threaten the survival of some organizations, especially those whose finances are marginal.

But as leaders of mission-driven organizations—we are nonprofits, after all—most of the community foundation heads I know and admire are focused on a larger question of purpose. They care about growth and keeping the doors open, of course, but what they really care about most passionately is *why* that matters. This is a classic business model question. A business model describes how an organization creates value and, as Harvard's Michael Porter (1985) might put it, addresses the unique role that organization plays in the value chain.

Now, if we are being honest with ourselves, we will acknowledge that no question exposes the Jekyll-and-Hyde split personality of our field faster than this one. For our communities, we most often state that value in terms of *our* ability to deliver impact, leadership, and change. For our donors, at least as expressed in our single largest product offering, the donor-advised fund (DAF), we tend to state that value in terms of *their* priorities, wishes, and discretion. I will leave it up to you to decide which of these personalities is Jekyll and which Hyde. No judgment—consider it your own personal bias test.

That tension was perfectly captured in a 2012 study by FSG (formerly known as Foundation Strategy Group) and CF Insights (Graves et al. 2012) on how community foundations engage with donor-advised funds. As a field, we often rationalize the two halves of our being—the donor-centric side and the community-impact side—by suggesting that DAFs open a door to engaging donors in the community issues we care about. Unfortunately, the FSG/CF Insights study found that, as a rule, that's not actually what we do. The study found little alignment, or even attempts at alignment, between the priorities community foundations think are important and the giving patterns of donor advisors.

I am not entirely comfortable with that finding, since most of us who are attempting this alignment take an exceedingly long view about bringing donor advisors along a continuum of trust whereby they ultimately cede greater discretion to the foundations where their funds are housed. But here is what that study confirmed for me: As a field, we are still struggling to articulate and abide by the unique value proposition that we bring to the world of philanthropy. Our business model may not be broken, but studies like this suggest we are not exactly clear on what it is either, at least as manifested in our actions.

That is a terribly dangerous position for us to be in at a time like this. We are operating in a dynamic, fast-paced, fiercely competitive, Darwinian landscape. That shifting terrain is forcing us to vie for relevance in two races simultaneously: the race for new donors, who have more options and broader interests today than ever before; and the race for impact, in a world where our resources seem perpetually outmatched by the ever-expanding scale of need.

As I see it, the dual nature of this struggle is precisely what defines us. These two strands are the double helix of the community foundation species, the strands of DNA that, wrapped tightly one around the other, represent the core of the community foundation model and the very essence of our value proposition. More than a bridge between donors and community, we are the peculiar alchemy that happens when they meet and transform simple charity into purposeful philanthropy. If that is true and this is in fact our distinctive niche in the philanthropic ecosystem, then we need to be crystal clear on it, guard it jealously, and work constantly to keep updating its relevance into whatever new era is coming.

So how might we think differently about this whole question of our model and our place in the world? What would be a more productive response than either going on about our business as though we are immune to the changes around us or panicking hysterically over our imminent demise?

Not long after I arrived home from that 2011 conference, a man named Neil Alexander came to the Pittsburgh Foundation to meet with me. Just before that meeting, I was sitting at my desk working on a TEDx talk about what our society can learn from people who are facing consequential, life-altering countdowns. Neil, it turned out, had just been diagnosed with ALS, Lou Gehrig's disease, an unpredictable but certain countdown to an early and terrible death. I marvel at the timing of his visit—and at the courage he and his wife displayed in that meeting. Still in their early forties, parents to two young children, they refused to be undone by the difficult hand life had dealt them. They wanted the end of Neil's life, however long that might be, to be about helping others, and they wanted to do it through us because that way his legacy would be woven into the community he loved.

Every community foundation leader could share a similar story and many others like it, but here is why I share this one. What I learned from studying the example of people like Neil, people who face terrible countdowns with amazing courage, is how they find a way to triumph in a way by reacting with what I came to call "fierce acceptance." To me, this reaction is radically different from the passive resignation we typically think of as acceptance. It seems to be characterized by four distinct responses, which I summarize as:

> Life has changed.
> Time has changed.
> But I can still . . .
> . . . Act.

The first response is a sudden, sharp focus on the situation at hand. People like Neil, when faced with a truly consequential countdown, move quickly past denial and acknowledge their situation for what it is, how their lives and circumstances have changed. Whatever hard new shape reality has taken for them, they name it and own it. However much they would like to be somewhere else or someone else, they are absolutely clear on what is happening to them and what the stakes are.

The second response is to get very serious about time and what Martin Luther King, Jr., called the "fierce urgency of now" in his historic 1963 "I Have a Dream" speech. No matter the countdown they have been given—to the end of a life, the death of a marriage, the loss of a dream, the certainty of a future—these individuals suddenly measure time differently than most of us do. They are totally and completely present in *this* place and *this* moment in their lives. The concept of "now" has a power for them that most of us can hardly comprehend.

The third response is to reframe their situation around what is still possible. Yesterday's dreams may no longer seem possible or relevant. But rather than define themselves by the hopes they have lost, these individuals focus instead on a new set of possibilities, representing the outcomes they still might affect. They somehow shift their thinking from what they can no longer do to what they still can.

The fourth and final response is simply to act on these new possibilities. Whatever these individuals have identified as still possible for them to do, they do. They behave bravely. They stand up for a principle, help a friend, write a manifesto, or deliver a globally celebrated last lecture. They offer up an overdue apology, provide for their loved ones, or whisper a long-forgotten prayer. Some even start a fund at a community foundation. The actions are as varied as the circumstances and people involved, but what they all have in common is the transformation that happens when people move beyond their perceived powerlessness and act.

Since meeting Neil and learning from his example and others, I have often wondered what it would look like if our community and country were to apply this concept of fierce acceptance to the major societal countdowns we encounter every day. These are the countdowns measurable in lives lost to senseless violence, futures ruined by failing schools, health destroyed by environmental toxins and inadequate health care, coastline lost to global warming, and on and on—all the countdowns we experience where the costs of denial and inaction pile up a little higher each day, like grains of sand at the bottom of an hourglass threatening ultimately to bury us beneath the consequences of our indifference and inaction. What would it be like if we took these countdowns as seriously as the ones many of us face in our personal lives and that some heroically transform through fierce acceptance?

I find this to be a helpful filter for me when I assess our community change work at the Pittsburgh Foundation. It grounds us in time and space in a way that all the lofty ambitions and grandiose plans never can or will.

The same filter could be helpful to community foundations as we confront our own existential angst on the verge of a second century. What would happen if we, as institutions and as a field, applied this notion of fierce acceptance to this moment in our history?

I think the first step we would take is to see our situation more realistically. We would acknowledge that we are experiencing an extreme period of what Clayton Christensen (1997) at Harvard University terms "disruptive innovation," when so much is in flux that almost all the old models are being challenged to find their way in an evolving world. Commercial competitors, new technologies, social media, shifting community loyalties and donor habits, the unbundling of philanthropic services—all of these are disrupting our model not because we are broken, but because that is the world we are living in. This is today's normal; this is how life has changed, and not just for us but for every industry with a pulse. None of our natural human impulses—to wish it away, ignore it, or curl up in a corner sucking our collective thumbs—will help. The situation is perhaps best captured by the cliché: It is what it is.

The second step we would take is to treat time differently. We would act as though what we do now really matters. When I speak about this point publicly, I illustrate it with a wayfinder sign pointing off to destinations like "Bewildered," "Disoriented," and "Perplexed." The community foundation field has been standing at that intersection for years. Questions about the future of the field's business model were clearly laid out in *On the Brink of New Promise: The Future of U.S. Community Foundations* (Bernholz, Fulton, and Kasper 2005), a seminal report informed in part by concerns being expressed at the time by Emmett Carson. That was a full six years before his Big Speech, so why was it such a shock to the system to be reminded of those concerns in 2011?

In a period of disruptive change, every moment counts. The issue is not whether community foundations are going to wither up and die. The issue is whether we are going to persist as robust and growing centers of meaningful philanthropy. Will we be as relevant as we possibly could be in the years ahead? Will we be making the sort of difference we could be in our communities? Or will we be content to play whatever diminished role is left after the innovations happening around us rob us of the growth and impact opportunities that might have been ours? The answers to these questions lie very much in what we do today. We can no longer be patient with the voices in our ranks, and in our own heads, telling us that everything will be okay—that all we have to do is just continue on as we always have.

That, of course, leads us to the third step that fierce acceptance might prod us into taking: We would shift and reframe this conversation from what we can no longer do to what we still can. If this is our moment, then let us accept that, as a field, we can no longer take our place in the philanthropic ecosystem for granted; the supposed halcyon days when we were the default choice for donors, if they ever existed, are gone for good. But what we can still do is fight for our rightful place in that ecosystem. If the changes happening around us represent the threat, then the only viable answer is to counter those changes with innovations of our own. We need to stop viewing this as a rescue mission to fix a broken model and start viewing it as an innovation challenge, a call to continuously rethink, reimagine, and reinvent our way forward.

Here we will need to acknowledge a hard truth about foundations in general, and this applies even to community foundations, although I would argue less so: We are not inherently designed to respond nimbly to a changing environment. Those of us blessed with endowments meant to endure in perpetuity are sitting on a great big pile of what got us here. Lofty though that perch might be, it is always a difficult place to peer out from if you want to see the road ahead instead of the road behind. At the same time, those of us who for the most part are not endowed—either because we are too new or have donors who want to spend down their wealth in their lifetimes—theoretically should be more nimble; we tend, however, to lack the long view that would allow us to escape the whims and vicissitudes of immediacy.

This is where fierce acceptance differs so radically from resignation. Its last and most defining impulse is to actually do what one still can, to take action, regardless of how difficult or unpleasant or unnatural that might be.

And that leads us to the fourth step we would take if we applied this thinking to our field. No, we are not ideally suited for innovation, but we can innovate, and so that is what we need to do. Organizations that emerge successfully from periods of disruption, it seems to me, are invariably the ones that advance to the reframing and action stages of their own moments of fierce acceptance. The idea is not to find a single fix to the challenges we face, but to create, as many companies and industries have done, a process and culture of change that allows our institutions to remain in step with the donors and communities we serve and that together make our mission possible. In a changing environment, the point is not to have a perfect crystal ball that points us to a predictable outcome; it is to start making educated guesses and experimenting with them.

I suppose all of this could sound very grim, but I do not see it that way. I think this is probably the most exciting time in the history of our field. Change is inevitable; survival, or at least staying where we are, is not. But why are we so afraid of that? Community foundation leaders today have an unprecedented chance to reframe our institutions around a new set of possibilities and to strengthen the unique role we play in our communities. We have the opportunity to make our business model more robust than ever before by fashioning it more explicitly around impact and more aggressively connecting donors with the opportunity to share in the results.

These institutions are an extraordinary gift that have been placed in our care, not to put on a dusty shelf somewhere with the hope of not breaking them, but to keep as vital and healthy and relevant as they were when they were created. Using this period of disruption to help community foundations and this field become better off than we found them is not only our opportunity but our obligation.

I take my cue in our work at the Pittsburgh Foundation from the human-centered design movement, a process of innovation created at places like Stanford University's "d-school" and popularized recently in Peter Sims's book *Little Bets: How Breakthrough Ideas Emerge from Small Discoveries* (2011). The key elements of design thinking are *empathy,* which simply means engaging the people you are trying to help in a process of discovering what they really want and need; *prototyping,* which means offering up little experimental solutions; *testing* those solutions and *failing* fast, which means letting the flaws in those experiments be exposed quickly; and *repeating* the process often enough until you get it right. In Pittsburgh, we have used this thinking, although not always so logically and certainly not so elegantly, to launch a host of innovations in recent years, including experiments in collaborative grantmaking with our donors, tackling tough advocacy agendas, staking out difficult leadership roles in our community, opening up our investment platform to third-party advisors, converting private foundations, engaging in civic journalism, helping nonprofits become more self-sufficient through new technology and social media, and several others. Every one of these initiatives has evolved, and many still are, through a process of listening, prototyping, experimenting, failing, refining, and moving on.

The good news is that we are far from alone. In fact, as the stories shared elsewhere in this book attest, we are just one of many colleague foundations that have begun experimenting in similarly ambitious ways. Many community foundations around the country are demonstrating that we have gotten the message: This is a time for creativity.

The Council on Foundations' Community Foundation Leadership Team, a group tasked by our peers to look out for the field's broader interests, recently arrived at the same conclusion as we dove into this question of the future of the community foundation business model. After considering a traditional study process, the members of this group decided such an approach would be just one more trip inside the echo chamber in a field that has already had plenty of those. Instead, they chose to partner with the Monitor Group on a fieldwide design initiative, intended to engage people inside and outside the field in crafting a broad range of innovations that might help shape the community foundation of tomorrow.

We are motivated by a conviction that community foundations are not some tired, broken-down philanthropic appliance waiting either to be restored to the mint condition they enjoyed in some mythic better days or, worse, kicked to the curb for their final journey to philanthropy's scrap bin. They are, rather, a great and noble idea that many of us would argue has yet to reach its real potential.

One of the people I considered in my study of countdowns and fierce acceptance was Randy Pausch, the late Carnegie Mellon University professor whose famous "last lecture" became a global Internet sensation and then a bestselling book published as he was dying of pancreatic cancer. In that book, Pausch wrote of the obstacles, the "brick walls," that stand between us and our dreams. "The brick walls are not there to keep us out," he wrote. "The brick walls are there to give us a chance to show how badly we want something. Because the brick walls are there to stop the people who don't want it badly enough" (Pausch 2008, 52).

Community foundations are not broken. We just have a wall to climb. What lies on the other side is an opportunity to deliver on our missions more powerfully, and with greater resources, than ever before. The only question is whether we want that badly enough.

Bibliography

Bernholz, L., K. Fulton, and G. Kasper. 2005. *On the Brink of New Promise: The Future of U.S. Community Foundations.* New York: Monitor Group. http://www.monitorinstitute.com/downloads/what-we-think/new-promise/On_the_Brink_of_New_Promise.pdf.

Christensen, C.M. 1997. *The Innovator's Dilemma: When New Technologies Cause Great Firms to Fail.* Cambridge, MA: Harvard Business Press.

Graves, R. et al. 2012. *Do More Than Grow: Realizing the Potential of Community Foundation Donor-Advised Funds.* Report. Washington, DC: Council on Foundations. http://cfinsights.org/Knowledge/ViewArticle/ArticleId/25/Do-More-than-Grow-Realizing-the-Potential-of-Community-Foundation-Donor-Advised-Funds.aspx.

Pausch, R. 2008. *The Last Lecture.* New York: Hyperion.

The Pittsburgh Foundation. 2012. http://pittsburghfoundation.org.

Porter, M. 1985. *Competitive Advantage: Creating and Sustaining Superior Performance.* New York: Free Press.

Sims, P. 2011. *Little Bets: How Breakthrough Ideas Emerge from Small Discoveries.* New York: Free Press.

5

The Digital Age Foundation

Mariam C. Noland
The Community Foundation for Southeast Michigan

Eric Newton
The John S. and James L. Knight Foundation

For generations, the mission of community foundations has been remarkably stable. They are a "special double trust," honoring the wishes of thousands of benefactors and advancing new visions for communities (Noland 1989). In this new century, while the basic idea of pooling money to improve community life has not changed, nearly everything else has.[1]

American society has entered a new digital age (Bernholz 2007). Our emerging information economy is accelerating the "creative destruction" of key industrial-age institutions. Almost everything that matters to community foundations—flows of information and money, behavior of citizens and consumers, models of business and leadership, even the way we define community—is changing. We have swiftly entered a new era of philanthropy, "so new, its implications and opportunities have yet to be fully described" (Fulton and Blau 2005).

Some community foundations see this metamorphosis as an opportunity to strengthen the "special double trust." They believe digital tools can help them increase impact by engaging the whole community. They see a networked, digital society as one in which they might more easily lead. Lacking, though, is a sense of urgency to match the accelerating forces of change. This chapter will explore ways a Digital Age Foundation, one that takes up the digital transformation in earnest, would better fulfill its historic mission.

The first step requires an acknowledgement that the world is indeed in a profoundly new age of human communication, changing society "so fundamentally there is absolutely no going back" (Prensky 2001). At the heart of this change are two developments: (1) content once exclusive to mass media now can be created and shared by anyone, and (2) mobile devices, along with the Internet, have created a world connected by one digital network. As a consequence, news and information have become "personal, portable, and participatory" (Purcell 2011). Because media is "an extension of the human mind," it shapes who we are and what we do (McLuhan and Fiore 1967). A new kind of post-institutional digital age society is evolving, moving from the exclusivity of expert and elite governance to the inclusivity of "participatory culture" (Jenkins 1992). Many important trends—immigration, resegregation, population shifts, distrust of civic institutions—are accelerating within the rapidly transforming media ecosystem. We face an increasingly unfamiliar and fluid world, one in which our polarized digital cocoons make data easier to find yet agreement harder to achieve, in which government is shrinking and leadership seems scarce.

Suddenly, venerable community institutions fear for their very existence. Among the oldest of those is the daily newspaper. Its story as an institution in decline is one community foundations should heed. For two centuries, dailies have been America's leading local news source. Now they struggle to survive. From 2007 to 2011, some 15,000 local journalism jobs were lost. Reporting is back to 1970s levels; there are large gaps in "local accountability journalism" (Waldman et al. 2011). In major cities like Detroit and New Orleans, the daily printed home-delivered newspaper is history. There, citizens get a print version only three or four days a week. This is but the beginning. If current patterns hold, one study projects that the nation's last daily printed newspaper will roll off the press in the first quarter of 2043 (Meyer 2004).

A good newspaper's mission can mirror the mission of a good community foundation. As editor and publisher Jack Knight wrote: "We seek to bestir the people into an awareness of their own condition, provide inspiration for their thoughts and rouse them to pursue their true interests" (Knight 1969). That goal infused the Knight Ridder company, a bastion of journalism excellence until, in the digital age, it was dissolved. Both newspapers and community foundations seek to know their communities intimately to help them succeed. Given this, it is not surprising that the John S. and James L. Knight Foundation (funded by Jack, his brother Jim, and their mother, Clara) works to improve both journalism and community foundations. Neither foundations nor democracy itself can function well without healthy information flows; in recent years, community foundations have increased media funding. To some, filling the news gap is becoming a leadership issue. The idea: A community needs healthy flows of news and information just as much as it needs good schools, safe streets, or clean air. In fact, it is difficult to see how any problems in a self-governing community can be solved without communication (FSG 2011a).

The same digital revolution upending institutional media is disrupting the way we spend and give money. Today, 71 percent of adult Americans use their credit cards online, and 20 percent have made charitable contributions online. Some 90 percent of U.S. adults own cell phones, and 10 percent have made mobile contributions (Smith 2012a). Though e-commerce is only 10 percent of national commerce, its growth rate is four times that of offline commerce (comScore 2012; U.S. Census Bureau 2012). As early as 2020, experts believe that cash "will have mostly disappeared" (Smith, Anderson, and Rainie 2012).

Technological shifts are producing new competitors to community foundations. Since Fidelity Charitable started the trend in 1991, commercial charity funds have grown rapidly. Just two commercial entities, including Fidelity, have collected or distributed a total of $23 billion in charitable funds (Fidelity Charitable 2011a; Vanguard 2012). Even newer are Internet-based *crowdfunding* platforms, developed in the past decade and growing exponentially. As of 2012, Razoo claimed $98 million in funds raised (Razoo 2012), Kiva (2012) reported $333 million in loans, and Kickstarter (2012) recorded $289 million in donations. MobileCause, saying it serves 40 percent of U.S. nonprofits, predicted mobile giving will soar to $17 billion a year by 2017 (PRNewswire 2012). Many digital age–donor relationships are starting with simple text messages.

Community foundations have a local mission, whereas these generic technological platforms do not. This could lead one to think that local foundations have a competitive edge. After decades of strong growth, however, the expansion of community foundations in the United States appears to be leveling off. Endowment reserves peaked at $56.7 billion in 2007; annual giving topped out at $4.5 billion in 2008, and the highest number of community foundations recorded, 737, came in 2009 (Lawrence 2012). A combined endowment of $56.7 billion is a significant achievement in a field that, compared to other community institutions, is relatively new. Yet most of this success has come without harnessing the power of digital media.

Today, computer-based technology does more than transport information and money. It affects how society fixes problems. Media "shapes and controls the scale and form of human association and action" (Mortensen 2008). Even when new technology is disruptive, in the end it can be a "positive force," turning complex and expensive systems into simple, easy, accessible, and affordable ones (Christensen 2003). Community foundations do complex work that could be done easier with better tools. They face myriad balancing acts. Foundations seek creative solutions but respect prevailing norms; they stay flexible but keep a long-term perspective; they quickly identify new needs and opportunities but move cautiously; and they serve individual donors but also the entire community. Community foundations deal with multiple constituencies, choosing "doable" activities that are right-sized for impact, and leverage that support with "positive visibility" (Noland 1989).

A Digital Age Foundation would not shy away from technology; it would seize it as a new opportunity to advance community. Technology, in theory, both breaks and fixes the community foundation model. A Digital Age Foundation would understand its media ecosystem, be a fluent communicator, and help the community get the information it needed. It would enlist digital tools to help local nonprofits learn how to better manage their constituencies, finances, and boards. It would be a respected convener in both physical space and cyberspace, bridging social fault lines to help people solve problems and seeking to master the science of engagement and impact. Perhaps most important, it would create a culture of continuous change, both within the community and its own walls. A Digital Age Foundation would use this new capacity to lead, to remain relevant, to honor its benefactors, and to help its community prosper.

The transformation to becoming a true Digital Age Foundation may not be easy. There are historical, cultural, and philosophical roadblocks. Foundations will need to invest in new tools and new staff as they seek to improve community information, engagement, and leadership.

The argument for better technology grows larger when one considers the many different styles of foundation grantmaking. They range from the reactive to highly prescriptive, from banker to venture capitalist, from independent to collaborative, from minimal to continuous contact, from basic tracking to formal evaluation, from limited community involvement to direct involvement. Further increasing in complexity are the grants themselves, often tailored to the wishes of local donors, ranging from general support to specific projects, from small to large, from one-time to long-term (Noland 1989).

Digital tools can handle this kind of complexity. They can empower even the smallest community foundation to enhance its effectiveness. A program officer could write into the dynamic database once and watch that prose emerge in whatever formats are needed: grant summaries, press releases, grant agreements, website stories, and so on. Yet the technologies so common to competitors are not widely used at community foundations. "We will never be the Jetsons," said one foundation president, "because when I got here we were the Flintstones." This suggests change requires additional or different staff, newly trained and differently equipped.

A Digital Age Foundation would automate its routine tasks to allow more time for strategic discussions. Many new debates loom: Are program-related investments needed to harness the power of markets? Can intellectual property policies help maximize public benefit and avoid inappropriate private benefit?

Can the digital age value of transparency be balanced with donor desires for anonymity? If the first strategic decision is not to become more digital, how will we meet increasing demands for clarity, accountability, and impact?

All community foundations are independent. Some are quite small. In the digital age, these can be advantages. Small can mean nimble. Independence can mean a problem could be as simple or complex as foundation leaders wish to make it. In that spirit, the mantra of our imagined Digital Age Foundation is just three words: Inform. Engage. Lead.

Informing Communities

Each community has its own unique information flow. Networks of civic leaders, clergy, schools, business, unions, and voluntary associations all contribute. Yet no American institution has been more important to informing communities than the press (Commission on Freedom of the Press 1947). The lessons of its erosion are illustrative. Some 100 years ago, newspapers were the "schoolhouse of the masses" (Council on Foundations 2013). From World War II on, however, they fell behind as each generation saw new technologies emerge: radio, television, computers, the Internet, smartphones, and tablets. In the mid-1940s, American households each bought an average of 1.2 newspapers; today, that number has dropped by two-thirds. Most printed newspapers embraced neither the technology nor the concurrent digital age values of immediacy, transparency, and interactivity.

Today, as printed newspapers shrink, other institutions are rising to take on its agenda-setting leadership function. Universities are building on the "teaching hospital model" of journalism education to become community content providers. Public broadcasting is trying to shake its own sluggish history and become more locally relevant. Community foundations are funding media. In some communities, these three groups represent the same people: A major donor might give equally to a university, a public broadcaster, and a community foundation in the same city. Such donors may prefer the old assembly-line form of mass media even as their communities are networking and going digital.

To be a trusted communicator, however, a Digital Age Foundation must avoid both the slowness to change and the arrogance that plagued the worst newspapers: the notion that knowing a city's leaders means knowing what is good for the community, no matter what the people themselves say. It is difficult for legacy institutions to replace elite leadership models with new ones based on immediacy, interactivity, and transparency. To become a fluent communicator, a foundation would keep these elements of transformation in mind.

Discovery

Discovery of the facts can save money and time. Foundations need to understand modern information flows. This can be accomplished by mapping the community media ecosystem on a key issue or issues. Some communities are information deserts; others are rain forests. Mapping education news flows, for example, goes beyond the obvious conclusion (the local newspaper has laid off the education reporter). Expert websites or blogs might be major sources, or social media, or public databases, or mobile applications. Mapping can be as sophisticated as a major study or as simple as a scavenger hunt (Knight Foundation 2012a). Foundations can gather community leaders to map media around a key issue, strengthening their role as neutral conveners.

Know-How

Know-how separates success from failure in the digital age. This means foundations must increase their communications capacity. In the digital age, everyone can tell his or her own story. Everyone includes community foundations. Foundation websites should be easy to change in real time from any location, offering opportunity for public comment. Foundations need to hire more digital people. A *digital lieutenant* will help choose vendors and translate the technology world. Interns are needed. *Digital natives,* the children of digital age technology, "think and process information fundamentally differently from their predecessors" (Prensky 2001). Most important is ongoing digital training for the entire staff. This is what helped NPR make the transition from radio to multimedia (TCC Group 2011).

Vision

Vision is required to increase and improve digital information flows. Winners of the Knight Community Information Challenge showed this. The challenge, a $24 million project launched in 2008, matched community foundation investments in news and information. The projects were as different as the communities themselves. In a survey, community foundation leaders said these different projects were united by a single vision: They needed better information flows to make progress on the issues they cared about (FSG 2011a). Though overly broad projects and those without digital media expertise struggled, in general, funding (or being a source) of accurate, contextual nonprofit news not only helped the communities but increased the community foundation's visibility and impact as well as the community's trust that the foundation knows the landscape.

Whether their Knight Challenge projects were for neutral content creation, supporting media outlets, influencing policy, increasing digital media literacy, or running advocacy campaigns, community foundations saw the value. Originally, few foundations said "media funding" was part of their mission; by the end of the four-year project, nearly one in four were converts: "To a great extent," they said, news and information grants had provided them "a unique opportunity to play a leadership role in their community," and they planned to increase such grantmaking in the future (FSG 2011b).

Courage

Courage is required to be a true digital age content provider, particularly in the areas of interactivity and transparency. Today's participatory culture demands two-way communication, supporting, even mentoring, those who wish to carry on a conversation, showing them their contributions matter, and helping provide some degree of social connection with each other (Jenkins 2006). In this context, donors to media projects, unlike others, should be known to the community. This and other elements of a foundation's information ethic, such as social media policies, should be available to content users so they have standards by which to judge the foundation or grantee.

Significant trust can be garnered by those who replace the straightforward, factual information being lost in the decline of printed newspapers. People need facts to solve problems. Stories that expose *negative* situations are in the long view *positive*—admission of a problem is the first step toward its solution. This philosophy departs from a traditional foundation view that media means public relations and every item must be positive. Foundations will need thicker skins to be able to handle an influential donor who does not like a foundation-funded information project. Frank discussion of the roles and responsibilities of information providers in advance of such moments would serve foundation leaders well.

These should not seem like simple steps. The Knight Foundation adopted these four elements—discovery, know-how, vision, and courage (and a fifth, tenacity)—as the essential ingredients of transformation. They have been applied not only to Knight's grantmaking, but to the ongoing project that is the transformation of the foundation itself (Knight Foundation 2012a). This five-step process could apply to community foundations as they build new modes, networks, and institutions to increase local information flows.

Engaging Communities

Informing communities is essential, but it's not enough. Information by itself does not change behavior. Only when a person, group, or whole community engages with a piece of data (or with a news story of an event, or a debate on a larger issue) does something change (The Knight Commission 2009). To know what is getting traction in a community, foundations need relationships. A Digital Age Foundation defines community engagement as the process of building lasting relationships with others who also seek a better community. This is a traditional community foundation mission; the digital age gives it new dimensions and requirements. Increasingly, two major values drive engagement—inclusiveness and place-making.

Scholars considering *social capital,* the value to society of the social relationships between people, are concerned about decreasing trust in institutions, less volunteering and charitable work, and lower expectations of others (Putnam 2000). Yet many fail to consider the effect of cyberspace on these real-world activities. The important point is not that bowling leagues are fewer, but that much larger groups are flocking to multiplayer games such as *World of Warcraft* and continuing their relationships offline. Digital foundations would expand the term *social capital* to include both online and offline activities.

Engagement requires inclusiveness and mutual respect. This is especially true when bridging the social fault lines and fissures of "gender, race, generation, geography and class" (The Maynard Institute 2012). As Henry Jenkins (2006) of UCLA explains, a sense of open invitation is essential: "Not every member must contribute, but all must believe they are free to contribute when ready and that what they contribute will be appropriately valued." People are more likely to engage when they think it matters. Interfaces like SeeClick-Fix.com work best when users see the potholes repaired. Providing metrics on projects, showing what they are really accomplishing, should increase engagement.

The same principles apply to seeking new donors. When a foundation meets people "where they are" to raise money, it begins a relationship, whether that is in a face-to-face meeting or via cell phone. In time, the foundation can help show the donor what it knows about the community, draw them into local issues, into a sense of what community means to their business, their children, their future. Foundation leaders do this now in physical space. The challenge is expanding that into cyberspace.

Examples of early community foundation use of digital technology are *giving days,* where donors are asked on a given day to contribute to a group or cause, or *flash philanthropy,* in-the-moment fundraising. In 2009, for example, a giving day was sponsored by the Community Foundation for Southeast Michigan (CFSEM) in the hopes of raising $3 million for arts and cultural groups. Despite software problems, it secured $4.9 million. One new donor, attracted by friends through social media, described the effort as "a ray of sunshine" (CFSEM 2009). Other examples, from Minnesota to Kentucky, use platforms like Razoo and GuideStar to help citizens learn about nonprofits and donate by credit card. Though few community foundations have done them, a Digital Age Foundation would consider giving days and flash philanthropy to be only very early versions of what's coming.

The digital age offers new ways of taking advice from a cross-section of the entire community. Public Insight Network, developed by Minnesota Public Radio (MPR), provides open source software used to contact large groups of citizens from a variety of disciplines to help with news stories. This *crowdsourcing* method is being used by scores of newsrooms (MPR 2012). Before it needs specific help, the news organization enlists an army of volunteers who have agreed to be interviewed. The same software could be used by foundations to crowdsource topics of interest, a type of "public insight philanthropy." Coupled with another piece of free software, the proportional voting system Selectricity, a foundation could find out from several thousand community members how they ranked community issues or solutions to a particular problem. Popular understanding of and support of a solution translates into greater impact.

A Digital Age Foundation would become expert at place-making, using the global medium of the Internet to help build community. Though technology "greatly enlarges the potential public sphere," it has not freed us from geography. "Most of us are social creatures who would still rather go to the ballpark once in a while than watch every game on TV" (Meyer 2004). America's political system is geo-tagged. A resident of Detroit can't (at least not yet) vote for the mayor of San Francisco. The digital age has enlarged the notion of community, made it more elastic, but has not eliminated geographic communities. We may commute to work, but most of us still worship, educate our children, eat, sleep, and live in just one place at a time.

Community attachment is linked to local GDP growth. The *Soul of the Community* study in 26 U.S. communities examined what makes people feel connected to where they live (Knight Foundation 2012a). It found that community attachment is linked to social offerings, openness, and aesthetics more than it is linked to work or schools. This mirrors economic development philosophies emphasizing "creative class" workers from technology, entertainment, journalism, finance, high-end manufacturing, and the arts who are looking for "acceptance, diversion, and beauty" (Florida 2012). In this sense, place-making means supporting programs in public spaces, like the arts, that bring people together and strengthen their attachment to community.

In short, by respecting inclusiveness and place-making, by making connections between cyberspace, the Digital Age Foundation would engage its community and avoid making the same mistakes others, particularly newspapers, have made. Community foundations, in fact, are uniquely positioned to combine digital and traditional face-to-face networking strategies between and among leaders from different local sectors.

Leading Communities

Leadership opportunities abound as disruptive technologies dissemble local institutions. For a foundation to take advantage of those opportunities, however, it must be able to harness the very forces that are creating them. This is the largest challenge to leadership: How does one engage community members in positive change while at the same time enlisting one's own colleagues to accomplish the task of creating a Digital Age Foundation?

Universities struggle with this as they hope to become stronger local leaders but must cope with students taking digital classes from other universities, with in some cases as many as 160,000 students in a single class. Businesses struggle with it when they would like to lead locally but instead end up chasing new revenues all over the globe. Community foundations struggle with it when they seek to lead without using the new tools.

Who should lead? Of the dozens of conflicting theories and models, one of the most attractive for Digital Age Foundations is that of the transformational leader. Such leaders aim to create major change, redesign perceptions, and alter expectations and aspirations. They lead by example, coaching and inspiring through an energizing vision and challenging goals (Bass and Riggio 2006). In a community-wide context, helping communities adopt such goals requires clarity.

Traditionally, foundations have found they lead best on issues in which they have standing. They earn standing in traditional ways: through their history of funding, or the size of their grants, through staff expertise or inside connections. In the digital age, standing can come equally from being an "honest broker," the authentic desire to inform and engage a community and to join in the search for a solution to whatever problem emerges as important. Both the expert approach and the engagement approach can work. The important point is not whether leadership happens behind-the-scenes or in a meeting hall of 2,000, but rather that leaders must clearly and transparently express their methods and goals.

Clarity helps define a foundation's focus. This in turn helps potential donors understand the foundation's value. It helps community members see where they can join with the foundation to make positive change. If program staff can't explain in clear and jargon-free terms what a grant will accomplish—how this advances donor strategy and how that helps the community—it will be difficult for anyone to honestly evaluate that grant, help improve it, or want to add to the dollars supporting it. For the modern community foundation, clarity is a key element of leadership.

A more traditional type of digital age leader is *adaptive*. These leaders can see changes and opportunities early on in their community and quietly influence those who can address those challenges (Crutchfield, Kania, and Kramer 2011). But such leaders face a dilemma: a multiplicity of donors on the one hand and community desires on the other can create a mosaic of interests that may or may not, in the foundation's judgment, align to deal with the community's true interest. The ability to be transformative or adaptive but also supportive—serving and protecting donor intentions—is perhaps the greatest balancing act of all. Today's community foundation leaders face the daily reality that many donors—some elderly, some not— may in their lifetimes use mobile technology not as an electronic wallet but to make phone calls. No matter how donors communicate, community foundation leaders still must reach them to seek the resources a foundation needs to serve the community.

The more a foundation focuses, the more difficult the balancing act may become. Creative solutions are needed. Here's one: *Crowdfunding*—many people using digital platforms to make micropayments—allows traditional donors to selectively match only the community programs and ideas that fit their funding strategy. This allows for independent leadership at the same time as engagement.

Another major leadership issue is foundation aversion to risk. The risk-reward tension increases as foundations want more social change for their dollars. Giving out fish is not enough, that's charity; teaching people to fish is not enough, that's routine philanthropy; reinventing fishing is what foundations want to do today. Yet innovation is not easy. It is based on a messy system of *failing forward,* the art of quickly failing, learning, and trying again immediately. Foundations that fund such efforts will find they cannot guarantee every dollar will get maximum social return; some experiments must fail in order to produce insights that lead to greater gains down the road. When a foundation's project of research and development, for example, pays off in an approach spread by government or business, the foundation has a clear argument that it and its work matter. Working with their boards, foundation leaders will need to find ways to get past the paralyzing embarrassment that today often accompanies any report of failure.

In the digital age, foundation leaders must transform their organizations before their organizations can best lead communities. They will need to staff up to meet more ambitious goals, add technology and communication staff to expand reach, and retrain everyone to increase productivity. Transformational leaders encourage such creativity and independent thinking, treating unexpected situations as opportunities to learn (Bass and Riggio 2006). Thus, the Digital Age Foundation will be a *learning organization.* Such organizations train nonstop. They are more adaptable, flexible, creative, and effective. Writes Peter Senge: "The organizations that will truly excel in the future will be the organizations that discover how to tap people's commitment and capacity to learn at all levels" (Senge 1990).

In a learning organization, "certain basic disciplines" are mastered by everyone. The challenge to community foundations: What are those disciplines? Grantmaking, certainly, in its myriad forms. But in a Digital Age Foundation, there are the new values to consider: the clarity and transparency of informing communities, the inclusiveness and place-making of engaging communities (including donors), and the clarity and vision needed for community leadership.

Conclusion

Community foundations once were revolutionary—and can be again. They mushroomed to counter the negative impacts of what lawyers call "the dead hand" constraining distributions from trusts. When donors were gone and their last wishes had become impossible, impractical, or unnecessary, a "living hand" had to reach in and help. The value proposition: You can't take your money with you, but if you care about this community, you can leave your wealth with an institution that will make it count. This seems elementary now, but was, nearly 100 years ago, a new idea: that local citizens could have the right to re-deploy bequests. From that pioneering notion, after the tax reform that began in 1969, the role of banks housing distribution committees gave way to the proliferation of modern community foundations (Magat 1989).

Foundations need to expand their vision. If railroads had seen themselves as being in the transportation business, they would have changed faster. If newspapers saw themselves in the information business, they would have changed sooner. If community foundations see themselves in the business of leadership, they will change more quickly. Community foundations that don't expand their vision may find the digital world has passed them by, their growth has vanished, and, despite what they may have promised donors, they have lost their standing as agents of the community.

How likely that is no one can say. If one takes the long view, it is reasonable to expect community foundations will eventually evolve, shaped as is all of society by larger forces. The industrial revolution sparked industrial philanthropy a generation later; the service industry created niche-oriented service philanthropy, including venture philanthropy, about a generation later; now, the digital revolution in commerce is sparking digital age philanthropy.

In addition, so many fundamental functions in the information economy are carried out through media, that it seems all organizations are starting to operate as a type of media (Kramer 2010). The time period of "eventually," however, may not be soon enough for some communities. When communities lose their way, bad things happen. In Bell, California, for example, a little city without a newspaper, officials paid themselves salaries so high they made away with more than $5 million before out-of-town reporters caught them. A community lost can quickly become a community ruined.

Innovation experts offer this recipe for technological change: (1) convince an organization that the new technology is a threat, so the dollars will be committed to change, then (2) create a new autonomous organization to make the changes, staffed with employees who see the new technology as an opportunity, not a threat (Christensen and Raynor 2003). This argues for the creation of a research and development center beyond anything currently in existence, specifically for the digital transformation of community foundations. Such an enterprise could easily be supported on $22.5 million a year, one half of one percent of the annual distributions of community foundations. On day one, its innovations would make giving days look passé. The center, partnering with existing groups such as the Nonprofit Technology Enterprise Network and the Technology Affinity Group, could help foundations reach millions of digital natives in ever-changing forms of media, and assist in designing the engagement systems that sign up new donors and help communities better solve problems.

"We must grasp the authentic beginnings of what information networks have enabled," writes strategy consultant Lucy Bernholz (2010), "and be prepared for faster, smarter, farther-reaching, and more innovative opportunities—for a philanthropy that's truly effective."

The dawn of the digital age offers a unique opportunity for community foundations to transform, differentiate their product, grow their business, expand their markets, and drive the health and vitality of their communities. What's more, digital tools provide the best chance yet for community foundations to know their constituents and communities as least as well, if not better, than everyone else. Yes, new tools and constant training will be needed to create the Digital Age Foundation. But the good news is that size doesn't matter as much in this world as it did in the old one. Caring about communities is what matters, and of their many attributes, community foundations have that in abundance.

Note

1. This view places us between foundation leaders such as Douglas Kridler (Columbus), Jennifer Leonard (Rochester), and Carleen Rhodes (Minnesota), who talk about community foundations "recalibrating," and Emmett Carson (Silicon Valley), who says "our financial model is broken" (Council on Foundations 2011).

Bibliography

Bass, B.M., and R.E. Riggio. 2006. *Transformational Leadership.* 2d ed. Mahwah, NJ: Lawrence Erlbaum.

Bernholz, L. 2007. "'See(ing) Through' Philanthropy." Philanthropy 2173. Blog, May 21. http://philanthropy.blogspot.com/2007/05/seeing-through-philanthropy. html.

Bernholz, L., with E. Skloot and B. Varela. 2010. *Disrupting Philanthropy: Technology and the Future of the Social Sector.* Durham, NC: Center for Strategic Philanthropy and Civil Society, Sanford School of Public Policy, Duke University.

Bernholz, L., K. Fulton, and G. Kasper. 2005. *On the Brink of New Promise: The Future of U.S. Community Foundations.* New York: Monitor Group. http://www. monitorinstitute.com/downloads/what-we-think/new-promise/On_the_Brink_of_ New_Promise.pdf.

Burke, A. 2012. "$123 Million Crowdfunding Market Nearly Quadrupled in a Year, Report Says." *Forbes*, March 30. http://www.forbes.com/sites/techonomy/2012/03/30/123-million-crowdfunding-market-nearly-quadrupled-in-a-year-report-says.

Christensen, C.M., and M.E. Raynor. 2003. *The Innovator's Solution: Creating and Sustaining Successful Growth.* Boston, MA: Harvard Business School Press.

Commission on Freedom of the Press. 1947. *A Free and Responsible Press: A General Report on Mass Communication.* Chicago, IL: University of Chicago Press.

Community Foundation for Southeast Michigan (CFSEM). 2013. http://cfsem.org.

———. 2009. "Detroit-Area Arts Organizations Praise CFSEM's Fundraising Challenge." News release, September 15. http://cfsem.org/media-center/articles/detroit-area-arts-organizations-praise-cfsem-s-fundraising-challenge.

Community Foundations. 2012. http://www.communityfoundations.net.

comScore. 2012. *State of the U.S. Online Retail Economy in Q1 2012.* Presentation, May 17. http://www.comscore.com/Insights/Presentations_and_Whitepapers/2012/ State_of_US_Online_Retail_Economy_Q1_2012.

Council on Foundations. 2013. *The IRS and Nonprofit Media: Toward Creating a More Informed Public.* Report of the Nonprofit Media Working Group. Arlington, VA: Council on Foundations and the John S. and James L. Knight Foundation. http://www.niemanlab.org/pdfs/IRSandNonprofitMedia-CouncilofFoundations. pdf.

———. 2011. "Is the Community Foundation Business Model Broken?" Twitter chat. Storify, November 14. http://storify.com/cof_/is-the-community-foundation-business-model-broken-twitter-chat.

Crutchfield, L.R., J.V. Kania, and M.R. Kramer. 2011. *Do More Than Give: The Six Practices of Donors Who Change the World.* San Francisco, CA: Jossey-Bass.

Fidelity Charitable. 2011a. "Fidelity Charitable Reports Record-Breaking Volumes for First Half of Year." News release, July 20. http://www.fidelitycharitable.org/ about-us/news/07-20-2011.shtml.

———. 2011b. *2011 Annual Report.* http://www.fidelitycharitable.org/2011-annual-report/annual-letter.shtml.

Florida, R. 2012. *The Rise of the Creative Class: Revisited.* New York: Basic Books.

The Foundation Center. 2012. Aggregate Fiscal Data by Foundation Type, 2010. Table. http://foundationcenter.org/findfunders/statistics/pdf/01_found_fin_ data/2010/02_10.pdf.

————. 2011. Change in community foundation giving and assets, 1981 to 2009. Table. http://foundationcenter.org/findfunders/statistics/pdf/02_found_ growth/2009/00_09.pdf.

FSG. 2011a. *Impact: A Guide to Evaluating Community Information Projects*. Report, February. Miami, FL: Knight Foundation. http://www.knightfoundation.org/ publications/impact-practical-guide-evaluating-community-inform.

————. 2011b. *2011 Reports from the Field: Community and Place-Based Foundations and the Knight Community Information Challenge*. Report, February. Miami, FL: Knight Foundation. http://www.knightfoundation.org/media/uploads/publication_pdfs/13511_KF_REP_FROM_FIELD_2–25-web.pdf.

Fulton, K., and A. Blau. 2005. *Looking Out for the Future: An Orientation for Twenty-First Century Philanthropists*. New York: Monitor Company Group. http:// www.monitorinstitute.com/downloads/what-we-think/looking-out-for-the-future/ Looking_Out_for_the_Future.pdf.

Heifetz, R.A., and M. Linsky. 2002. *Leadership on the Line: Staying Alive Through the Dangers of Leading*. Boston, MA: Harvard Business School Press.

Jenkins, H. 2006. "Confronting the Challenges of Participatory Culture: Media Education for the 21st Century (Part One)." Confessions of an Aca-Fan: The Official Weblog of Henry Jenkins, October 20. http://www.henryjenkins.org/2006/10/ confronting_the_challenges_of.html.

————. 1992. *Textual Poachers: Television Fans and Participatory Culture*. New York: Routledge.

The John S. and James L. Knight Foundation (Knight Foundation). 2012a. "Lessons Learned from Using the Community Information Toolkit." KnightBlog, February 21. http://www.knightfoundation.org/blogs/knightblog/2012/2/21/lessons-learned-from-using-the-community-information-toolkit/.

————. 2012b. http://www.knightfoundation.org.

————. 2010. "Got Love for Your Community? It May Create Economic Growth, Gallup Study Says." News release, November 15. http://www.knightfoundation.org/ press-room/press-release/got-love-for-your-community-it-may-create-economic/.

Kickstarter. 2012. Kickstarter stats. http://www.kickstarter.com/help/stats?ref= footer.

Kiva. 2012. Statistics. http://www.kiva.org/about/stats.

Knight, J.S. 1969. "The Philosophy of the Knight Newspapers." Remarks made by John S. Knight of the Knight Foundation, July 12. http://www.knightfoundation. org/press-room/other/philosophy-knight-newspapers.

The Knight Commission. 2009. *Informing Communities: Sustaining Democracy in the Digital Age*. Washington, DC: Aspen Institute.

Kramer, L. 2010. *C-Scape: Conquer the Forces Changing Business Today*. New York: HarperBusiness.

Lawrence, S. 2012. *Foundation Growth and Giving Estimates*. 2012 ed. Report, June. New York: The Foundation Center.

Leighninger, M. 2006. *The Next Form of Democracy: How Expert Rule Is Giving Way to Shared Governance . . . and Why Politics Will Never Be the Same*. Nashville, TN: Vanderbilt University Press.

Levine, P., and J. Youniss, eds. 2009. *Engaging Young People in Civic Life*. Nashville, TN: Vanderbilt University Press.

Magat, R., ed. 1989. *An Agile Servant: Community Leadership by Community Foundations*. New York: The Foundation Center.

The Maynard Institute. 2012. *Fault Lines: Cultural Diversity Training in the Work-place.* Workshop and further readings. Oakland, CA: Robert C. Maynard Institute for Journalism Education. http://mije.org/faultlines.

McLuhan, M., and Q. Fiore. 1967. *The Medium Is the Massage: An Inventory of Effects.* New York: Random House.

Meyer, P. 2004. *The Vanishing Newspaper: Saving Journalism in the Information Age.* Columbia: University of Missouri Press.

Minnesota Public Radio (MPR). 2012. "Public Insight Network: Frequently Asked Questions." MPR News. http://minnesota.publicradio.org/publicinsightjournalism/faq.shtml.

mobiThinking. 2013. "Mobile Subscribers Worldwide." In *Global Mobile Statistics 2013 Part A: Mobile Subscribers; Handset Market Share; Mobile Operators.* http://mobithinking.com/mobile-marketing-tools/latest-mobile-stats/a#subscribers.

Mortensen, C.D., ed. 2008. *Communication Theory.* 2d ed. New Brunswick, NJ: Transaction Publishers.

Newton, E. 2011. "A History of the Future of News: What 1776 Tells Us About 2100." Speech, November 15. http://knightfoundation.org/press-room/speech/history-future-news-what-1767-tells-us-about-2100/.

Noland, M.C. 1989. "Grants: Giving Life to the Public Trust." In *An Agile Servant: Community Leadership by Community Foundations*, ed. R. Magat. New York: The Foundation Center.

Perry, D.K. 2003. *The Roots of Civic Journalism: Darwin, Dewey, and Mead.* Lanham, MD: University Press of America.

Pew Internet & American Life Project. 2012a. Trend data (adults): Usage over time spreadsheet. August. http://www.pewinternet.org/Static-Pages/Trend-Data-%28Adults%29/Usage-Over-Time.aspx.

———. 2012b. Trend data (adults): What Internet users do online. September. http://pewinternet.org/Trend-Data-%28Adults%29/Online-Activites-Total.aspx.

Prensky, M. 2001. "Digital Natives, Digital Immigrants." *On the Horizon* 9, no. 5. http://www.marcprensky.com/writing/prensky%20-%20digital%20natives,%20digital%20immigrants%20-%20part1.pdf.

PRNewswire. 2012. "MobileCause Leads Mobile Giving Market with 40% of Nation's Top Nonprofits Moving from Disaster Relief to Fundraising." Press release, January 12. http://www.reuters.com/article/2011/01/12/idUS168747+12-Jan-2011+PRN20110112.

Purcell, K. 2011. *Grounding Digital Information Trends.* Presentation at the Museums and the Web conference, Philadelphia, PA, April 7. http://pewinternet.org/Presentations/2011/Apr/Museums-and-the-Web.aspx.

Putnam, R.D. 2000. *Bowling Alone: The Collapse and Revival of American Community.* New York: Simon & Schuster.

Razoo. 2012. "What Is Razoo?" http://www.razoo.com/p/overview.

Schumpeter, J.A. 1943/2003. *Capitalism, Socialism, and Democracy.* Oxfordshire, UK: Taylor & Francis e-Library. http://books.google.com/books?id=UFWS5hAbUuEC&printsec=frontcover&source=gbs_ge_summary_r&cad=0#v=onepage&q&f=false.

Senge, P.M. 1990. *The Fifth Discipline: The Art & Practice of the Learning Organization.* New York: Doubleday/Currency. http://books.google.com/books?id=b0XHUvs_iBkC&printsec=frontcover&source=gbs_ge_summary_r&%20cad=0#v=onepage&q&f=false.

Smith, A. 2012a. *Real Time Charitable Giving.* Report, January 12. Washington, DC: Pew Internet & American Life Project. http://www.pewinternet.org/~/media//Files/Reports/2012/Real%20Time%20Charitable%20Giving.pdf.

———. 2012b. *17% of Cell Phone Owners Do Most of Their Online Browsing on Their Phone, Rather Than a Computer or Other Device.* Report, June 26. Washington, DC: Pew Internet & American Life Project. http://pewinternet.org/~/media//Files/Reports/2012/PIP_Cell_Phone_Internet_Access.pdf.

Smith, A., J. Quintley Anderson, and L. Rainie. 2012. *The Future of Money in a Mobile Age.* Report, April 17. Washington, DC: Pew Internet & American Life Project. http://pewinternet.org/~/media//Files/Reports/2012/PIP_Future_of_Money.pdf.

TCC Group. 2011. *News Improved: NPR's Transition from Public Radio to Public Media.* Report, August 26. Miami, FL: The Knight Foundation. http://www.knightfoundation.org/media/uploads/publication_pdfs/Knight-Foundation-NPR-Assessment-2011.pdf.

U.S. Census Bureau. 2012. "Quarterly Retail E-Commerce Sales, 1st Quarter 2012." Press release, May 17. ftp://ftp.census.gov/retail/releases/historical/ecomm/12q1.pdf.

Vanguard Charitable Endowment Program. 2013. https://www.vanguardcharitable.org.

———. 2012. "Charitable Giving Up 4% in 2011, Giving USA Reports." News release, June 25. https://www.vanguardcharitable.org/giving/news/news_charitable_giving_up_4_percent.html.

Waldman, S., and the Working Group on Information Needs of Communities. 2011. *The Information Needs of Communities: The Changing Media Landscape in a Broadband Age.* Report, July. Washington, DC: Federal Communications Commission.

Wheatley, M.J. 2006. *Leadership and the New Science: Discovering Order in a Chaotic World.* 3d ed. San Francisco, CA: Berrett-Koehler.

Zaccaro, S.J. 2007. "Trait-Based Perspectives of Leadership." *American Psychologist* 62, no. 1, 6–16.

6

Future Shock

The Case for Endowment

Lorie A. Slutsky
The New York Community Trust

Ani F. Hurwitz
The New York Community Trust

In an age that demands instant gratification and teems with controversial matters, community foundations raise the patient capital that allows them to stick with issues, even difficult ones, over the long haul. Entrenched poverty and environmental degradation will not be solved during our lifetimes. Fixing the schools, creating jobs for all who need them, and reforming health care will take years of hard work and perseverance—and reliable, patient capital. It's no accident that philanthropy often focuses on "intractable" problems.

But the "perpetual" foundation has been called into question. When Warren Buffett and Bill Gates announced the Giving Pledge in 2010 (Frank 2010)—urging America's richest individuals and families to commit the majority of their wealth to philanthropy—it was front-page news. Organized philanthropy, long ignored by the media and little understood by most Americans, had become a hot topic as extremely wealthy individuals—many of them young entrepreneurs and celebrities—began "investing" in charitable causes in highly visible ways. In addition to money, these donors have brought much-needed attention to dire problems such as crushing global poverty, the education crisis at home, and the impact of climate change.

Giving away money is always a choice, and it is always personal. Many of today's "new" donors devote their considerable wealth to a limited number of causes, and often, their commitment includes more than money: they may sit on a nonprofit's board, bring in staff, help write business plans, and insist on rigorous measurement. Many invest in developing countries, often supporting efforts to provide clean water, improve public health, and develop microenterprise.

And an awful lot of them want to do it during their lifetimes. "Giving while living" is being sold by spend-down foundations and mega-donors as the new and improved way of making a difference and leaving a legacy (although, of course, "it's not for everyone") (The Atlantic Philanthropies 2012). As a trustee of the Beldon Fund, which closed in 2009, said: "John [Hunting, its founder] and two senior staff people did a lot of speaking road shows. That was all very intentional because they wanted to promote the giving while living concept" (Ostrower 2011). And Atlantic Philanthropies, founded by Charles Feeney and closing in 2014, cites its founder's purpose on its website: "to put to good philanthropic purpose an endowment created by his life's work and to promote Giving While Living as an approach for those who have accumulated wealth to make a difference, sooner rather than later" (Oechsli 2012).

It "sharpens the focus," say these donors, maintains the present value of assets, spends the maximum amount of money when it's needed, and doesn't allow for "mission drift." It implies that "perpetuity" equals the "dead hand" and those donors who want permanence are old, tired, and hamstrung by the need to keep their institutions going.

But in addition to sticking with difficult issues over the long haul, endowment enables us to respond to emergencies and unpopular causes. Where would we have been after the market crash in 2008, with millions of people in need and donors, hurt by sizeable financial losses, less able to give to charity? Community foundations substantially increased support to nonprofits providing emergency food to families pushed to the brink, cash to pay the rent, and job training to get them on their feet again. Who would stand up for immigrants at a time when they are unfairly blamed for taking Americans' jobs? Community foundations, who cherish the diversity of their cities and towns, have long supported integrating their immigrant residents, and fought for the rights of those without papers. Who would have supported advocacy for same-sex marriage? Again, it has been community foundations that have supported advocacy for equal rights for all.

It is the American community foundation that weaves the varied charitable interests of its donors into a giving pattern that deals with the totality of its community's needs and opportunities.

Community foundations help today's donors carry out their charitable goals through donor-advised funds, which we started in 1931. We vet the nonprofits they wish to support to ensure they are programmatically and fiscally sound. We give as much—or as little—advice as they want. We tell them about urgent needs in our communities and introduce them to nonprofits they may not know. We show them why and how they can leave charitable legacies. We, in turn, learn from them.

But endowment—gifts most often left by donors in their wills—is our particular specialty, and indeed, the raison d'être of our beginnings 100 years ago when Cleveland bankers created the first community foundation in their city. Over the years, we've become expert in honoring a donor's intent and dealing with contemporary problems.

Examples abound, but here are three. The support for these projects came from three different kinds of permanent funds: the first from a somewhat flexible field-of-interest fund; the second, a narrow field-of-interest fund; and the third from a variety of funds that are unrestricted, broadly defined, and for education.

What is noteworthy is that these projects are not at all sexy, nor have they attracted the attention of the new mega-donors. Even in education—which is the passion of a number of powerful investors—our grantees spent years looking at an obscure issue—the state funding formula—and many more devising a new one and promoting it to constituencies with differing agendas. Who but a community foundation would pursue the daunting task of making our public schools give a decent education to all our children?

How a Fund to Help Isolated Elders Also Improved the Lives of Home Health Aides

Katherine Park lived a charmed life. She met her husband Sam in 1927 on an ocean liner heading back to New York from Europe. When he died in 1976, Katherine, who had no children, found herself feeling isolated and alone. As she walked around her neighborhood she began to notice the number of elderly people who were alone and in obvious financial distress. So she volunteered in a senior center. When Katherine died in 1981, she left the largest part of her estate to create the Katherine Park Fund in the New York Community Trust "to assist the elderly . . . with the problems of loneliness and boredom" (NYCT 2012a).

For years, we made grants to senior centers and other nonprofits that took elders to concerts, plays, and other outings. But by the mid-1990s, with many elderly New Yorkers being cared for by poorly paid, unhappy home health aides rather than family, we started to use the Park Fund differently. While their employers were socializing at senior centers, our grants paid aides to learn better ways to do their jobs. At the same time, we funded other agencies to develop those jobs into careers. The result has been more satisfied and qualified home health aides—and better care for their patients.

How a Sophisticated Donor's Trust Used Technology to Fulfill His Mission

Leprosy, one of the oldest recorded diseases, still afflicts nearly one million people around the world. Perhaps more surprising, there are several thousand infected people in New York City. Dr. Victor Heiser died in 1972 at the age of 100, and through his will established the Heiser Gift to research the prevention and control of leprosy. It is one of only two funds in the world created to fight the disease.

The first grants awarded were for fellowships to encourage scientists early in their careers to research leprosy, and grants to laboratories studying the disease. For 15 years, the fund helped more than 200 young scientists develop their careers and study leprosy.

But Heiser also instructed the Trust to make grants "for purposes, closely allied to, or of the general character of [leprosy]" (NYCT 2012b). This broader purpose allowed the Trust to begin giving grants to researchers studying tuberculosis (TB) in 1991. Leprosy and TB are caused by closely related bacteria that share common characteristics and stimulate similar immune responses in humans. Scientists believe that a vaccine for tuberculosis will prove useful against leprosy as well. At the time, TB had reemerged around the world as a serious health problem—8 million new cases and 3 million deaths were reported each year. We had the opportunity to help fight a growing problem and continue to learn about other ways to fight leprosy.

The fund continued to support direct research into leprosy, funding tests of new treatments for the disease through the World Health Organization. In 1995, we helped fund a five-year project to map the leprosy genome (a technology developed after Dr. Heiser's lifetime), which resulted in an increased understanding of the bacterium and pointed to new ways to identify and fight it. This knowledge prompted our support of another large-scale leprosy project: developing the first diagnostic test for the disease. Leprosy incubates in people for up to a decade before symptoms are noticed, by which time serious irreparable damage has been done to the victim's nervous system. Creating a test to identify it early on will save lives and help stop its spread, just as Dr. Heiser hoped, but in ways he never could have imagined 40 years ago.

How Patient Capital Brought Financial Equity to New York City Schools

New York City has a number of excellent public schools that are models for the country. But too often, the neediest kids receive the least help.

For decades, the Trust used a number of flexible endowed funds to improve the city's schools for all students. In the late 1970s, we funded research to document how the state's education funding formula shortchanged the city and other high-needs districts in New York. But an unsuccessful lawsuit by a Long Island district challenging the inequitable funding set a seemingly insurmountable precedent.

In the early 1990s, New York City was still receiving 12 percent less aid per pupil than the statewide average, even though it enrolled 70 percent of the state's low-income students, 60 percent of those in remedial programs, 50 percent of kids with severe disabilities, and 80 percent of immigrant students. A community school board president and parent of a public school student, along with a lawyer for the District 6 school board in Washington Heights, decided they'd had enough. They founded the Campaign for Fiscal Equity (CFE), a coalition of New York City education and advocacy groups, to revive efforts to get sufficient money for the city's schools. Our first grant to CFE supported research to determine whether a new legal challenge was possible. In 1993, CFE brought a lawsuit claiming that the system denies city students their rights under the state constitution to an adequate education (CFE 2012b).

Subsequent grants to CFE—more than $3 million over 15 years—included support for litigation, activities to build city and statewide constituencies for reform, and research to develop accountability measures. The Trust also supported other groups working with CFE to build citizen support for the lawsuit and proposed remedies, and to advocate with elected officials.

Ultimately, the lawsuit was successful. The Court of Appeals established that children in New York have a state constitutional right to "a sound basic education" and ordered an additional $2 billion per year targeted to needy kids (CFE 2012a). Because of advocacy by CFE and other education organizations, the law also introduced a new accountability that requires these funds to be invested in proven strategies.

For 15 years, the Trust stuck with CFE to get better schools for New York City's kids. From the beginning, we knew there was no way to predict the outcome of the lawsuit. Had we looked for short-term results, or even measured the impact of our grants over a few years, we might have ended our support prematurely. Grantmaking is in part hardheaded judgment, part instinct, and part passion, which sometimes means doing what needs to be done even if progress is slow, and even in the face of possible failure.

The Donor-Centric Mantra

Despite Google and a host of other web-based options for research, not all charitable individuals have the time to vigorously investigate their options for giving. Indeed, many people just want to give back, improve their communities, or help the poor. Others have specific areas of charitable interests, but don't know the best places to put their money. Potential donors want to do good but often lack the expertise, the time, or the inclination to do the research necessary to inform their decisions. New York City's five boroughs alone are home to more than 42,000 nonprofits!

Community foundations can help donors refine their charitable goals, delineate problems needing solutions, identify effective nonprofits, and tailor entire grant programs. For individuals who know exactly what they want to support, we offer efficient service. We are unique because we are able to take the diverse passions of living donors, mix them with broad and narrow interests of past donors, and develop grantmaking programs that take coordinated approaches to improve our communities.

But in order to build assets, many of us have become overly donor-centric, shifting the balance from community philanthropy to individual giving. We've all learned to use the word "you" in our communications, perhaps too well, neglecting to talk about our collective grantmaking to tackle community issues.

"Giving while living" may be exactly what is called for if an issue can be resolved within a proscribed time with an infusion of money. If, like Brooke Astor, donors want the joy of spending money during their lifetimes, terminating a private foundation is surely the right thing. But "giving while living" is not a strategy for solving a problem; it is another way of giving. In the paper cited earlier, Ostrower (2011) finds some promise for small foundations because it enables them to become bigger players in the arenas they fund. Joel Fleishman and Tony Proscio of the Duke University Center for Strategic Philanthropy & Civil Society (2012) are documenting the final years of two large private foundations. As yet, there is simply no evidence we could find that spend-down foundations have any greater impact on the issues they supported than have endowed ones. Most assessments focus on end-game investment strategies and the scramble to find other funders to carry out the work.

Some of those who would spend all their charitable money while they are alive assume that tomorrow's philanthropists will do the same. But not all generations can count on surging economies, peaceful times, and plentiful jobs—the ingredients of a thriving philanthropic sector. We rely on the generosity and foresight of people who want to make sure that their grandchildren and great-grandchildren, and generations beyond, have the resources to make the world they live in a better place. These are people who trust that those who come after them will have the intelligence and the passion to make effective use of their legacies and will take advantage of new technology and opportunities; who want to ensure that the causes they care about will continue to get support; who understand that they can't predict the future and want their successors to have flexible resources, both to take on unpopular causes and to continue to chip away at those that abide.

In 2005, Lucy Bernholz, Katherine Fulton, and Gabriel Kasper released *On the Brink of Promise: The Future of U.S. Community Foundations,* writing, "The purpose of [community foundations] is to build a permanent nonprofit institution that both honors donor intent and flexibly responds to community needs over the long term" (2005, 13). They then go on to challenge this "original principle," questioning the very notion of community philanthropy by asserting that people now (1) identify in ways other than by their geography, (2) have "alternatives for long term estate planning," (3) live in a world where "credibility of institutions of all kinds has eroded," and (4) see themselves as "a new generation of donors . . . interested in making an impact today." Furthermore, the authors say: "What's clear is that in the coming years, community foundations will face a far greater challenge than they have in the past to define and act on their distinctive value to their communities" (2005, iii).

While true, these are not earth-shaking thoughts. Individuals have always sought identity in a number of ways, not only through where they live or work. We are tribal. We are parents, we are environmentalists, we are members of congregations. We're young, we're old, we're in between. We're arts lovers, avid fisherman, and science buffs. Since community foundations began offering donor-advised funds in 1931, we've helped donors support all their communities of interest. And since commercial gift funds, hospitals and universities, and large nonprofits began to offer this "product," we've been all too aware of the "far greater challenge" that we face.

But each of us wants to live in a place that is safe, that educates our kids, employs our people, preserves open spaces, one that is culturally vibrant, and takes care of those of us who need help. It is the community foundation that weaves the varied passions of individual donors into grantmaking that contributes to the whole community in ways no individual donor can. It is we who help find the balance between individual giving and collective giving. It is the community foundation that promises—and fulfills—a donor's legacy to support the arts, or preschool education, or immigrants, or scientific research, or finds the best nonprofits doing the work.

It's easy to look at our radically and quickly changing environment and decide that we, too, must make swift, major change. Yes, we must keep up with technology, understand what interests our donors, be flexible, and do all the other things demanded of us by those who find the community foundation model "broken." But we should all have learned by now that predicting the future is a fool's game (and not coincidently the reason community foundations were invented in the first place). Some of today's philanthropy has more than just a whiff of the trendy, and we know that trends come and go.

It is just as possible that those community foundations focusing primarily on endowment are simply too rigid to accommodate change—that they are old foundations relying on endowment raised years ago, ignoring what others see as the handwriting on the wall. But community foundations rely on multiple approaches to problems—and multiple approaches to philanthropy. We tout our flexibility, our ability to help donors of all kinds, our capacity for quick response, and our patience. We don't believe in silver bullets or single answers. We know that much of what we accomplish today has been enabled by the money and vision of past donors. We believe that our generation, and those who follow us, will again appreciate the wisdom of legacy and the need for real community.

Given that the only thing predictable is that things will change, we should be careful not to fall prey to the next new thing. We should hold on to the sense of place and pursuit of the common good that community foundations fostered in the first 100 years as we prepare for the next 100.

Bibliography

The Atlantic Philanthropies. 2012. "What We Believe: Giving While Living." http://www.atlanticphilanthropies.org/giving-while-living.

Bernholz, L., K. Fulton, and G. Kasper. 2005. *On the Brink of New Promise: The Future of U.S. Community Foundations.* New York: Monitor Group. http://www.monitorinstitute.com/downloads/what-we-think/new-promise/On_the_Brink_of_New_Promise.pdf.

Campaign for Fiscal Equity (CFE). 2012a. "A Brief History of the Lawsuit." http://www.cfequity.org/static.php?page=historyoflawsuit&category=resources.

———. 2012b. About us. Web page. http://www.cfequity.org/static.php?page=about_us.

Center for Strategic Philanthropy & Civil Society. 2012. "Reports on Spend-Down at AVI ChAI and The Atlantic Philanthropies." Philanthropy Central, Sanford School of Public Policy, Duke University. http://cspcs.sanford.duke.edu/content/reports-spend-down-avi-chai-and-atlantic-philanthropies.

Frank, R. 2010. "More Billionaires Sign the Gates-Buffett Giving Pledge." *Wall Street Journal,* August 4. http://blogs.wsj.com/wealth/2010/08/04/40-billionaires-sign-the-gates-buffett-giving-pledge.

The New York Community Trust (NYCT). 2012a. "Katherine Park: Caring for the Elderly." Honoring Our Donors. http://www.nycommunitytrust.org/KatherinePark/tabid/344/Default.aspx.

———. 2012b. "Victor Heiser: Searching for a Cure." Honoring Our Donors. http://www.nycommunitytrust.org/CurrentDonors/HonoringOurDonors/VictorHeiser/tabid/342/Default.aspx.

———. 2012c. http://www.nycommunitytrust.org.

Oechsli, C.G. 2012. "30 Years of Giving While Living: Our Final Chapter." The Atlantic Philanthropies, July 10. http://www.atlanticphilanthropies.org/news/30-years-giving-while-living-our-final-chapter.

Ostrower, F. 2011. *Sunsetting: A Framework for Foundation Life as Well as Death.* Report, September 14. Washington, DC: Aspen Institute.

Part II

Connecting Community and Prosperity

7

Community Foundations as Impact Multipliers

Carleen Rhodes
The Saint Paul Foundation and
Minnesota Community Foundation

Our communities are changing. Fast. We're aging, inequities in opportunity are widening, and public resources to meet our neighbors' needs are shrinking. Demographics and crystal balls do not suggest that these dynamics will lessen in the decades ahead.

Community foundations have some of the resources required to adapt to changing needs, but the current speed and scale of change will hamper our effectiveness. Collaboration is second nature to how we do our work as community foundations, but the current model of collaboration will not be able to keep pace. We need our collaborations to be exponentially more powerful—not solely in volume or size but in terms of impact. We need to be *impact multipliers.*

We often focus our discussions on the future of donor-advised funds (DAFs), the return on investment of our other product lines, and the challenges of our business model. While all those warrant attention, we also need to think afresh and work beyond our current frameworks to find the best ways we can amplify our impact—and the outcomes for our communities.

We have an opportunity to reconsider collaboration—to create a fresh approach that multiplies our effectiveness—and to rethink how we define the mix of people we bring into the circle. We will need to be more purposeful in adding to the table decision makers who represent a variety of interests. We will need to align ourselves with new people and groups that have different resources to wield.

In our organization, we have taken some significant strides—and some smaller steps—to move in this direction. Our network of foundations, funds, and organizations gives us a unique space and some flexibility to experiment with old and new approaches. The following eight strategies to multiply our impact point to what we see as potential for us all.

Sharing Services

Community foundations were created with the idea of sharing and pooling resources and services to amplify the effectiveness of individual donors. Over time, success led to success; as people trusted us and became our partners, we gained more knowledge, and the value we provided grew proportionately. As we grew, our investment expertise also increased. We became the institutions where donors came to establish donor-advised funds as alternatives to setting up their own foundations. Sharing services has been an essential part of our long history and rich tradition.

Minnesota Philanthropy Partners (MN Partners 2013e) is a network of foundations, funds, and organizations. We are anchored by four main institutions: the Saint Paul Foundation and Minnesota Community Foundation, the F.R. Bigelow Foundation, and the Mardag Foundation. The first two are community foundations and the latter two are private foundations supported by our staff yet operating with their own boards and grantmaking policies. Our network also includes more than 1,600 affiliates across the state of Minnesota.

We created the MN Partners brand in 2011 as an improved way of talking about how we do our work. Our approach has always been to identify and implement new ways to align the work of our many foundations and funds when appropriate, but we lacked a way to talk about this shared work as a whole with our constituents. The new MN Partners "connector" brand was designed to help us describe the unique affiliation of community foundations, private foundations, organizations, and funds that are powered by our boards, staffs, and operations. Finding a smarter, more cohesive way of talking about who we are and what we do is enabling us to magnify the impact we have as individual affiliates of the MN Partners' brand—and as a whole.

For example, the Saint Paul Foundation and Minnesota Community Foundation have shared a single board since 2007. Our ability to bring together these leaders and influencers and align them around a shared mission makes the most of an incredibly deep knowledge base for the maximum benefit of the communities we serve. Our affiliate private foundations still have autonomy and operate with separate boards, but the MN Partners' brand enables us and them to tell the story of our collective impact.

And that story adds up. Taken collectively, the assets of our four anchor institutions total over $1 billion (MN Partners 2013c), and annual contributions into the communities we serve exceed $77 million (Searson 2012). The total grantmaking that is informed and directed by our shared staff—about $20 million of the total—is twice what it would be if we relied solely on the unrestricted assets of the two community foundations. Our affiliate private foundations also contribute to overhead, diversifying our sustainable revenue and making all of our operations more efficient, yet retaining all of the individuality and flexibility that each foundation, fund, and organization in our network of more than 1,600 requires.

Beyond our own network, we identified an opportunity to collaborate with a colleague foundation. In 2013, we are moving our offices to a new location and co-locating with the Bush Foundation, a private, independent foundation also headquartered in downtown Saint Paul. Each organization is maintaining separate and private floors for staff, but we share the costs of the floor between us that includes a reception area and related staff, conference room facilities, a common kitchen, and other support space. Beyond the savings gained from sharing costs and facilities, we will continue to explore other shared services and programs and anticipate some unique opportunities for our staffs to learn together and from one another. Imagine the staffs of these large foundations coming together—every workday—to share space, ideas, and passion. We hope this becomes a powerful way to multiply both organizations' impact for years to come.

Influencing Through Communications

With the emergence of new technologies, we have an opportunity to position our communications as one of many tools to help us engage and align more people with our missions and community opportunities.

With the launch of the MN Partners' brand, we seized an opportunity to reimagine our publications. We saw an opportunity to reduce the number of our in-house publications and focus our efforts on a single, smart, and stylish publication that could speak to new partners and more donors. (It is interesting how reducing the number of something can actually multiply one's impact.) With the help of an expert publishing partner, we created *MNSights* magazine (MN Partners 2013a). We use the editorial space as a way to help more Minnesotans be more effective philanthropists. We fill it with our knowledge in the form of tips and tools that help individuals and families incorporate philanthropy into their everyday lives, learn about pressing issues facing our state, and connect with high-impact organizations they can support to make a difference. By positioning the magazine as a helpful tool for local philanthropists, we also make our expertise more visible (and more appealing) in an otherwise crowded field of information.

In addition, we created a new distribution strategy that expanded our usual mailing lists and focused on high net-worth individuals and households, including subscribers to the *New York Times*. We suspect this group is very philanthropic and a great audience for our expertise—and this strategy is another way we are able to multiply our opportunities to connect donors with nonprofits doing great work.

With the explosion of highly visual digital marketing, we knew we needed to find a way to create compelling content for our online communication channels. Some of the best stories we could tell are about the nonprofits we support. We launched Nonprofits to Know™ (MN Partners 2013b) as a way to share our expertise and create fresh, visual information to help donors be more effective in their giving while increasing the digital marketing capabilities of nonprofits.

We commission a professional videographer to produce the Nonprofits to Know™ series that tells the story of select nonprofits through the eyes of a client, volunteer, or organizational leader. The featured organizations are given free use of the video for their own marketing materials, and we provide training workshops to help them create promotional plans to use it effectively. Our program officers select the featured nonprofits with an eye toward diverse issue areas and Minnesota geographies. We have been told that the series has brought additional attention and resources to organizations.

We are just beginning to explore the full potential of strategic communications, especially as technology empowers an increasing variety of communications methods. We can imagine exciting possibilities such as using social media tools to allow more voices to participate in conversations around community issues, or to help donors to connect with each other around shared interests, or to enable grantees and community leaders to ask us and each other for tips, perspectives, and solutions. Online brainstorming could improve upon people's best ideas and build ownership leading to action.

Donors in our communities want to achieve impact and improve their communities. Some of our best work ahead may be with people and organizations who never affiliate with us formally, but whom we reach with information and messages that inform their philanthropy.

Increasing Online Donations for More Nonprofits

In 2008, we saw both a competitive threat and a mission opportunity. We understood that we could use technology to dramatically expand the scope of our work and that we would lose the opportunity to other players if we didn't do so quickly and effectively.

Inspired by trailblazing e-philanthropy ventures such as Kiva (2013) and DonorsChoose (2013) that were using technology to create powerful personal giving experiences for donors, we had an idea for expanding giving in Minnesota by moving more of it online. We also were attuned to the impressive results our peers were producing by promoting *giving days* to connect their donors with nonprofit organizations.

We introduced GiveMN.org in 2009, and since then it has transformed giving for our state. The online giving site was created as a one-stop shop for donors to do all of their charitable giving. To celebrate its launch, we created the first Give to the Max Day—a 24-hour giving extravaganza designed to rally excitement for Minnesota nonprofits and help more Minnesotans become donors, no matter how big or small their gifts. It is now an annual event that has become a sort of philanthropic holiday for our state (West 2011).

GiveMN became one of the nation's leading web portals for charitable giving, outpacing the donations made on Facebook Causes. To date, GiveMN has helped raise over $70 million in donations. Philip Vassilou, managing director of Legatum, the organization that built the Razoo platform on which GiveMN operates, says, "GiveMN has played a huge role in helping to show the world what can be achieved when technology is leveraged to facilitate life changing experiences for donors" (Vassilou 2013).

The success of GiveMN is not the technology itself. It was a result of a collaboration of more than a dozen foundations and the Greater Twin Cities United Way, who together funded the development of the platform. By aligning our efforts to harness online giving for Minnesota (not just for ourselves), we established a common space for donors to give online and multiplied the impact nonprofits can make by enabling them to easily and inexpensively reach more donors.

GiveMN's success is not in spite of the fact that it is local, but rather because it is local. Today, nearly half of Minnesota nonprofits report that GiveMN is their primary online giving vehicle. Although there are many national giving platforms for people to use, GiveMN is unique in its local focus. The result, we hope, is that more money ultimately is given to Minnesota nonprofits and supports our communities.

Surely, online giving will continue to be a growth area for community foundations. In a 2012 donor survey, 76 percent of donors indicated that online was their preferred method of giving compared to 46 percent in 2009. The same survey showed that the percentage of those preferring to give by check dropped from 83 percent to 22 percent.[1]

Inspiring Individuals to Action

Many challenges facing our communities can be addressed if we energize and engage people. We talk about the importance of community engagement, but mostly in an institutional way, defined by meetings, task forces, surveys, and reports. Our approach often is to bring these established processes and structures to the same groups. But a more powerful definition of engagement is emerging—one that places the ability to shape the conversations and the solutions in the hands of individuals.

We have a unique opportunity to think about new ways of involving individuals in helping to solve problems. One possibility is to explore new staff positions—like engagement specialists—who work in communities to ignite individual participation and action. Institutions alone cannot solve many of the issues we face. Problems like obesity, for example, will not be solved with an expert task force and white papers but through actions designed and driven by individuals.

Our role as community foundations can be larger. We can help individuals multiply their effectiveness by providing incentives to more people to work together on the same problems. We also have the ability to influence how this work is done. The issues are serious, and our work on them is serious. But how can we make such seriousness appeal to more people? Is there an opportunity to infuse our problem-solving efforts with some fun?

Enter the Minnesota Idea Open (2013), a fresh and entertaining way to engage more individuals in solving critical issues facing our state. The Idea Open hosts an annual ideas competition that invites all Minnesotans to learn about an issue and share their ideas for solving it in a race to "win" the funds to implement their winning idea. With support from the John L. and James S. Knight Foundation to create the Idea Open platform, we have administered several "challenges" and made the technology available to other organizations to administer their own idea competitions.

The Idea Open essentially functions as a public education campaign. The goal is to inspire conversation and thinking in classrooms and coffee shops and at dinner tables, and to move from bemoaning problems to enacting solutions. Anyone can enter an idea—online or off—and everyone is encouraged to vote to determine the winner. We have addressed obesity, water stewardship, and interfaith/intercultural issues. Through the Idea Open website, we have collected more than a thousand ideas and engaged tens of thousands of individuals through public voting to select the winning ideas. The implementation grants are typically around $15,000, which may seem small, but the impact has been significant.

We have expanded our own networks, reaching individuals we otherwise never would have touched through our traditional grantmaking and engagement efforts and inspiring them to turn their ideas into action. We have lifted up ideas from "unusual" suspects; many of them have told us that exposure through the Idea Open enabled them to secure funding and supporters even if they did not have the winning idea. And we have addressed serious issues but made the process of problem solving more inviting. In 2013, we are stretching the boundaries, offering $1 million to inspire great ideas to make Saint Paul strong.

Improving the Impact of Public Investments

The financial assets available in the public sector, even in an era of diminishing resources, absolutely dwarf what the philanthropic sector has to invest now or will have to invest in the decades ahead. Seizing the opportunity to influence how these public funds are allocated must be a priority for community foundations. We must learn to use our David-sized resources to affect the Goliaths, and to help ensure that the dollars spent enable our communities to thrive.

All of a community foundation's tools and assets, including financial assets, can be brought together to magnify public policy development and implementation. Our knowledge of community is first and foremost a critical asset. Our staffs and nonprofit partners have a frontline view of what is and is not working. We also benefit from the long view, which allows us to focus on issues over time without the disruption of changing legislatures or other leadership changes. We bring a degree of neutrality to discussions. While we may have a solutions agenda, we are likely to work across political boundaries and with a wide variety of partners. Our involvement and influence is especially important as government tries to do more with less—a problem facing all of our communities.

Many community foundations have a distinguished track record of working successfully to influence public-sector priorities and programs. For example, in 1996, the New Hampshire Charitable Foundation (NHCF) founded the New Hampshire Civic Leadership Initiative that unites public and private funders in nonpartisan, apolitical, information-gathering and policy analysis for the sole purpose of improving the quality of life for residents of the state (New Hampshire Charitable Foundation 2012). Longtime president Lewis Feldstein championed this effort, and it has inspired many in our field to find ways to influence public-sector investments.

Current NHCF president Dick Ober and his team continue to engage proactively in public issues ranging from substance abuse to land use to energy to corrections spending. Their approach is apolitical and nonpartisan and focused on improving quality of life. They see their role as helping find common ground, keeping stakeholders moving in the same direction, using private funds to leverage public dollars, and informing public policy.

In Minnesota, we are just beginning to crack the surface of efforts like New Hampshire's. Building on the success of the Central Corridor Funders Collaborative (explained later in this chapter), we are participating in Corridors of Opportunity (Metropolitan Council 2013a), an effort that aims to build and develop a world-class regional transit system that advances economic development and ensures people of all incomes and backgrounds share in the resulting opportunities. The work is guided by a 24-member policy board that represents local government, foundations, business, community development organizations, and advocates. The project directors, who work together on a daily basis, are housed at the Saint Paul Foundation and Metropolitan Council, the region's planning and transit operating agency.

Since participating in Corridors of Opportunity, the Metropolitan Council (2013b) established a $32 million grant program and is developing a strategic plan titled *Thrive MSP 2040*. The plan will be a very different guide than in decades past—addressing broader policy areas such as fair housing and economic development, and launching a more robust public engagement process. Our staff and policy board members will be working directly with the Metropolitan Council to develop policies and strategies that will shape the region for years to come.

Supporting Donors' Drive for Impact

We need to partner with donors to shape and achieve the impact they seek—for both the near term and the long term. When we think about our role as fundraisers—after all, we need to meet the public support test—it is easy to slip into the language of "case development" and "prospect cultivation" when talking about how we work with donors and how we hope they respond to our requests. Many of us have worked on campaigns to raise funds for annual, special, or capital projects. In those instances, our job was to help prospects recognize the merit of our projects and the important purposes their gifts would achieve.

Fundraising at community foundations is fundamentally different. We really can make the "case" that we are here to achieve donors' goals—supporting communities they love and issues close to their hearts or fulfilling estate or tax planning objectives.

Like many nonprofit organizations, we prefer unrestricted gifts. These gifts enable us to be flexible and move quickly when community solutions require resources. But today, donors want to be more creative and may be less likely to grant us these types of assets. They want us to help them achieve their charitable goals—and they increasingly want that to happen during their lives in a hands-on environment where they are involved in the grantmaking process.

The Transformational Fund (MN Partners 2013d) is an example of the impact that donors talk about today. We shaped it with a donor who wanted to create a sizeable impact for a single organization rather than spread it across multiple organizations with small grants. The Transformational Fund is a single $500,000 grant designed to transform an organization that works to ameliorate poverty in Hennepin County, Minnesota. Our staff facilitated the process, working in tandem with the donor family every step of the way. The culmination was a selection process that allowed the donor to select the grant recipient with the input and expert counsel of our staff.

Two things were especially exciting about the Transformational Fund. We received calls from several nonprofit leaders to thank us for encouraging them to think big. It inspired one organization to rethink how it uses resources and put into action some of the ideas originally proposed to the donor. The donor, who originally requested anonymity, was so encouraged by the outcome that he became willing to have his name associated with the Fund, renewed his commitment for a second year, and is recruiting others to work with us in this bold way.

Joining Efforts and Interests to Address Changing Needs

Community needs evolve over time, and grantmakers sometimes find themselves facing a gap that their current grantmaking strategies do not fulfill. Many of us employ a familiar tool to address this need—we create a new community partnership or initiative.

The impetus for launching a new initiative may come from a community partner or from us. For example, our affiliate F.R. Bigelow Foundation was the spark for what became a longtime focus on literacy—first adult, then early childhood—by Bigelow and the Saint Paul Foundation in the early years, later joined by the Mardag Foundation. Similarly, our 30-year effort of providing emergency help to individuals through small grants—known as the Community Sharing Fund—was launched with an early investment from the McKnight Foundation. And Arts Lab, an effort to build the capacity of small arts organizations across the state, was encouraged at first by our affiliate the Mardag Foundation. Through the years, we have helped lead and form coalitions that focused on riverfront redevelopment and downtown revitalization. In all cases, multiple foundations aligned their commitment and resources to increase the common good—allowing us to collectively generate more than four times the annual funding that one foundation could have invested.

When construction of a new light rail line connecting downtown Saint Paul and Minneapolis was announced, the Saint Paul Foundation partnered with the McKnight Foundation to create the Central Corridor Funders Collaborative (2013), made up of 13 local and national funders working together to identify economic opportunities that the rail line could provide. A key goal is to ensure that all members of the community, regardless of race or economic status, experience the benefits of the $1 billion in infrastructure investment.

The Funders Collaborative has raised and distributed more than $5 million to help community organizations and businesses along the route sustain and strengthen their commercial, residential, and neighborhood vitality. It also is providing grants to support affordable housing near the new light rail line and has worked to make stations attractive and reflective of their individual neighborhoods. The Central Corridor is home to a large number of independent small businesses, many owned by Asian Americans, African Americans, and recent immigrants, so the collaborative also funded mitigation strategies for the construction phase.

Such agreements do not stop here. Today, with each new funding partnership, we realize gains that enable us to serve our communities in ways we could not have achieved alone.

Activating the Power of Convening

Since their inception, community foundations have used *convening* as a tool to gather the community to discuss common concerns and inform grantmaking. Our involvement in grantmaking and community initiatives puts us squarely in the middle of what is happening in our communities. We often are at the table when issues are being analyzed and implementation plans are put in place. Increasingly, we are involved in cross-sector, regional discussions about addressing systemic issues and closing gaps. Convening is one of the most important and effective impact multipliers we can use.

Saint Paul leaders today celebrate the results of a two-year convening effort—actually an intervention—that led to the creation of the Arts Partnership (2013). This new organization grew from the effort that the Saint Paul Foundation and other community leaders invested to address a bitter and longstanding feud between one of our signature arts organizations, Ordway Center for the Performing Arts, and its resident arts organizations.

It all started with a few simple phone calls, asking both parties to come together and address the problem. The approach was to ask, Can we do more than study this problem—can we solve it? Through the Saint Paul Foundation, we led the formation of a task force that included board members from each organization, civic leaders, funders, and leadership staff. Funders brought neutrality to the table; the implied leverage of future philanthropic support was applied very subtly. Early meetings were filled with contention and posturing, but the collaborative spirit grew as we focused on shared aspirations: predictability, affordability, and sustainability. More than two years later, the new way of working together was established and the Arts Partnership was formed.

The results of the Arts Partnership exceeded everyone's initial hopes. By patiently pursuing an imaginative and permanent solution and keeping everyone at the table (and withstanding four CEO changes during the process), we were able to create an operating model that is now being studied by performing arts facilities around the United States.

Conclusion

Community foundation leaders must reimagine how our foundations can adapt and grow to become even more relevant and dynamic community assets. Much more important than documenting our past achievements is the need to chart our future. Because our visions for our communities will outstrip our available resources, we will need to become impact multipliers, proactively bringing all of our tools, capacities, and resources to bear on our communities' most pressing problems and most promising opportunities.

No doubt, there are more avenues to pursue in our field's second century than the strategies detailed here. Our continuing relevance depends on our seeking and testing new ideas and ways of making a difference—to continue to learn and focus on the greater good—to multiply the impact of the resources and expertise we steward.

As community foundations, we are situated at the relatively uncommon intersection of wealth and poverty, privilege and obstacle, and of doors open and closed to opportunity. We work regularly with the wealthiest individuals in our communities and with organizations that serve the least advantaged. We support the first group with their philanthropy, providing counsel and context when asked. Our knowledge is informed by our interactions and work with the second group.

We are in a position to serve as a more intentional broker—not just a neutral party creating connections. With widening economic gaps and pronounced racial divides, we must advocate for ideas that strengthen our communities and give more people greater access to resources and information. Tools like GiveMN help break down barriers to access by equalizing every organization's ability to reach prospective donors online. New initiatives like the Transformational Project or Minnesota Idea Open also level the playing field and allow open competition from likely and unlikely sources based only on the best ideas.

In the future, we will need to continue to innovate. We will need to face the inherent contradictions in points of view that will arise from our varied customers—the advantaged and the disadvantaged—and at the end of the day, we will either help find common ground and shared aspirations or take stands based on what the community requires of us.

Place matters. Philanthropy matters. For a century, community foundations have played a valuable role in local places by bringing these two powerful concepts together. And as we've grown and developed, we've recognized that our work goes far beyond our grantmaking. We are dynamic agents in our communities, agents that multiply impact and make our communities ever better places to live, work, and thrive.

Note

1. The survey is hosted on http://givemn.razoo.com/giving_events/GTMD12/home.

Bibliography

The Arts Partnership. 2013. "History of the Arts Partnership." http://www.artspartnership.org/artspartnership/History.html.
Central Corridor Funders Collaborative. 2013. http://www.funderscollaborative.org/about-us.
DonorsChoose.org. 2013. "How It Works." http://www.donorschoose.org/about.
Kiva. 2013. "How Kiva Works: The Long Version." http://www.kiva.org/about/how/even-more.
Metropolitan Council. 2013a. "Corridors of Opportunity." http://www.metrocouncil.org/planning/COO/.
———. 2013b. *Thrive MSP 2040.* http://www.metrocouncil.org/ThriveMSP/index.htm.
Minnesota Community Foundation. 2012. http://www.mncommunityfoundation.org.
Minnesota Idea Open. 2013. "The Story." http://www.mnideaopen.org/thestory.
Minnesota Philanthropy Partners (MN Partners). 2013a. *MNSights: The Magazine for Minnesota Philanthropists.* https://www.mnpartners.org/mnsights.
———. 2013b. "Nonprofits to Know™." https://www.mnpartners.org/nonprofits_to_know.
———. 2013c. "Our Impact." https://www.mnpartners.org/about_us/our_impact.
———. 2013d. "Transformational Fund." http://www.mncommunityfoundation.org/transformational_fund.
———. 2013e. https://www.mnpartners.org.
New Hampshire Charitable Foundation (NHCF). 2012. "About Civic Leadership." http://www.nhcf.org/page.aspx?pid=556.
The Saint Paul Foundation. 2012. http://www.saintpaulfoundation.org.
Searson, C. 2012. Vice president of finance and operation, MN Partners. Personal communication with the author.
Vassilou, P. 2013. Personal communication with Dana Nelson, Executive Director of GiveMN.

8

Merging Money and Mission

Becoming Our Community's Development Office

Jennifer Leonard
Rochester Area Community Foundation

Imagine the surprise of Cleveland Foundation founder Frederick Goff were he to encounter today's community foundation. Far from serving merely as a passive distributor of endowment income, community foundations today finance their community missions with current gifts, grants from government and foundations, online fundraising, major gift solicitation, community campaigns, and more. To a core function of personalized funds for individuals and businesses we have added giving circles, project management, disaster and memorial accounts, computerized match days, and countless configurations of financing for philanthropic collaborations.

We are the money we raise. More than any other place-based entity outside of United Way, dollars are our destiny—and the destiny of our communities. Not just any dollars: dollars that can galvanize change. The dollars we raise reflect our chosen roles as grantor, agent, or leader (Leonard 1989). They enable or constrain our ability to meet changing community needs.

Perhaps because we were born of banks, community foundations became trusted stewards for contributed dollars, a strength we market worldwide. In the future, our ability to raise, manage, leverage, inform, and distribute these funds can complement and expand our community leadership work. To maximize this opportunity, community foundations will need to become more like other nonprofit organizations by raising funds directly, from an expanding array of potential donors and partners (Bernholz, Fulton, and Kasper 2005).

Community foundations are often the largest broad-purpose private entities focused solely on our chosen regions. We can act with (or without) the countless local political entities; we can flex our focus overnight to respond to disasters or opportunities; we can help our communities make the tough trade-offs to invest in the future rather than submit to short-term thinking.

Many case studies in this volume showcase our agility as a community partner, convener, collaborator, instigator. But at the core we bring money to the table. We are a community financing resource. We are the development office for our communities. And that means we need to think about whether we are raising the right kinds of money for our communities to prosper.

From Bequest Stewards to Advised Fund Platforms

Many community foundation staff and trustees learn the following history: In the beginning was the bank. Donors left charitable bequests with their favorite banker, then "distribution committees" of knowledgeable local leaders made grants according to donor intent in the context of current needs. The bank invested the funds. As other banks' clients sought these services, and banks fell from favor during the Great Depression, community foundations became multibank and ultimately freestanding corporate entities rather than bank-backed community trusts.

Recent history is often less clear, especially to those living through it. Three in four U.S. community foundations have formed since 1980, the overwhelming majority as nonprofit corporations. Most chose to raise funds from living donors to ensure a fast start, many through "advised" funds that maintain donor involvement in grant selection.

Community foundations invented donor-advised funds at least as early as 1931, at the New York Community Trust. Their popularity surged following the Tax Reform Act of 1969, which drew a bright line between private foundations and public charities. As public charities, community foundations could offer tax-free flexibility to donor-advisors and even anonymity, which was impossible under the new private foundation rules.

By 1987, gifts to community foundations from living donors surpassed gifts from deceased donors (Leonard 1989). In the United States alone, community foundation assets doubled, tripled, and more than quadrupled, from $2 billion in 1980 to more than $50 billion today.

Meanwhile, larger and older community foundations pursued ever-better investment results and continued to wean themselves from banks. Some trust-form community foundations, like the California Community Foundation in Los Angeles, successfully won court approval to sever their ties with founding banks.

Community foundations were stunned in 1991 when the Brooklyn IRS office approved a new bank-charity arrangement that strangely echoed the original Cleveland Foundation: Fidelity Investments' nonprofit Charitable Gift Fund would make grants from donor-advised funds, while Fidelity would continue to invest the dollars. Only this time, there was no community foundation involved.

From Transaction Agents to Philanthropic Advisors

Just like the original banks that wanted to hold on to the charitable bequests of their patrons, America's burgeoning financial sector wanted to keep the funds from leaving for other philanthropic destinations. A McKinsey speaker at one fall conference for community foundations explained that the United States had produced too many financial professionals for the amount of money available to invest, which put our asset management in head-to-head competition with financial firms.

Having grown exponentially through donor-advised funds (DAFs), many community foundations fought back. The emergence of commercial DAFs had the positive, if ironic, effect of making us better marketers. Some community foundations developed local and regional partnerships with financial firms that echoed the original bank relationships; the ambitious but now-defunct Community Foundations of America formed in part to orchestrate these arrangements, as well as to develop technology that could compete with the financial firms' platforms.

Nurtured by the Community Foundations Leadership Team of the Council on Foundations, the Merrill Lynch Community Charitable Fund successfully married that financial firm's marketing prowess with community foundations' grantmaking expertise. Built on the promise of an earlier partnership between Merrill Lynch and individual foundations, the national partnership raised a remarkable $480 million and granted $325 million nationwide before disbanding in 2012 following the Bank of America acquisition of Merrill Lynch. The program's creation of a joint investment platform and common national service office will inform future national efforts (Collis Townsend & Associates 2012b).

Yet, despite the community foundation movement's sharpened focus on donor service, technology, and financial service partnerships, it became clear by the early 2000s that the major financial institutions could outmarket us to their captive clients. Meanwhile, the IRS showed no inclination to revisit its decision to approve the commercial DAFs, despite widespread belief among community foundations that the funds violated the "organized and operated exclusively for charitable purposes" principle. Fidelity's Charitable Gift Fund now ranks third in the United States for total contributions received.

The glow of DAFs dimmed further when Foundation Strategy Group (FSG) consultants, working with community foundations, discovered that many advised funds cost more than they paid in fees. Others in the field questioned advised funds' largely transactional and pass-through nature. Former Minneapolis Foundation development VP Stuart Appelbaum wrote a compelling article contrasting community foundation roles as "charitable transfer agents" or "community change agents" (Appelbaum 2005). "I didn't sign up for this work to become a banker," Appelbaum later explained.

This made it even more important that community foundations understand what they were offering to donors, and why. Did it fit their mission? How could we establish a compelling case for donors, so that we could continue to grow while also serving our communities?

Fortunately, the National Marketing Action Team (NMAT), organized by the Community Foundations Leadership Team under Managing Director Suzanne Feurt, did a masterful job of defining the community foundations' niche as a powerful combination of personalized service, local expertise, and community leadership. The first challenged the one-size-fits-all efficiency of the commercial firms; the second and third called on community foundations to highlight and enhance their community-centered knowledge and activities, again distinguishing them from the commercial funds.

The first response was a flurry of donor education and support services designed to draw donor-advisors to community giving. Some community foundations that had long been attracting DAFs, like the New York Community Trust, already had hired specialized donor services staff like pioneer Bob Edgar, brought on in 1984 to administer the exploding DAF work. His job description and department evolved to bring donor-advisors into the life of the Trust and connect them to the Trust's local expertise. Using targeted newsletters about grant opportunities, donor education events, and personalized staff outreach to connect donors to exciting new projects, the Trust attracts a million dollars a year from donor-advisors for its core community mission, thus supplementing its unrestricted funds.

Rochester Area Community Foundation hired its first donor services director in 2000. After several years of disappointing turnouts for donor education events, staff hit on a successful model: a donor breakfast "hosted" by a passionate fellow donor. These modest events build donor connections to each other while showcasing good grantees or initiatives. In response to this and other techniques similar to the Trust's, a record 175 of Rochester's 500-plus DAFs gave last year in response to staff recommendations, including $30,000 for sand and water tables, math manipulatives, and simple instruments to prepare city classrooms for a new, developmentally appropriate kindergarten curriculum approved after the school district budget had been adopted.

How Can Advised Funds Better Serve Our Community Mission?

Just two decades after the launch of the Fidelity Charitable Gift Fund, DAFs have become commodities, with universities, Jewish federations, and other large nonprofits joining most major banks in sponsoring them. Their relative success has drawn attention from Congress, which inserted numerous donor-advised fund provisions into the 2006 Pension Protection Act and has considered imposing private foundation payout requirements on advised funds.

Our assets continue to rise and community foundations still manage a plurality of DAFs in the United States. However, the shift from endowment manager to transaction agent to philanthropic advisor has exacerbated the challenge of sustainability for DAFs, with the need for additional staff to provide enriched services (as our competitors in private foundation services and family offices have also done, it should be noted).

We can definitely distinguish ourselves from the commercial funds, even though our interface with donors is not as seamless as their own. In the breakup of the Merrill Lynch Community Charitable Fund program, some 75 percent of donors chose to stay with community foundations rather than migrate to Bank of America's gift fund (Collis Townsend & Associates 2012a). But we still face the challenges that modern donors want control over their dollars, are mobile with multiple or even global interests, and are disinclined to tie up their dollars during life in permanent endowments.

In retrospect, our strenuous effort to engage donor-advisors in local grant-making brings up the question of whether or not we raised the right money in the first place. The philanthropic services department, as essential and successful as it is, is still a work-around for a donor-advised program that, in many community foundations, has been more about bringing in dollars than aligning them with community needs. As we refocus on community leadership—the third leg of the NMAT tripod (personalized service and local expertise being the other two legs)—this mismatch between money and mission becomes even more glaring.

This is not to say that investing in donor-advisors won't pay off. Just like the banks with their client relationships, our existing donor relationships can result in community support not only if they give to community programs during contributors' lifetimes but also if they turn into planned gift donors—a key premise of the original efforts to attract living donors.

In a seminal 2012 study of 31 community foundations with one-third of the field's advised assets, CF Insights found that community foundations *do* want their advised funds to "do more than grow." Some of the study respondents successfully raise current and planned discretionary gifts through their donor-advised fund program; break even or make money on fees; and augment their own grantmaking and community leadership. However, success varied widely and almost always lagged aspirations. The study authors identified key strategies and practices associated with success in each area; for example, "increasing relationship intensity" led to more donors funding recommended grantees, co-investing, contributing to flexible funds, and pledging planned gifts (Graves et al. 2012).

The Primacy of Unrestricted Endowment

A key question for many community foundations should be whether they are asking the right questions of their donor-advisors as they come in the door—and whether the rules they establish demonstrate the community foundation's dedication to its community. You might say that our rules illustrate whether we "walk our talk" about our community mission.

Yes, we will grow more quickly if donors can set up pass-through funds to give anywhere, for any purpose, at rock-bottom fees. But this service is now widely available, even for no fee at all at some nonprofits (including the local United Way and Jewish Federation in Rochester, New York). And growing fast is not our only goal. That frees us to ask the question, What kind of money do we want for our communities?

For most community foundations looking for flexible dollars for local grants and community initiatives, unrestricted endowment would top the most-wanted list. In the past, DAFs often became unrestricted after one or two generations, which provided a pipeline for such funds in the future. Yet surprisingly, in a recent informal survey of 13 urban community foundations, only two limited the number of generations that could advise on their donor-advised endowments.

Limiting the inheritability of DAFs may look traditional, but it's also practical. Most small private foundations stumble by the third generation, as families expand both in numbers and geographically. By limiting DAFs to one or two generations, this can be avoided, while providing a source of future unrestricted or broad field of interest endowment for our communities. For the exceptional family who stays local and involved, exceptions are easy to make. The Rochester Area Community Foundation also exempts supporting foundations, which start at $2 million and thus are more likely to retain family involvement.

We need the courage of our convictions to decide what kind of money we need for our communities, and then to raise it. If we are the development office for our communities, we need to ask for unrestricted gifts. No other development office would neglect to do so. A donor-advised endowment that eventually gives in the family name for changing community needs is a double gift—one that involves the family, and one that enshrines the family's values far into an unseen future for both family and community.

From our first days in Cleveland, endowment for the future has prepared communities and nonprofits for the vicissitudes of an unknown future. Unrestricted endowment provides for the community's future; that is a key reason the National Standards for U.S. Community Foundations require that a community foundation have a long-term goal to raise unrestricted endowment. Rather than giving up because unrestricted endowment is hard to wrest from modern donors, we owe it to our communities to try our hardest. It may pay to study the examples of community foundations, like those in Hartford, Connecticut, and Grand Rapids, Michigan, which never completely bought in to the focus on DAFs. They continued to foster community leadership and unrestricted funds, with positive results that others may wish to study and emulate.

What is the case for unrestricted endowment? Love of place, combined with the inevitability of change. If community foundations want to meet the changing needs of communities, they need to deliver flexible funds for future decision makers. These aren't the unrestricted operating funds other organizations request—this is community capital for everyone's use.

Asking donors to imagine 80 to 100 years into the future, past their own and their children's lifetimes, can illuminate the uncertainty of extending our philanthropic views far into the future. It also helps to point out that many current grantees weren't around 25 years ago—and how even trusted, 100-year-old institutions can stumble and need outside assistance. Promoting our own impact with unrestricted funds can then seal the deal.

The long-serving, remarkable California Community Foundation president Jack Shakely once declared that unrestricted giving was dead—not worth fighting for, he opined, in a universe of modern donors no longer attached to place or institutions. Yet after his retirement, that same foundation received one of the largest-ever community foundation gifts—a $200 million bequest from philanthropist Joan Palevsky. The gift reflected a lawyer's recommendation, estate plan needs—and the foundation's own clearly communicated, exciting community projects.

Endowment in general should be reframed as a mainstay of community foundation strategy, even though we may grow more slowly in its pursuit. While not included in the NMAT pillars, permanent stewardship continues as a critical strategic niche for community foundations—one that others (including the United Way) would be happy to wrest from our grasp. Lawyers, accountants, and other professional advisors will continue to need our assistance for clients who want to create scholarships, leave designated gifts, or honor the community or a chosen cause through a more flexible fund. We can do that; we always have.

Community foundations like the Oklahoma City Community Foundation have also become the repository of a large number of nonprofit endowments, which free agency resources from unnecessary investment committees while promoting their participation in planned giving. The spreading of more strenuous government investment guidelines (such as those stipulated in the Prudent Management of Institutional Funds Act) has made community foundation management even more attractive to nonprofits. This is a key competency for community foundations that serves a local purpose.

One of the reassuring signs that endowment fundraising is still alive and well in the community foundation field may be found in a 2009 Aspen Institute survey on geographic affiliates, which have grown rapidly in recent years, especially in rural areas. Aspen identified more than 1,400 affiliates holding $2 billion in total assets. The lead community foundations reported that a majority of affiliates (71 percent) held more endowed than nonendowed assets, and four out of five were actively fundraising. Younger and smaller community foundations held significant portions of their endowments in these geographic divisions. It would be possible to hypothesize that the sense of place in smaller communities may lead to easier endowment fundraising (Aspen Institute Community Strategies Group 2011).

Moving Beyond the Fund

Individual philanthropic funds, reflecting the organizing principle of bank-trust departments, have remained at the core of the community foundation business model for a hundred years. Our accounting software neatly organizes all dollars into funds for endowment and grantmaking, for operations and projects.

Yet the geographic affiliates' research reminds us that many community foundations start out with a campaign for general endowment, seeding unrestricted grantmaking power for the future. This direct fundraising often falls to the wayside as people and organizations create named funds, particularly (in recent years) donor-advised funds. Then the ability of the community foundation to make competitive grants is often limited to the original pool of unrestricted funds, disappointing community expectations for rising grant awards.

What is the solution to raising unrestricted endowment for our communities? One possibility is to consider the *virtuous cycle* articulated some years ago by the Toronto Community Foundation, in which limited unrestricted funds are leveraged for maximum impact. The impact is then marketed to the community to attract donations to, rather than merely through, the foundation, as Jack Shakely used to put it. As donations increase (many would still be planned gifts, so this evolves over time), the added donations can be invested for added impact, marketed, and serve again to attract more donations. And so on.

The maxim in fundraising is that nobody gives if they aren't asked. Community foundations must move beyond the passive, "donor takes all" approach to fund creation and assert community needs when asking for funds. Sometimes this can be done by establishing areas of work for community support; sometimes multiple areas of work; and sometimes, the ask needs to be for pure unrestricted endowment. After all, what will be lost if the donor declines, but settles on an arts or education fund?

The Columbus Foundation under former executive director Jim Luck hired a seven-person development department and built a case statement for community investment to present to donors in their homes and offices; that foundation grew exponentially in subsequent years. Today, increasing numbers of community foundations are exploring or conducting traditional endowment campaigns for unrestricted funds, which may reach far beyond the usual fund donor by soliciting small as well as major gifts. A group of community foundation development professionals began meeting in 2012 to exchange ideas for raising unrestricted funds.

Expanding Resources for Community Leadership

Meanwhile, community foundations are experimenting with a great variety of tools for increasing current giving for community needs—even though those gifts may not form a fund, may not be endowed, and may not even go to the community foundation. In these innovations lie many stories yet to be written about the new directions of the second century of community foundation leadership.

Direct fundraising for current use flies in the face of much community foundation tradition. "That's the province of United Way," many say, even though United Way's focus is usually limited to human service organizations. Or, "We'd be competing with other nonprofit organizations." (Just as they compete with us for planned gifts, perhaps?)

Certainly, most community foundations need to increase staff skills to be successful in direct fundraising, but that can be done. Founded in 2003, the Boston Foundation's Civic Leadership Fund has become a tantalizing beacon of what can be accomplished if the old rules are set aside. Nearly $1 million per year comes in from corporations, foundations, and individuals to finance current leadership work by the foundation.

That is the point of current fundraising: to expand on our available endowment income and get more work done now. Referring back to the virtuous cycle, that should also allow us to create added impact, leading to donations of more unrestricted funds and more unrestricted income for leadership work in the future.

Increasing numbers of community foundations are experimenting with annual campaigns, either for community leadership purposes or for operations badly damaged by two recent recessions and the challenge of paying for additional donor services and community leadership work (neither of which is covered by our traditional bank-trust fee structure). One solution to sustainability has been community foundations working together through shared back-office services, leaving the enriched community services in place at home.

Raising annual dollars through campaigns and even special events seems much like other nonprofits, as Lucy Bernholz and her coauthors predicted in 2005. So is raising grants for our leadership work, increasingly a core part of the community foundation development toolkit.

For several decades, national foundations have turned to community foundations to extend their local presence with "feet on the ground." Frequently, the national foundations challenged community foundations to raise funds for their joint programs. Rochester Area Community Foundation has arts, early childhood education, and environmental endowments created from these national partnerships, in addition to having raised current funds to match national foundation grants for telemedicine, civic engagement, father involvement, and more. All were areas in which the foundation already had a focus, and the national grants helped underwrite leadership work and often provided professional development through peer learning as well.

Most recently, the Rochester Foundation applied for Ford Foundation grant support on behalf of Rochester's high-needs school district, to experiment with extending the school day and programs as an avenue to student achievement. Ford expects the community foundation to bring other local foundations to the table in the future.

Foundation fundraising is a little closer to home than annual campaigns, but the realm of government grantseeking continues to separate some community foundations from the herd. In New Haven, Connecticut, community foundation CEO Will Ginsburg is a former Commerce Department assistant secretary, so government grants were a comfortable option when he arrived in 2000. In 2009, he helped attract $4.5 million in federal funds to reduce infant mortality through New Haven Healthy Start (The Community Foundation for Greater New Haven 2012). Kathy Merchant in Cincinnati was at the table for the original STRIVE initiative to strengthen children "cradle to career," about which FSG authors coined the term "collective impact." STRIVE was the only community-based effort to receive an inaugural grant from the federal Fund for Social Innovation.

Many more community foundations have involved themselves in cross-sector community collaboratives that have sought regional and national funding, from the original Rochester AmeriCorps Collaborative, to Say Yes to Education in both Buffalo and Syracuse, New York, to Promise Neighborhoods that replicate the Harlem Children's Zone and 21st Century Community Learning Center grants for after-school programs, to the dozens of STRIVE replications nationwide, and many, many others.

In these efforts, community foundations have had to be the "agile servants" (Magat 1989) that provide what is needed from our expanding leadership toolkits as conveners, grantmakers, grantseekers, project managers, advocates, and coaches. Our ability to provide grant support brings us to the table—and brings others. After that, we are learning the ropes for a whole host of additional roles in making our communities better, with the help of CFLeads (an independent nonprofit helping community foundations strengthen their leadership skills and impact, formerly known as the Coalition of Community Foundations for Youth), Aspen Institute, FSG Social Impact Advisors, and other consulting groups working with community foundations.

Much of this work requires us to raise money from our own donor-advisors as well as from the community as a whole. At any given time, the Rochester Area Community Foundation is typically raising the match for one or two major challenge grants; the Rochester community brings even more requests of this type than the community foundation can accept, especially following announcements such as the Robert Wood Johnson Foundation's Local Funding Partnerships opportunity.

Which brings us back to Bernholz's prediction (Bernholz, Fulton, and Kasper 2005) that, to thrive in a competitive and complicated philanthropic environment, community foundations would have to behave more like other nonprofits. Our growing evolution as fundraising entities certainly fits that mold. It also creates a staff recruitment and training challenge.

Earlier in this young century, as community leadership began to reassert its place and the selling of donor-advised funds receded as a primary goal, executive directors hired for their fundraising prowess wondered who was to lead these community leadership efforts. "My background is entirely in fundraising, in development," they would say. "I don't know how to run programs or initiatives in the community."

In reality, these leaders should be in hot demand because they are able to raise funds for the community's present and future, using a wide variety of fundraising approaches. Both fundraising and program skills are needed in

the modern CEO, who of course can also complement his or her strengths
with those of other staff.

The Community Foundation Fundamentals course taught by the Council on Foundations presents community foundation asset development as
a matter of "attracting assets" rather than "raising dollars." Our longtime
marketing to professional advisors falls in this realm, since we provide the
solution for their clients who want to create philanthropic funds. However, as
we discovered with financial services firms, other professional advisors are
increasingly competing to provide both asset management and philanthropic
advice. Direct fundraising seems inevitable in our future, and perhaps our
Fundamentals curriculum will evolve to include training on grantsmanship,
major gifts fundraising, and more.

Raising Money for Others

Raising money to support our community leadership makes a lot of sense,
particularly when our impact then stokes the virtuous cycle of grants–impact–
gifts. But what if money is the community need? Community foundations
can serve as the engines, not just the stewards, for community resource
gathering.

Our own credibility to raise money or build endowments for other nonprofits or causes, or to strengthen the ability of others to raise funds, is an emerging
arena with considerable opportunities for community leadership. Rather than
raising money only for the community foundation, these programs stimulate
gifts that build endowment or current income for a wide swath of community
needs. And all of them build on better fundraising and marketing skills.

A familiar role for community foundations has been to serve as the single
point for gifts for disaster relief, as we saw in New York City after 9/11 and
Oklahoma City after the federal building bombing. Other community foundations were relieved to be able to direct their donors to the Baton Rouge and
New Orleans community foundations after Hurricane Katrina (Baton Rouge
showcased colorful online donor communications). This may be one of the
few areas in which community foundations are working together nationally
to address community needs, and they are doing it through a fundraising
mechanism.

Another opportunity that leverages community foundation fundraising
skills has been to help nonprofit organizations raise endowment funds, often
to be housed at the community foundation. In the 1994 Arts Tomorrow Initiative, Rochester Area Community Foundation responded to a fiscal crisis at
three major arts groups by issuing a public challenge. For every two dollars
the public put into endowment for these organizations, we would put one

into their operations, provided a quarter of that went toward technical assistance or capacity building. All three organizations completed the challenge and went on to thrive institutionally, while their new endowments provided continuing support.

After the Community Foundation for Southeast Michigan announced that its region was underendowed, the Kresge Foundation helped the foundation strengthen area nonprofits with endowment challenges and fundraising skills. Kresge, led by former Rhode Island Foundation president John Marshall, found the results so compelling that it offered a similar program to community foundations nationwide, which included a challenge for unrestricted endowment in addition to the agency funds.

Civic engagement is measured in part by levels of volunteering and giving in our communities, and fostering both has become the province of community foundations and United Ways alike. Community foundations with deep local roots are often asked to receive memorial gifts or provide a platform to build scholarship and other funds for local purposes. Because so many of the Rochester community foundation's funds now raise money through dinners and golf tournaments, the foundation has established strict limits on these fundraising events, instead facilitating their fundraising.

Similarly, Rochester Area Community Foundation rejects many requests to serve as a fiscal sponsor except for projects in which we have a direct connection. Yet, even being selective, the leadership activities we embrace have mushroomed to about two dozen relationships. For example, Rochester's 25-year-old Early Childhood Development Initiative keeps spawning important activities that raise money for projects such as early childhood scholarships, parent leadership training, or the developmentally focused kindergarten curriculum that so excited the foundation's donor-advisors in 2011.

This openness to community fundraising, with its large number of small gifts as well as small grants from many donor-advised funds, results in Rochester placing very high (sixteenth) on the CF Insights survey for number of transactions. But for community foundations willing to step up as the community's development office, community leadership can mean raising money the community needs, not stopping all small gifts and grants at the door. Finding new efficiencies then becomes critical; improved technology has become a strategic goal for Rochester's community foundation.

Community foundations across the country have made a similar decision in creating increasingly popular match days. Called PowerPhilanthropy in Columbus, Give to the Max Day and GiveMN at the Saint Paul and Minnesota Foundations, and giveGreater in New Haven, these fundraising challenges and platforms help area nonprofits raise funds in one-day, online fundraising extravaganzas.

Interestingly, match days and their software emerged from a community foundation desire to demonstrate local expertise through online content for donors. The Arizona Community Foundation developed Dotche to profile programs and organizations, allowing nonprofits to fill in their own information using the self-serve power of the web. But nonprofits weren't always cooperative. In Milwaukee, former community foundation president Doug Jansson hired a reporter to write up stories for that foundation's Dotche site. On the other hand, in Columbus, community foundation CEO Doug Kridler chose to incentivize nonprofits to complete their PowerPhilanthropy profiles by offering matching gifts on a single day; this may have been the first actual match day.

All consuming operationally, if only temporarily, match days won't be right for every community foundation. Some community foundations may prefer to raise funds for themselves or feel that such current giving trends better suit the United Way. The Rochester, New York, United Way initiated a 2011 match day called ROC the Day, which raised $500,000 in its first year. Other United Ways may follow suit.

Match days cater to the modern donor's interest in choosing gift recipients, just as donor-advised funds do. Giving circles similarly speak to donors' passions but also provide a social experience, a group connection. First held up as a model during the New Ventures in Philanthropy initiative run by the Forum of Regional Associations of Grantmakers, giving circles offer the opportunity to expand the populations we serve using a device similar to a stock investment club.

Members provide $1,000 (or another set sum) each year, engage in peer learning about their chosen focus area, request applications and select grantees, then promote the impact to prospective members. In Rochester, a strategic goal to "broaden our circle" of community foundation donors resulted in giving circles for young professionals, women, African Americans, and the LGBT community. The New Britain, Connecticut, community foundation has a longstanding Catalyst Fund of area adults that also learns together and does its own grantmaking.

These communities of identity take a bit more staffing than an average endowment fund, but they reach a lot of prospective donors who help govern the group and build relationships that may ultimately be beneficial to the community foundation. The Rochester Women's Giving Circle has raised and granted $355,000 in five years, which would have required a $1.4 million endowment to equal; they do the grant screening, selection, announcement, and monitoring. Rochester's African American Giving Initiative has raised additional money to publish a *State of Black Rochester* book, while introducing growing numbers of prospective donors to the Community Foundation (RACF 2012a, 2012b, 2012c).

Will this work pay off for future gifts as well? The relationship building is key. Many existing planned gift donors have joined these giving circles as a hands-on opportunity in philanthropy during their lifetimes. And in Rochester, the first known bequest prompted by the five-year-old giving circle experiment was written into a will in early 2012.

Go Boldly Where No Community Foundation Has Ever Gone Before

These innovations demonstrate that community foundations are more focused than at any time in the past 25 years on our basic mission of community betterment. We still faithfully carry out the hopes and dreams of charitable donors, though we have moved far from being just a passive recipient of planned gifts. Instead, we are in the process of moving from asset attraction to active fundraising for our communities.

Our fascination with a growth model based on donor-advised funds has slowed with competition and regulation, but our ability to engage our donors in meeting local needs has increased remarkably. So has our commitment to raise the community's flag in attracting unrestricted funds, both to meet changing needs and to underwrite the increased costs of donor service and local leadership. We are using the virtuous cycle to position community foundations as a destination for charitable giving, not just a way station.

More than ever before, fundraising and development have become critical skills for community foundations. With our financial credibility and agility, we can also use fundraising and asset development tools in our community leadership toolboxes. Like other nonprofit organizations, we must speak for the needs of our communities—and raise the money we need to address them.

Frederick Goff would surely approve.

Bibliography

Appelbaum, S. 2005. "The Cost of Sticking Your Neck Out." *Foundation News & Commentary* 46, no. 5.

The Aspen Institute Community Strategies Group. 2011. *Growing Local Philanthropy 2009 Survey: Community Foundations and Geographic Affiliates.* Washington, DC: Aspen Institute. http://www.aspencsg.org/survey/AspenCSGGrowingLocal-Philanthropy2011.pdf.

Bernholz, L., K. Fulton, and G. Kasper. 2005. *On the Brink of New Promise: The Future of U.S. Community Foundations.* New York: Monitor Group. http://www.monitorinstitute.com/downloads/what-we-think/new-promise/On_the_Brink_of_New_Promise.pdf.

Collis Townsend & Associates, LLC. 2012a. *Merrill Lynch Community Charitable Fund Program: A Decade of Successful Service.* Legacy Report. Kennett Square, PA: Collis Townsend & Associates, LLC.

————. 2012b. "Merrill Lynch Community Charitable Fund Program to Dissolve." Press release, June 1.

The Community Foundation for Greater New Haven. 2012. "Leadership Activities." http://www.cfgnh.org/About/LeadershipActivities/tabid/290/Default.aspx.

Graves, R., E. Nico, C. Wendel, et al. 2012. *Do More Than Grow: Realizing the Potential of Community Foundation Donor-Advised Funds.* CF Insights Report. Washington, DC: Council on Foundations. http://cfinsights.org/Portals/0/Uploads/ Documents/Do%20More%20Than%20Grow.pdf?cpgn=CFI%20WP%20DL%20 Do%20More%20Than%20Grow.

Leonard, J. 1989. "Creating Community Capital: Birth and Growth of Community Foundations." In *An Agile Servant: Community Leadership by Community Foundations,* ed. R. Magat. New York: The Foundation Center.

Magat, R., ed. 1989. *An Agile Servant: Community Leadership by Community Foundations.* New York: The Foundation Center.

Rochester Area Community Foundation (RACF). 2012a. "African American Giving Initiative." http://www.racf.org/GiveToAFundHere/AfricanAmericanGivingInitiative/tabid/323/Default.aspx.

————. 2012b. *Rochester Area Community Foundation Investment Policy.* February 8. Rochester: RACF. http://www.racf.org/Portals/0/Uploads/Documents/RACF%20 Investment%20Policy%20Approved%20by%20Board%20020812%20Final%20 _2_.pdf.

————. 2012c. "Rochester Women's Giving Circle." http://www.racf.org/GiveToA-FundHere/RochesterWomensGivingCircle/tabid/305/Default.aspx.

————. 2012d. http://www.racf.org.

9

Ensuring There Is "Community" in the Community Foundation

Alicia Philipp
The Community Foundation for Greater Atlanta

Tené Traylor
The Community Foundation for Greater Atlanta

What makes a community foundation unique is its connection to multiple nonprofits and donors; however, it is the ability to be knowledgeable about the local community at a granular level that makes it a viable entity for credible community solutions. In other words, community foundations, for the most part, are oftentimes at the heart of bridging major resources (human, social, intellectual, and financial) with community needs. The social capital and networks that are fostered by a community foundation typically indicate its level of development and engagement. But what happens when the issues and solutions are not championed by a nonprofit service delivery leader or engaged donor? What role does a community foundation play in neighborhoods or issues affecting an entire region—issues such as housing, water, green space, air quality, transportation, etc., with a true understanding of the effect on local residents?

As a place-based funder, community foundations are not only conveners, caretakers, and grantmakers but they are also a conduit for public funds, national philanthropic resources, and local partnerships, all of which can directly support the needs of developing and transforming communities and neighborhoods. An obstacle for many communities is the inability to efficiently organize local and regional institutional resources. Given the bond between a community foundation and the area it serves, engaging in the complexities of community development is necessary for it to remain competitive and relevant for future generations of donors.

Community development is a process based on how people live, work, and play in a specific neighborhood, region, or place. It can be best described as the interplay of infrastructure (housing, transportation, green space) and human (strengthening families, neighborhoods, and citizen engagement) progression (and in some cases, regression). The ways in which communities are developed is based solely on the balance of power (government, business, philanthropy, etc.), access to resources (food, jobs, housing, etc.) and equity (fair and just practices) in relationship to the members of the community it represents. Community foundations can formalize their ability to organize the intellectual, social, and financial capital to substantively collaborate and influence decisions and resources with, and sometimes on behalf of, community.

Since 1991, the Community Foundation for Greater Atlanta has managed a small grants program called the Neighborhood Fund. The program has allowed the Community Foundation to be invited to kitchen tables, living rooms, backyards, gardens, and playgrounds in a way most funders are not granted. Being "invited" does not make an institution like a community foundation an equal member of a community, but it does provide us with a lens to see how decisions affect the community served. For us, the time spent working in the neighborhoods helps us understand the changing dynamics of the region. It also helps us prioritize what issues we should be paying attention to and when to pay attention to them. This chapter will explore this definition of *community,* collective decision making, and the evolution of a changing philanthropic community.

"Won't You Be My Neighbor?"

"Won't you be my neighbor?" is the famous invite that shapes how we live and interact in our communities. It is also a question explored by community foundations when developing clear strategies to address regionwide (macro) and neighborhood-deep (micro) challenges and opportunities. But who and what makes up this *community* of which we speak? Traditionally, it is the local institutional leaders of nonprofits, business, and governmental institutions (Guo and Musso 2007). Albeit efficient, at times, it can be difficult to discern if the representatives are substantive or symbolic agents of their constituents (Guo and Musso 2007). The community is also greater than its constituents. It is geography, history, and subtext enriched by multiple parties over time.

If community foundations are going to effectively fill this bridging role, then the connections need to be deep and wide. We cannot be on automatic pilot and reach out to the same "leaders" each time. We have to be able to find those emerging voices that truly have a constituency and a desire to create good beyond their boundaries. These leaders are often in unlikely places, thus community foundation staff need to be in living rooms as much as board rooms. The social capital strength of an organization is where this begins. *Social capital* is most famously defined and critiqued by author and professor

Robert Putnam (2000). In summary, it is the networks, norms, and social trust that facilitate coordination and cooperation for mutual benefit.

Knowing what affects the lives of the everyday person, then connecting or rolling up that knowledge to issues affecting that region, is the role for community foundations. Community foundations must delve beyond grant applications from nonprofits to understand the community it serves. This act must also be institutionalized, practiced, and realized throughout the organization.

> A local story is a community in a predominantly African-American neighborhood, named Adamsville, on the west side of Atlanta, Georgia. Like so many other neighborhoods deemed an urban blight, the community experienced crime, unemployment, and deteriorating economic and social conditions. Today, it is a symbol of "possibilities" and a replicable model for resident-led change in neighborhoods throughout Atlanta. Adamsville residents continue to work on critical issues impacting their community's families, but they have also come a long way from where they once were.
>
> During a Neighborhood Planning Unit meeting, residents discussed the lack of enrichment opportunities for Adamsville's youth and began to brainstorm ways to better support its young people. As a result of that discussion, a resident-led non-501(c)3 group created the Youth Leadership & Community Engagement Project funded by The Community Foundation's Neighborhood Fund. In fact, the Youth Leadership & Community Engagement Project was the first time the community received resources from outside its community. The project facilitated mentorship and leadership/life skills workshops for 12 students from the local Benjamin E. Mays High School. The students recruited were not currently enrolled in leadership positions but demonstrated great potential. The project sought to demonstrate to the 12 students and Adamsville's residents that young people are a community's most valuable asset and should be protected and nurtured.
>
> During the same time, the community's confidence was mounting, which led to a newly constructed Adamsville Recreation Center & Natatorium. The recreation center was a community effort advocated by residents directly to their city council members and mayor. Additionally, there was a nearby park underutilized and overrun by truant students, illegal activity, and illicit behavior. That is until Mrs. Harris and her fellow neighbors started the Friends of Collier Heights Park and set their sights on "taking the park back." In concert with The Community Foundation's philanthropic services department and a donor interested in parks and green space, the Neighborhood Fund's program officer was successful in securing funds to support a preschool playground and life trail for seniors.

What started as a small grant to support Adamsville's youth development activities led to six-figure investments from foundations, local government, businesses, and local/national nonprofits (e.g., Park Pride, KaBoom, and others). Residents' capacity to leverage additional resources on behalf of their community is largely due to the ongoing consultation, tools, resources, networking opportunities and training/technical assistance offered by funders supporting community development at the neighborhood scale.

Last year, Adamsville's residents did a little grantmaking of their own. Modeled after and supported by the Neighborhood Fund grant, Adamsville created "Building Blocks for a Better Community," a six-phase Community Leadership Training and Engagement Series for the 26 community clubs throughout Adamsville. Every club that attended each of the six Building Blocks sessions received a mini-grant of $150 to support their community club projects. Community Club members developed community organizing, leadership, stakeholder engagement, and resource development skills.

Adamsville has gained a reputation for being "A Community of Possibilities" and inspires so many of us to give a little of ourselves to make our homes and communities a brighter place.

Knowing people at all levels helps shape the sphere of influence for community foundations. However, knowing is half the battle; it is the ability to employ and maintain social capital to meet community needs that community foundations must demonstrate moving forward.

Collective Decision Making

In the 35 years I [Alicia Philipp] have been in Atlanta, I have seen decision making change dramatically. When I began my career at the Community Foundation, it was comprised of five white men meeting for lunch at the Commerce Club. The men represented two sectors—government and business—and all lived in the same neighborhood. Progressive thinkers, bottom-line oriented, but not diverse.

Over the ensuing years, decision making became more inclusive but also somewhat messy. African Americans and women began to dominate in local politics, including the office of mayor and other top business and political positions. While deep tensions grew in the business/government coalition, it also created an opportunity for other voices to be at the table. What was once homogenous and safe became different and uncomfortable for everyone involved. During this era, there was a rise in neighborhood organizations and involvement. In 1974, Mayor Maynard Jackson, the city's first African American mayor, created Neighborhood Planning Units, citizen advisory councils that make recommendations to the mayor and city council on zoning, land use, and other planning issues.

All this was happening with a very Atlanta city-centric focus. Comparatively, the city's geography and population size is not a complete depiction of the multicounty metropolitan region. As a region with a myriad of municipalities (county, city, school, etc.) and no regional government, decision making reached a new level of uncertainty.

There stood yet another challenge before us, namely, How do we have an inclusive table large enough to represent various voices on a particular issue but not so large that it is unwieldy? The de facto representative for government became the Atlanta Regional Commission, the regional planning and intergovernmental coordination agency for 10 county governments; the Metro Atlanta Chamber of Commerce represented the business community; and increasingly the United Way of Metropolitan Atlanta and the Community Foundation for Greater Atlanta became the go-to agencies to speak on behalf of nonprofits, community-based organizations, groups, etc.

In order for the de facto representative to be effective and solutions-oriented, the group needed to have access and a shared understanding of the same data and information pertaining to the region. This was not available during these early days. Metaphorically, not having the same data would be similar to some members of a book club reading *War and Peace*, while other members read *Moby Dick*. How could the book club have a discussion about the plot of *To Kill a Mockingbird*? They couldn't. In the same way, we need to be reading from the same book about community for the conversation to have impact and relevance. We need to make sure everyone has access to the book, as well as ensure everyone has the ability to read and comprehend the text.

One opportunity for the Atlanta region is a community indicators initiative, Neighborhood Nexus, that hosts our regional and neighborhood data and helps frame issues (health, housing, income, transportation, and community assets) for residents, government, business, nonprofits, and higher education institutions. But Atlanta is not unique. Currently, indicators are used by many constituencies across the country. Community indicators represent a valuable mechanism to improve monitoring and evaluation in planning. Information-led decision making, combined with a sense of the people in a community, strengthens its members.

Along with sponsoring community indicator projects, community foundations can be the institution that represents, acknowledges, and strengthens the grassroots leaders in order to be their own champions. Grassroots leaders are often the PTA president, the local leader who speaks on behalf of his or her neighbors for safety needs, or the community leader who organizes the annual festival or garden club. If we invest the time to know who to bring to the table, and we can ensure that they are authentic and engaged leaders, then we need to guarantee there is high-quality, easily accessible data at a level that matters so that collective decision making can start there. We also need common methods of reaching decisions; the parliamentary procedure set forth in *Roberts Rules* is not always the best way to reach collective decisions and actions. Through the development and intentional support of grassroots leadership programs, bonds are developed, decision-making methods become second nature, and success is experienced. The future is about collective decision making, fairness, and transparency. That is our charge.

A Changing Philanthropy

If community foundations have a strong core of genuine community knowledge and leadership, these assets can be connected in ever-widening circles that include local business, government, nonprofits, and funders. The community foundation can connect at all levels. This is the true, unique value of a community foundation for all stakeholders, including the donors that entrust us to help guide their philanthropy.

It is this relationship with the donors and their families that is changing as well. In 2005, the Charles Stewart Mott Foundation and the Ford Foundation funded a report entitled *On the Brink of New Promise: The Future of U.S. Community* (Bernholz, Fulton, and Kasper 2005). The report explored several trends facing community foundations in the present and explored the shifting dynamics in the future. A significant highlight pointed to the shifting relationship of the community foundation donor from isolation to inclusion—from asking the question: What did our grant accomplish? to How do we work with others to contribute to community improvement?

In an age of information overload, donors have many philanthropic options, including supporting smaller projects that directly influence a change in the local community. For some, this is one rationale for starting a donor-advised fund. The fund is a symbol of allegiance to grow, advance, and further this place called home, and to do it now, in collaboration with others. The value proposition of community foundations is the substantive knowledge of both the micro (neighborhoods) and macro (regional) community geography over the long term. Such knowledge makes community foundations more viable than other philanthropic tools and is the reason why these foundations must know how to adapt to changing philanthropy.

To do so, community foundations need to play four major roles: that of *investor, convener, partner,* and *supporter.* As an *investor,* the community foundation can expand on its traditional role of grantmaker and provide grants and other financial resources to advance community solutions and innovations. This may also include mission-related investing or building upon our amassed social capital to move forward a specific issue, conversation, or organization. The *convener* role involves on the one hand being a neutral party to gather and connect, while on the other taking leadership responsibility related to inclusion and representation of voices and issues that may be different but necessary for authentic dialogue. Being a *partner* requires the community foundation to be an active participant in an identified effort, but also acknowledging the thin line it plays as a funder. This role may be the most difficult of all because of the traditional expectation that foundations are simply funders. But with cultivated relationships and continued presence, this will likely become a less challenging role—and perhaps the most vital. Finally, as a *supporter,* the community foundation will be a collaborator, thought leader, and advocate. Separately, these roles may seem familiar to many community foundations and other funders, but it is the combined and simultaneous interaction of these roles that defines the future for community foundations.

Conclusion

As stated in *On the Brink of New Promise* (Bernholz, Fulton, and Kasper 2005), the future of community foundations has begun. In the twenty-first century, tradition is captured by characters instead of sentences. We measure access to information by the number of screens one has versus the number of hours spent reading a newspaper or book. However, it is the mutual assistance and shared responsibility that will not change. Community foundations have to stay up-to-date with advanced technology while maintaining a simplistic, open-door approach to community leadership.

The knowledge and contacts from our deep community work are now an integral part of all our work—arts, education, community development, etc. Each new project taken on by the Community Foundation for Greater Atlanta is viewed and structured from an asset-based model. This level of community work has also positioned this community foundation to be even bolder in our strategies as we work to develop a cooperative business in one of our most underdeveloped neighborhoods. The business effort will be enhanced by our deep neighborhood knowledge and broad donor engagement.

Community foundations and their staffs must understand and be adept at all methods of communication and relationship building. These multifaceted and real relationships, developed over time, make us a valuable link to all sectors. Taking this approach will ensure that the *community* in our name means something and reflects the true work we do.

Bibliography

Bernholz, L., K. Fulton, and G. Kasper. 2005. *On the Brink of New Promise: The Future of U.S. Community Foundations.* New York: Monitor Group. http://www.monitorinstitute.com/downloads/what-we-think/new-promise/On_the_Brink_of_New_Promise.pdf.

The Community Foundation for Greater Atlanta (2012). http://www.cfgreateratlanta.org.

Guo, C., and J. Musso. 2007. "Representation in Nonprofit and Voluntary Organizations: A Conceptual Framework." *Nonprofit and Voluntary Sector Quarterly* 36, no. 2, 308–326.

Putnam, R.D. 2000. *Bowling Alone: The Collapse and Revival of American Community.* New York: Simon & Schuster.

10

The Community Foundation as Borderland Institution

G. Albert Ruesga
The Greater New Orleans Foundation

Some critics have argued that it's no accident that grand philanthropic gestures coincide with moments in our history when wealth becomes concentrated in very few hands and the gap between the rich and the poor grows unmanageably large. Consider, for example, the founding of the first great American foundations around the time of the Robber Barons, or the Gates Foundation's contemporary vow to eradicate malaria. Now, as in ages past, observers contend that philanthropy has functioned as a social safety valve, redistributing just enough wealth to keep people in low-income communities from becoming uncontrollably militant. In contexts such as these, they ask, is it really possible for foundations to become the snakes that bite their own tails, to be effective agents of change, challenging and reforming the structures from which they draw their power? (See, for example, Cubeta 2008.)

Foundations—and community foundations in particular—typically straddle two worlds that frequently come into conflict: the world of wealthy trustees, whose power is rooted in the stability of an economic system that creates and sustains their wealth, and the world of grantees who may have little appetite for sustaining the status quo. The role that community foundations play in redistributing wealth is well understood. The role they play in creating bridges of understanding between the social classes, less so.

How, short of civil war, does a nation typically work through periods of intense social polarization? In the United States, we face persistent racial and ethnic divisions as well as stark income and asset inequalities. In 2013, we are experiencing these differences in the context of some very uncivil post-presidential election rhetoric and the emergence of a new kind of American class consciousness characterized by the Occupy Movement.

Given these polarizing forces, what is the glue that keeps contemporary American society from spinning apart? Is it simple inertia, a kind of consumerist satiety? Do we ever, in fact, learn to resolve our differences, or do they come into greater or lesser focus depending on the whims of the news media? If we manage somehow to work through our divisions, where does this bridging work happen?

It's not the first time in recent history that we've come to a perceived boiling point. In a book titled *Beyond Individualism*, Michael Piore (1995) wrote about a "social deficit" created in the 1980s and early 1990s that eventually led to increased political mobilization and social instability. A pivotal event of that era, according to Piore, was President Reagan's crushing of the federal air traffic controllers' strike of 1981, an action that "galvanized anti-union managerial factions in a whole variety of industries and occupations where union organization had previously been unassailable" (Piore 1995, 14). It was open season on organized labor. The wealthiest Americans saw a marked increase in their standard of living while the incomes of blue collar workers declined. The savings and loan crisis and its attendant bailout presaged our contemporary financial market meltdown and moved some commentators to dub the period between 1985 and 1995 the "Looting Decade" (Sherrill 1990). Political life also took a nasty turn. The Bush campaign's Willie Horton ads in 1988 alienated black Americans, while the family values rhetoric of the 1992 campaign unfairly targeted single mothers, feminists, and gays and lesbians. Against this backdrop of political turmoil, identity groups grew in visibility and pressed their claims on American society. According to Piore, we could not, during this fiscally lean era, opt to settle these claims through massive social spending. All of this created an atmosphere of tension and instability, perhaps not substantially different in feeling and tone from the one we're currently experiencing.

The Power of the Borderlands

To address this increased polarization, Piore suggested that politicians and policymakers champion the *borderlands*, institutions in which "social claimants" could cross group boundaries and communicate their needs and concerns to society at large.[1] Through dynamic give-and-take "political conversations" in these borderland institutions, marginalized identity groups could become agents in the creation of a new national culture, constituted not so much by erasing group boundaries as by increasing the acceptance of a more enlightened, more workable kind of pluralism (Piore 1995). Participants in these discussions would interpret their actions to themselves and others in ways that acknowledge the effects of one community of meaning upon another. Perhaps on occasion these discussants would even celebrate their differences.

There's so much that's compelling about Piore's vision of the borderlands, rooted, as it appears to be, in Aristotle's view of Man as the "political animal."

Somewhere between Wall Street and the Occupy Movement's encampments in Zuccotti Park, there would be a space where both bankers and activists could plead their cases. Ideally, the 1 percent would get a clearer sense of the effect of their actions on people with modest means, while the 99 percent would better understand the economic system that—for better or for worse—implicates us all. Unfortunately, in 20 years or so of nonprofit work, I've known only a handful of organizations that fit the description of a borderland institution.[2] First, most civil society organizations are segregated by race, ethnicity, class, and the other divisions that borderland institutions are expected to bridge. Even when these organizations are not segregated, they seldom make it their mission to champion give-and-take conversations across group boundaries. From my own experience of participation in diversity trainings, poverty summits, and other intergroup meetings, these bridging conversations are fiendishly difficult to pull off.

Of course the mixing of people from different backgrounds happens outside the context of civil society organizations, in such venues as grocery stores, sports stadiums, parade routes, and popular music concerts. But these are not typically places consecrated to boundary-crossing deliberation and the forging of new understandings. The fact that Piore dubs his institutions "borderlands" suggests how marginal this kind of discussion has become. Perhaps in some real or imagined past, we talked through our differences in the town square or the agora. In these nefarious times, however, we've pushed these conversations to the edges of civic life. We've made them exceptional rather than central to the political and other processes that shape our national character. To be clear, what's achieved through discussion and deliberation in the borderlands will often fall short of an identity-blurring synthesis of conflicting worldviews. Participants might instead discover shared values or ends. People on either side of the abortion debate, for example, might work together to prevent unwanted pregnancies, or they might find a way to move forward based simply on a clearer sense of their shared humanity.

Many of us who initially saw great promise in the ability of the Internet to provide virtual "bridging" spaces have been disappointed. Blogs, message boards, and other social media sites have self-segregated in predictable ways, and there are many characteristics of the Internet and its use that have gotten in the way of transforming loosely associated individuals into a community of people with shared understandings about the world. Consider, for example, an environmental advocate—call him Joe—who wants to use the Internet to discuss an upcoming election with people both inside and outside his ideological frame. Joe longs to engage others in an extended discussion of the candidates and their views, tactics for engaging the media, and other election season issues. If his experience is anything like mine, he'll face the following kinds of challenges when he goes online to his favorite social media sites:

1. *Light's on but nobody's home:* Joe submits a question to a message board here, a social media site there, but can't depend on getting a timely answer, or any answer at all. Sometimes it takes days to get a response. In any event, he wants something that feels more like a real-time conversation.
2. *The wrong people at the right time:* Joe has to contend with the usual trolls, flamers, and hyperpartisans who throw discussions off-topic. He visits his favorite sites, but, as is often the case, few people are present and contributing, and the best minds and moderators are absent.
3. *Drive-by comments:* He finds a few warm bodies willing to engage in a discussion of the upcoming election, but they keep straying off-topic. Because nobody really "owns" the discussion, it gets sidetracked easily.
4. *A million vases for a thousand flowers:* Nancy, a thoughtful conservative, likes to hang out on Facebook, but Mary, a dyed-in-the wool liberal, would never darken Facebook's cyber-door. She much prefers Change.org. And so it goes. Joe might need to visit 20 sites to have a prayer of finding what he's looking for.

I'm not here saying that there are no spaces on the Internet where meaningful bridging conversations can happen. There clearly are, but I suspect they're few in number, reflecting our limited appetite for this kind of online experience. Moreover, the Internet cannot be expected to save us from ourselves—our partisanship, our limited attention spans, our attenuated critical thinking and reading skills. We carry all of this baggage with us on our travels through cyberspace. There's a ghost in the machine, and that ghost is us, recreating in our virtual spaces the same barriers that keep us apart in the world where flesh encounters flesh.

Apart from the few civil society organizations specifically consecrated to abetting intergroup conversations, there is one American institution in which we consistently encounter the bridging work championed by Piore and others. This institution has the potential to demonstrate, in a powerful way, the value of the borderlands to our civic and political cultures, and perhaps even bring to scale intergroup work critical to our functioning as a multiclass, multicultural society. This institution routinely "translates" the language of one class, one racial group, one gender to the other. The institution I'm referring to is *the community foundation.*

Here's a gross simplification of how these translations work. Members of a marginalized community either plead their case directly to a community foundation program officer or, more commonly, through some proxy—the director of a nonprofit organization, for example—who submits a grant proposal on behalf of the community in question. The program officer, who has absorbed the middle-class norms of her institution, translates this request and its rationale into a form and language that will be acceptable to her largely upper-middle-class or wealthy trustees. The conversation doesn't just go in one direction—or at least ideally it shouldn't. There's a healthy back and forth as one class or group interprets its experience, its values, and its aspirations to the other. Since grant decisions are essentially about the allocation of scarce resources in a community, there's also discussion about economic constraints—their origin and ways to address them. The conversation is wide-ranging, including topics in education, the arts, health, economic development, the environment, and more. Unfortunately, in many community foundation board meetings we'll see a reflection of how class interdynamics play themselves out in the broader society. But if we're lucky, we might begin to see a model of what the ideal discussion should look like in a properly constituted borderland institution.

If we are to believe the rhetoric of many in the field of philanthropy, there is a growing movement of foundations—community and otherwise—predicated on the notion that "grantmakers are more effective to the extent that they meaningfully engage their grantees and other key stakeholders" (Bourns 2010, 1). This engagement takes many forms, and the crosstalk it can create between segregated communities about values, assumptions, and aspirations can help make the community foundation an effective engine of understanding and healing.

But for community foundations to become vibrant borderland institutions, they must first overcome several barriers.

Getting Inside the Black Box

I remember my sense of anticipation some 20 years ago when I landed my first community foundation job. None of my friends or colleagues had any inkling what happened inside these black boxes that consistently swallowed our proposals and issued polite rejections.

I had heard that foundations were about social change, that they were about marshaling private capital for the public good. I was excited by the idea of working with peers who had the time to think deeply about our community's greatest challenges, who were not constantly passing the hat to pay the light bill.

My first day on the job, I met former activists who knew what it was like to grow up black and poor. I felt an enormous sense of hope as I admired the view of the city I loved from my twenty-eighth story window. On my second day, I chided myself for my overly romantic idealizations of foundation work. Of course sexism, careerism, and other -isms could exist here as elsewhere. But still, foundations were anointed institutions, set apart to serve as the conscience of the community. On my third day, I was wondering what I had gotten myself into. There appeared to be a gulf between my institution's stated aspirations and its culture. This was not a place, in my view, where people of good will were united in a great purpose. We prided ourselves on our ability to listen to the community, but what the community said and how this got translated into foundation programs and initiatives seemed to be two very different things.

Most striking to me, however, were the middle-class values and worldviews that dominated the culture of the institution. For an organization so clearly focused on the concerns of the poor, poverty seemed a strangely distant phenomenon. The poor and the communities they inhabited became screens onto which we projected our favorite theories of change, knowing that if these were toothless enough, they would meet with the full approval of our senior managers and trustees.

Was I perhaps making too many assumptions about the character and role of a community foundation? After all, other community foundations I knew seemed to make it their purpose to *endure* or work with the status quo rather than challenge it. If my idealizations were so far off the mark, what then was a foundation supposed to be about?

One colleague recently addressed this very thorny question about the purpose and identity of community foundations:

> Should philanthropy uphold or challenge the status quo? I've always seen the role and purpose of [community foundations] as being one of brokerage between the two positions. We stand of necessity with a foot in both camps, and it is our specific function to interpret each side to the other and make them intelligible. A [community foundation] that plants itself squarely on one side or the other will betray its mission. . . . We serve mutually incompatible constituencies—proponents of social change versus upholders of the status quo. All over the world, I suspect, people in [community foundations] are deliberately muddying waters in order to satisfy both at once. It's what we're good at, and if we leaned too far in either direction we'd stop being [community foundations] and become something else.[3]

Here again we have a hint of the kind of borderland institution that Michael Piore championed. And yet the "interpreter" or "broker" in this passage stands outside or above the conversation. Is he supposed to have no feelings one way or the other about what he is asked to interpret, and if not, why does he bother? Does he interpret ultimately for the sake of a paycheck or for the sake of justice? And does it matter? Can an organization interpret the world

to everything and everyone except itself? It's not only community foundations that struggle to keep one foot in two camps, to broker between the lived
experience of poverty, say, and the privileged world of staff and trustees.
Small and large private foundations struggle with this as well, as does every
nonprofit intent on survival.

This identity crisis for community foundations is mirrored in fieldwide
conversations about the proper role of philanthropy in societies that face stark
racial and economic disparities. By some accounts, in the United States you
will currently find two armies battling against overwhelming indifference—
and against one another—for the soul of philanthropy (cf. Cubeta 2008). One
camp is arrayed under such banners as "metrics" and "evaluation," and has
a distinctly business-school cast. The other promotes a style of philanthropy
concerned with social justice and seeks to expose the root causes of our social
ills. These are caricatures, of course, but they're not entirely without foundation. Grantmakers in the social justice camp argue that most of the giving done
by mainstream foundations is based on an incomplete or flawed analysis of
what it takes to achieve goals like ending poverty or ensuring that all children
thrive. Mainstream foundations, they argue, content themselves with triaging
society's victims, never wondering about the causes of their victimhood, and
suspecting, perhaps, that they might themselves be implicated in the crime.

It's a rare community foundation that will come out squarely for social
justice, preferring instead to posit more neutral goals like "social change" or
"positive community impact." If they support advocacy or community organizing, they will sometimes describe these to their boards as grantmaking in
support of "citizen engagement."

Issues of translation aside, what is a community foundation's role in cities
and regions where significant racial and other disparities persist? How much
license is given to staff by trustees to develop an analysis of the origins of
these disparities? If, because of culture or by fiat, a community foundation is
obliged to pass over these matters in silence, then to what degree is it simply
making a show of addressing our social ills? And under these circumstances,
how can a community foundation hope to function effectively as a borderland
or bridging institution?

Community Foundations and Social Justice

You will rarely find a community foundation that fully embraces the analyses,
strategies, tactics, and values of social justice grantmaking, which I define
here simply as grantmaking that addresses the root and/or structural causes of
social, economic, or political injustice. A 2011 survey of community foundations suggests why this might be the case.

Barry Knight, director of CENTRIS (The Centre for Research and Innovation in Social Policy Ltd.), and I invited community foundation staff members to respond to a five-question survey on matters relating to social justice philanthropy. We received a little over 50 responses.[4] We found that 57 percent of respondents agreed or strongly agreed with the statement, "Many CEOs or trustees of community foundations resist social justice philanthropy because they fear alienating donors," while only 17 percent disagreed or strongly disagreed (see Figure 10.1).

Rather than guess at why social justice philanthropy might alienate donors, we included a question that would probe the roots of people's unease with the notion (see Table 10.1). There were two factors that stood out:

1. The term "social justice" sounds too radical for some.
2. The aims of social justice philanthropy seem too vague or too broad for others.

On the one hand, the radical connotations of social justice philanthropy might be a bit surprising, given that a quest for social justice is central to various mainstream Jewish, Christian, and other faith traditions. On the other hand, many people still associate calls for social justice with the politically charged language of the 1960s.

More troubling to practitioners should be the claim that the aims of social justice philanthropy are too vague or too broad. Is the goal fairness and equal access to opportunity? If so, how can this be sharpened? Or is the goal a fairer distribution of society's benefits and harms, something that might indeed cause a flutter in many a trustee's heart? Not too surprisingly, our survey uncovered a significant difference of opinion between the corner office and program staff members: 62 percent of respondents agreed or strongly agreed with the statement, "Program staff at community foundations are generally more supportive of social justice philanthropy than CEOs or trustees," as compared with 15 percent who disagreed or strongly disagreed.

When we asked survey takers to define social justice philanthropy, we saw a broad array of responses, the most popular involving, in some way or other, the attainment of "equity." Some respondents described *equity* as a leveling of the playing field; others as providing equal access to opportunity. None, apparently, thought of it as a post-earnings redistribution of wealth. If, as 11 of our respondents suggested, social justice philanthropy is simply a matter of helping those who are least well off, then the category suffers meaning inflation and comes to include just about every grantmaker in the United States and abroad (see Table 10.2).

Figure 10.1   Does Social Justice Philanthropy Alienate Donors?

Do you agree or disagree that "many CEOs or trustees of community foundations resist social justice philanthropy because they fear alienating donors"?

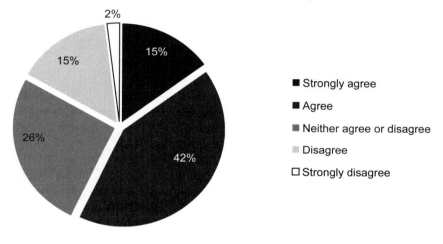

- ■ Strongly agree
- ■ Agree
- ■ Neither agree or disagree
- ▨ Disagree
- ☐ Strongly disagree

Table 10.1

Why Does Social Justice Philanthropy Alienate Donors?

A number of factors might contribute to a rejection of social justice philanthropy. Please rank the following factors in order of importance (1 = most important, 5 = least important).

Answer options	1	2	3	4	5	Rating average	Response count
The aims of social justice philanthropy are too vague or too broad.	13	18	16	3	2	2.29	52
The term "social justice philanthropy" sounds a bit radical.	22	5	5	6	6	2.30	44
The effects of social justice philanthropy can't be easily measured.	10	16	14	3	3	2.41	46
Social justice philanthropy is not generally considered effective.	1	6	11	19	8	3.60	45
Nonprofits that promote social justice are generally weaker than others.	1	2	6	17	25	4.24	51

Table 10.2

How Would You Define Social Justice Philanthropy?

Category	N
Achieve equity	18
Help people least well-off	11
Systemic/structural change	8
Not sure, no clue	5
Address root causes	4
All other responses	≤ 2

Pondering these survey results, I'm hopeful that community foundations will be able find the language—"fairness," "equality of opportunity"—that resonates with their donors and other stakeholders. The persistent racial and other disparities in many communities highlight, in my view, the shortcomings of philanthropy-as-usual and prompt us to look for a new kind of giving. To make the same kinds of grants year after year to the same communities, to see the same disparities persist and even widen, and not to question one's approach to grantmaking is, also in my view, to do philanthropy in bad faith. Social justice philanthropy offers us a way of recommitting ourselves to philanthropy's great aims. In practicing it, we acknowledge that what's good enough for us might not be good enough for the communities we purport to serve. And yet, if a community foundation chooses to hold itself accountable in this way, to what degree will it necessarily implicate itself in conversations that will be uncomfortable both for underserved communities and trustees?

Conclusion

In this essay I've concentrated on some of the purely cultural aspects of a community foundation's "bridging" work, ignoring the role it might play, for example, in using its convening power to forge a consensus on public policy or coordinate the efforts of other community actors. Speaking at a discussion hosted by the Philanthropic Initiative for Racial Equity, Rashad Robinson, executive director of ColorOfChange, made this observation:

> Oftentimes we miss moments to challenge the cultural conversation and we instantly go to policy. And I think that's where we lose. We can't have conversations outside of culture and where people are getting their information every day. We have to challenge that and hold those structures accountable the same way we want to hold elected officials accountable. (quoted in Villarosa 2012)

Robinson is right to say that many activists see policy change as the Holy Grail of social change efforts, or that, at the very least, they tend to underplay the role played by culture in keeping low-income communities marginalized. Activists and funders fall prey to the Systems Heresy: the belief that injustice is largely "structural," that it's the property of a system that regulates human behavior rather than a property of actors who are frequently all too human.[5]

In this essay, the bridging work of the borderland institution takes place much more in the arena of cultural translation than in the arena of public policy. But if policy change is difficult, the shifting of culture must seem impossible by comparison. It happens so slowly, so imperceptibly. We know from the history of large social change efforts in the United States—the ending of slavery, the achievement of women's suffrage—that shifts in cultural norms both precede and lag behind significant policy victories. Attitudes about African Americans and women, two groups who sought change, continue to evolve. Unfortunately, the time scale for these cultural changes makes them unlikely candidates for foundation funding, which is too often focused on the quick victory—or its simulacrum. Given that a cultural shift will take its own sweet time, is it even worth the attempt to accelerate the process, to encourage the community foundation's role as a borderland institution?

And what about the charge that a community foundation betrays its mission when it leans too far in the direction of social justice, or, alternatively, in the direction of elite interests? My own view is that a community foundation ceases to be a community foundation not when it sides with proponents of social change or those who resist them, but when it fails to understand what living in community requires of us; and that any foundation or charity betrays its purpose, its identity, when institutional imperatives completely trump moral imagination. I understand how fiendishly difficult it is for a community foundation, in particular, to give free rein to the moral imagination, to let it lead where it might. Community foundation staffers and CEOs can try to keep a foot in each camp, but unfortunately each camp—privileged or marginalized, the 1 percent or the 99 percent—has a narrative that implicates the other in some kind of moral failing. And for most community foundations, it's only one of these camps that pays the bills.

That is the irreducible tension presented by the community foundation, especially by one that serves a large and diverse constituency. The funds for these institutions typically rain down from above, while those who benefit from this largesse are not always simply content to play the role of grateful supplicant. They have a story to tell. They have questions to ask of a society in which poverty persists and afflicts one racially defined community more than another. And they have it on good authority that the game is rigged against them. Leadership requires that the foundation CEO do better than Buridan's ass, an animal that stood indecisively between two equally enticing bales of hay. If leadership requires that he move forward, rather than to one side or the other, what, exactly, would he be moving forward toward?

I offer, with fear and trembling, these words of advice to my colleagues, after having made every possible mistake in attempting to create bridges between the very different worlds served by a community foundation:

1. *Don't succumb to relativism.* While different communities have different ideas about truth, justice, and fairness, moving from this to the claim that we ought to tolerate all views will undermine rather than support your efforts to forge a deeper understanding between apparently incommensurable communities.

2. *It's not possible to be completely neutral and growth-encouraging.* You, your staff, your trustees, and your grantees all have points of view. Own them. And remember also Thomas Kuhn's (1962) famous dictum that there's no such thing as a theory-neutral observation: both what you choose to look at and what you choose to see are shaped by your worldview as much as anything else.

3. *Stick to your knitting.* The term *social justice* carries a lot of baggage, as does the term *equity.* Don't allow yourself to fall into a wordsmithing hole. If certain words offend, find new language and move on. From my own experience, more off-putting than these loaded words is the armchair sociology that often accompanies them. Concentrated poverty in the African American community is a complex phenomenon with a long history. Does anybody really have a perfect handle on it? Do your trustees and grantees need to agree on the forces that sustain it before you can agree to work together to eliminate it? Focus on the facts and hold yourself accountable to them.

Our experience of the world in many ways hides the contingency of what we know and believe. Social institutions and lifeways antedate our births and accompany us to our deaths without once appearing to change their essential natures. The community foundation, through its role as a borderland institution, can help move us outside of our class-constructed echo chambers, disrupting our sense of the "givenness" of what we encounter in our daily lives. It can help us model, perhaps like no other institution, a kind of civil discourse that is as powerful as it is rare.

Notes

1. Piore (1995) anchors his notion of a borderland institution in Renaldo Rosaldo's (1989) notion of a borderland culture, "in which people are led to reflect on their experience in ways that ultimately alter the interpretive framework of the culture itself"

(Piore, 148). Moreover, Rosaldo's concept of borderlands "yields new insight into how a society composed of communities of action might be integrated socially, . . . and into processes that might reconcile the conflicts among the claims of such communities and between those claims and the constraints imposed by the economy" (Piore, 167). Understood in this way, Piore's notion of a borderland institution is one of a family of concepts that might emerge from various versions of social contract theory or from theories of deliberative democracy—as described, for example, by Joshua Cohen (1991) in his essay "Deliberation and Democratic Legitimacy."

2. Re: "I've known only a handful of organizations that fit the description of a borderland institution": for example, the Public Conversations Project based in Watertown, Massachusetts, which was launched in 1994 when a televised debate on abortion moved one of its founders to explore "how family therapy practices could improve polarized conversations about abortion and other public issues" (Public Conversations Project 2013).

3. This is an excerpt from a longer comment left by Hilary Gilbert on a blog post by the author at Ruesga (2011). The excerpt is reproduced here with her permission.

4. The material in this section originally appeared in a blog post by the author at Ruesga (2011). The link to the survey instrument was distributed to Council on Foundation members, who then self-selected to participate in the survey.

5. For a discussion of this issue, see Ruesga (2008).

Bibliography

Bourns, J.C. 2010. *Do Nothing About Me Without Me: An Action Guide for Engaging Shareholders.* Washington, DC: Grantmakers for Effective Organizations.

Cohen, J. 1991. "Deliberation and Democratic Legitimacy." In *The Good Polity: Normative Analysis of the State,* ed. A. Hamlin and P. Pettit. New York: Basil Blackwell.

Cubeta, P. 2008. "Social Change Without Budgets or Permission." Gift Hub, June 12. http://www.gifthub.org/2008/06/social-change-w.html.

The Greater New Orleans Foundation. 2012. http://www.gnof.org.

Khun, T.S. 1962. *The Structure of Scientific Revolutions.* Chicago, IL: University of Chicago Press.

Piore, M.J. 1995. *Beyond Individualism.* Cambridge, MA: Harvard University Press.

Public Conversations Project. 2013. "History: The Beginning." http://www.public-conversations.org/who/history.

Rosaldo, R. 1989. *Culture and Truth: The Remaking of Social Analysis.* Boston, MA: Beacon Press.

Ruesga, G. Albert. 2011. "The Big Uneasy: New Data on Community Foundations and Social Justice." White Courtesy Telephone, November 7. http://postcards.typepad.com/white_telephone/2011/11/biguneasy.html.

———. 2008. "The Island of the Yooks and the Zooks: Notes on the Systems Heresy." White Courtesy Telephone, June 29. http://postcards.typepad.com/white_telephone/2008/06/the-island-of-t.html.

Sherrill, R. 1990. "The Looting Decade: S&Ls, Big Banks, and Other Triumphs of Capitalism." *The Nation* 251, no. 17 (November 19): 589–623.

Villarosa, L. 2012. *Continuing Dialogue Mobilizing Community Power to Address Structural Racism.* Report, April. Washington, DC: Philanthropic Initiative for Racial Equity.

11

Never Second-Guess the Locals

Chris Rurik
One Nation

Henry Izumizaki
One Nation

Nillofur Jasani
One Nation

What happens when a philanthropist from a third-tier city like Tacoma, Washington, decides that he's going to prevent a 100-year war? That by counteracting a festering nationwide fear of Muslims in the aftermath of 9/11, he's going to steer the whole world toward peace? Sounds like a well-intentioned prescription for some wide-ranging and ultimately futile work, right?

One Nation, the philanthropic collaborative resulting from George F. Russell, Jr.'s belief that ignorance and Islamophobia here in America were growing threats to peace the world over, could easily have taken the safe route into an oblivion of dubious impact and too-complex-to-counteract societal rifts, but for a variety of reasons that's not what happened.

One Nation ended as an entity in 2012, but its story ended in what seems an unexpected place—with community foundations. After seven years of wide-ranging efforts to find the most powerful avenue for its funds, One Nation came to the conclusion that the key to something so human and intimate as an individual's perceptions of other individuals could not be found at the national or regional levels. Only when local communities engaged on their own terms could fundamental progress be made toward erasing prejudice and building a more resilient society. Despite the normal temptation of national funders to invent silver bullet solutions and fire them every which way, One Nation was able to foster progress in dissimilar cities by counterintuitively ceding its authority as programmatic decision maker to locals, letting those who inherently knew their own communities invent the best ways to counteract misperceptions of Muslims locally.

When One Nation began concentrating its efforts on models of community engagement, it became clear that the seemingly intractable societal rifts that are woven into any diverse community are best bridged with conversations, and that the conversations are best housed in community foundations that can act as neutral conveners. Unfortunately, due to conservative financial stewardship and the paralysis that comes from intractable issues, most community foundations fail to host such diverse, open-ended conversations. A national funder can shock community foundations into that role, but only if the funder completely trusts the locals to make the strategy decisions about how best to exert an impact on their community.

Simple conclusions, really, to come from such a complex mission—that just getting people together provides the basis for a community with resiliency, that community foundations are perfectly positioned as forums for getting people together, that flexible national funders can instigate such community-building dialogues, and that the work is more critical now than ever.

But it was not a conclusion that came immediately or easily. After all, when your mission is as abstract as stopping a war by changing the minds of a nation of individuals, where do you start? What's your first move?

In business, Russell had a record of aiming high, making decisions quickly, moving fast, learning from the inevitable mistakes, and making more quick decisions. He also firmly believed in hiring people smarter than himself. These principles allowed One Nation to operate in a way that ultimately bypassed many of the conventions that dictate business-as-usual in philanthropy.

In addition, Russell had strong personal ties to his community of Tacoma, both professionally and personally, and his work previous to One Nation bore out the idea that the institutions and people that anchor communities are inextricable from their geography. From investment in local arts to the economic redevelopment of downtown, relationship-based local impact was the hallmark of his record. But this plan? This was different. Starting as broadly ambitious as One Nation did, it would take quite a bit of time and a significant shift in strategy before it could have that kind of local presence.

For its first four years, One Nation followed a more-or-less traditional organizational trajectory. Russell commissioned a report to identify and evaluate organizations across the country that were working with American Muslims. He then convened Muslim leaders from across the country in open dialogues to figure out how One Nation could work most effectively as a funder. A high-powered board was recruited. Eventually, four areas of work emerged as good areas for nationwide impact—*strategic communications, media development, civic engagement,* and *public policy.*

And over those four years, One Nation precipitated some exciting results. A network of Muslim spokespeople who had been trained in how to interact positively with the media began to offer journalists a more nuanced and moderate source of information when big stories broke. Four feature-length films designed to educate Americans about Islam were shown on public broadcasting stations and adopted into classrooms. Two digital film contests gave voice to creative American Muslims and launched several entertainment industry careers. A web page was developed that gave Hollywood writers access to basic information about Islam and life as a Muslim in America, that they might write less stereotyped characters. Capacity-building support was given to several organizations that were doing leadership training and civic engagement work. These are just a few examples.

Nonetheless, the civic engagement and public policy initiatives were dropped for a lack of actionable plans. Metrics for success were hard to come by. And more and more, the work that One Nation did felt like an uphill struggle on a hill that kept getting steeper. In fact, a 2011 report published by the Center for American Progress has since justified that impression (Ali et al. 2011). Despite their best effort to leverage their dollars, One Nation's modest budget was a fraction of the amount that had flowed from a small network of foundations into organizations that actively promoted Islamophobia in the decade after 9/11. Most discouraging? In the eight years between 2002 and 2010, the percentage of Americans with an unfavorable view of Muslims actually increased from 39 to 49 percent.

Something had to change. One Nation's impact was too slow—things were getting worse. But what could be done?

A new direction for the project revealed itself only when One Nation went back to struggle with the most basic question: "What is the most effective way of changing Joe America's ideas about what Islam represents and what Muslim Americans want?"

The answer, of course, was so simple as to nearly be dismissed. The best way to understand a Muslim is to meet a Muslim. When Joe America has a Muslim family as neighbors, he'll realize that despite a difference in religious ideology, most of the family's ideas about how to lead a fulfilling life are no different from his. Even if they're not his best friends, he'll know that they're not terrorists. They're American too. Then, when he sees news reports of anti-American riots led by angered Arabs, he'll be able to compare that side of Islam with his more peaceful neighbors, saving him from a stereotype-based view of those whose ideologies contrast with his. It won't erase his religion, but it will show him where his and his neighbor's religions overlap, allowing them to work together for the good of their greater neighborhood when the need arises.

The building blocks of resilient communities are conversations. One Nation had always believed that ignorance is the primary divisive force in society, and that education is the key to realizing true pluralism. Naturally, the best kind of education is personal interaction.

Once again, the question of where to start had to be addressed. For a national funder with a staff never greater than three, the idea that neighborhood-level work held the most powerful potential presented a logistical puzzle. Hiring staff around the country was out of the question. Who could they inspire with their vision? What institution had the resources and local ties to house the work?

Community foundations were the natural choice. What other institution exists solely to foster the growth and health of their community? Politicians are too enmeshed in a bureaucratic system. Individual philanthropists rarely represent all of the community's interests. Hospitals, libraries, and community centers each have their niche. At their best, community foundations have connections in all sectors—business, government, nonprofit—and the mobility to adopt any kind of project that is important for the community's well-being.

Here's where Russell's tendencies to move fast and trust others allowed One Nation to conceptualize a national-local partnership style that would have been too risky for most nonprofits. The strategy was based on an untested hypothesis: that local organizations would know far better than national organizations how to foster conversations within their particular communities, and that by ceding all programmatic authority to the locals, One Nation could instigate local solutions that took into account the individuality of communities and the forces of realpolitik. This even meant abandoning evaluation metrics and allowing the locals to measure their own success. Needless to say, it took a certain kind of staff to come up with a plan like that, and a certain kind of donor to agree to it.

In an effort to ensure that partnerships had sufficient local buy-in and would remain sustainable, One Nation also decided to require matches for all of their grants. It would partner with and cede programmatic authority to a community foundation, but only if that foundation matched them dollar-for-dollar, up to $500,000. This was another untested hypothesis. Would any community foundation be willing to put money on the table for such an ill-defined program?

To make a long story short, One Nation chose Chicago as the pilot city for its newly envisioned partnership scheme. Drawing on connections with the Chicago Community Trust and two Chicago-based, Muslim-led organizations—Interfaith Youth Core and Inner-City Muslim Action Network—One Nation proposed an initiative that would attempt to address misperceptions of Muslims in a manner specifically tailored to Chicago. With the help of a strategic planning consultant, representatives of the four organizations invented a program that became known as One Chicago, One Nation (OCON)

(2012). This program included a digital film contest, the formation of a Muslim donor circle, and the first ever Sharia-compliant fund. Most of the resources, though, went into recruiting what were called "community ambassadors," neighborhood leaders of every faith, age, and background that were trained to convene purposeful dialogues autonomously in their neighborhoods. If they wanted to host a larger event or support a community effort, mini-grants were available. After two years, nearly a hundred community ambassadors are working independently in Chicago, backed up by the network of like-minded leaders with whom they trained.

In planning a program like that, one might think there would have been a power struggle, with each organization pulling for its own vision. That's not how it worked. Since all four organizations had similar missions—strengthening the community—they were able to combine resources and invent a collective vision.

After Chicago, One Nation sought other cities in which to partner, cities in which the underlying mission and principles would be the same, but the program's manifestation might be quite different. By the time One Nation closed its doors, it had partnership initiatives running in Chicago, New York City, San Francisco Bay Area, Saint Paul, Santa Barbara, Los Angeles, Tacoma, Atlanta, and Baltimore. Each city has reinforced the idea that the people who know best about how to create conversations are the people who will be participating in those conversations.

Perhaps the most contentious moment in One Nation's life span came soon into the new civic engagement strategy, after it promised the organizations in Chicago that it would relinquish all decision-making power to the locals. Soon after the inception of OCON, the staff at One Nation realized that as long as they had a national advisory board that could dictate One Nation's participation in partnerships and define its desired outcomes, locals wouldn't feel like they had complete freedom to do what they determined best. One Nation staff laid the problem on the boardroom table and suggested that the board "retire," because under the new partnership model there were no real decisions for the board to make. Half of the board saw potential in the plan and were willing to trust the staff. The other half found it risky and wishy-washy and too sudden a shift—in cutting off all funding to existing grantees, much of the change they'd worked so hard for as an organization would be lost.

Of course, the vote that counted was Russell's. He had no patience for mixed results, especially when an untried alternative strategy presented itself. So the advisory board became the founding board, and One Nation became a nonorganization.

In Chicago, this step reduced One Nation's role to instigator and advisor. It precipitated the OCON initiative with its all-or-nothing fund-raising challenge, which then challenged business-as-usual for local organizations in several important ways. Though community foundations are uniquely poised to think creatively about solutions to local issues by convening a diversity of viewpoints, innovation continues to be rare. That's because innovation involves risk. Because of their position as philanthropic stewards, community foundations almost always play it safe by operating in a traditional framework of responsive grantmaking. Work remains in silos; most interaction with on-the-ground organizations occurs through the formulaic grantmaking process. They support solutions but do not help to invent them. A safe hierarchy exists between foundation and nonprofit, nonprofit and community.

With its premium on creating dialogue, One Nation was able to go in and say, "Look, you're already funding all the right people. Just get them together!" In building a resilient community, the same principle that applies to individuals applies also to organizations—conversations are key. In each city that met One Nation's challenge, the story was the same. Organizations with similar missions that had worked in the same space for years had never really collaborated. And when they did, their collective impact expanded beyond anything achieved while work remained siloed.

For example, in the One Nation Bay Area initiative, the San Francisco Foundation (2012), Marin Community Foundation, Silicon Valley Community Foundation (2012), and Asian Americans/Pacific Islanders in Philanthropy partnered by equally pooling vision and resources. The partnership has allowed each organization to expand beyond their normal jurisdiction, accessing a Muslim American community that sprawls throughout the Bay Area.

If One Nation let locals create the vision, make all the decisions, and house all the work, why can't community foundations do this work on their own? Is the national funder really necessary?

In almost every city, the answer was yes. Despite the capability of local foundations, this kind of dialogue-based, collaborative work usually does not happen. To make it happen takes a real, impactful change, like a local disaster, that forces a breakdown of stultifying normal organizational hierarchies. Alternatively, as One Nation learned, such collaborative change can be achieved at the instigation of an outsider. If someone "reputable" is willing to put their faith and money into trying a new system of action, it gives the locals the impetus to try something new. Otherwise, our experience requires us to ask quite rhetorically, why would a community foundation do something potentially controversial? Why take the risk?

One Nation made it clear in each city that it did not want to support business as usual. It wanted to bridge divides in the community, starting with organizations that ought to be working together and going on down to neighborhood-by-neighborhood rifts.

It was able to focus many cities' efforts on misperceptions of Muslims because its goal fit naturally with work that was already being done. Each of the community foundations had preexisting programmatic focuses—such as immigrant integration or interfaith understanding—into which anti-Islamophobia work could fall. It added inspiration and value to these programs, making the creation of local initiatives natural. This in turn contributed to the initiatives' ongoing sustainability.

With One Nation's instigation, lines of inquiry were ignited around the country that otherwise would have gone unexplored. Staff members at the Community Foundation for Greater Atlanta were intrigued by the idea of working with Muslim communities in their city. They estimated that they had 15 or 20 mosques in their service area. But they were wrong; after doing some research, they learned that there were over sixty.

Soon after Chicago, One Nation's open-ended desire to try new things by getting folks together led it to the true mother lode of division over cultural diversity—post-9/11 New York City. While planning its civic engagement strategy, One Nation had shied away from New York City as a place for partnership, intimidated by the city's size and complexity. But as the proposed "Ground Zero mosque" stirred up anti-Islam rhetoric nationwide and the tenth anniversary of the World Trade Center attacks approached, One Nation was compelled to act. They met with the New York Community Trust (NYCT) to discuss ideas for an initiative. Remembering the unexpectedly powerful support of Chicago mayor Richard Daley for OCON, they asked about the possibility of a partnership with the Office of the Mayor in New York.

One Nation was connected to Fatima Shama, leader of the Mayor's Office of Immigrant Affairs (MOIA). She told them that as a Muslim, she knew of their work. She thanked them on behalf of her family and children (Dolnick 2011).

That got them off to a fast start. In a city so tightly packed that any violent prejudice would be disastrous for everyone, the three organizations worked to strengthen the city through active integration. The program—One NYC, One Nation—hasn't invented much of anything; it has simply connected immigrant communities with existing programs and services in new ways, such as providing local leaders with formal training and then opening pipelines to established leadership positions such as neighborhood councils (The City of New York 2011). For One Nation, the formal partnership between the NYCT and MOIA, private philanthropy and government, epitomized vibrant, holistic civil society.

In each new city, One Nation was able to offer ideas and examples as to how other cities had gone about addressing misperceptions of Muslims. Then they watched as local community foundation staff engaged with local organizations to invent uniquely local ways of going about the work.

In Minneapolis, Minnesota Philanthropy Partners took the idea of giving decision-making power to the locals a step further by hosting a Minnesota Idea Open (2012b). They asked all Minnesotans, "What is your best idea to build bonds and work together across cultures and faiths in your community?" After everyday people submitted an avalanche of over 600 ideas, three winners were chosen and given $15,000 grants to make their ideas a reality. These included a traveling experiential art exhibit housed in tents, a multifaith barn-raising, and a group of girls who did several stunts to educate others about Islam, like teaching people how to tie head scarves in downtown Minneapolis (MN Idea Open, 2012a). More amazingly, though, Minnesota Philanthropy Partners heard from many nonwinners that though they would not receive any financial support, the process of inventing a plan to promote interfaith understanding in their community was all the motivation they needed to put their plan into action on their own.

This method of outsourcing a community's resiliency, giving the power for positive idea-generation to local individuals, was picked up on and affirmed by an unexpected entity—the American Psychological Association (APA). The APA cohosted with One Nation a symposium at their annual convention (titled "Psychology in Our Own Communities: Working Toward Structural, Sustainable Changes When We Are Part of the Problem, Process, and Solution" [APA 2011]) to better understand how psychologists might "change their image from lone office practitioners to citizen-experts who can help foster community well-being through psychological knowledge" (DeAngelis 2011).

At many of the partner organizations, programmatic staff was initially confused or annoyed with One Nation's seeming lack of direction. But One Nation stuck to their mantra: "Never second-guess the locals." A rigid program mandated by a national funder would suffer in fluid cities. By forcing locals to make the mental shift from seeing themselves as carrying out solutions to inventing solutions by working together, the programs in each city were able to listen more closely to the complex communities they were trying to empower, which then allowed them to respond quickly and flexibly to the needs of the day.

Internally well-connected cities are resilient cities. When connections are strong, communities are able to respond swiftly and positively to disasters. Perhaps more important, they are able to identify and proactively work to counteract more subtle systemic threats to the community's health.

The ultimate goal of a pluralistic society is not to erase differences in personal ideology. Instead, it is to realize a paradigm where acceptance and understanding counteract the many festering divisive sores that currently threaten our collective well-being. This has certainly been One Nation's vision. And their experience shows that ongoing dialogues are the most basic building blocks for a firm framework of pluralism.

Simply bringing together people who have never before talked with one another—like those at a "no proselytizing allowed" interfaith build hosted by Habitat for Humanity in Russell's hometown of Tacoma that then sparked further religion exchange events—allows people to understand others with a complexity that contextualizes differences in ideology and identifies common points of interest (Quinn 2009). In One Nation's experience, common interests nearly always supersede contention in casual conversation. While hammering together a house's walls, a Christian and a Muslim are much more likely to spend the time agreeing on the best hamburger in town or complaining about the poor quality of public education than getting into a vociferous debate on the evils of the other's religion. This then flows into a common vision for a healthy community. And it all starts, quite simply and naturally, with face-to-face interaction.

Again, since the goal is not to erase religious or other differences, but instead to provide a resilient framework of pluralism, top-down community planning will not work. The traditional, safe method of funder-determined and funder-implemented initiatives will continue to have disappointingly mixed results. Initiatives like these are like rigid recipes that cannot adapt to our complex, rapidly changing communities.

But if, after inciting focused self-reflection and connections in local communities, national funders and community foundations alike can relinquish creative authority to those on the ground and strengthen a network of local leaders, they will have created the basis for a strong, adaptable, resilient framework. All it takes is trust! Don't second-guess the locals.

Community foundations don't need to be told that the imperative for building strong, positive communities grows stronger every year. The issue of ignorance and Islamophobia in America is a good example of the great array of issues that plague our communities and threaten to infect our very lifeblood, issues like racism, same-sex marriage, equal opportunity, and health care. One Nation's community engagement strategy could have been applied to any of these, and in many cities, the One Nation-spawned initiative expanded beyond just the Muslim community.

In many ways, community foundations are in the eye of the hurricane. Their role is paramount as the United States experiences a sea change. We will soon be a majority minority nation, the stability of Social Security is unknown, health care is trapped in capitalism, environmental problems are intensifying—the future changes daily. Our melting pot has more ingredients than ever and threatens to boil over. Will there be disinvestment in our communities as the winds of change become gale force? Will we hole up, protect ourselves, and hope we can emerge all right? Or will we harness the wind? Embrace all the diverse forces in our country and be all for one and one for all? We have in this age tremendous energy, social capital at all levels that, if united, will turn the whole tide of the hurricane. Community foundations can do this. And when they do, the terrible storm will instead become a sublime expression of the promise of pluralism in America.

Bibliography

Ali, W., E. Clifton, M. Duss, L. Fang, S. Keyes, and F. Shakir. 2011. *Fear, Inc. The Roots of the Islamophobia Network in America.* Washington, DC: Center for American Progress. http://www.americanprogress.org/wp-content/uploads/issues/2011/08/pdf/islamophobia.pdf.

American Psychological Association (APA). 2011. "Psychology in Our Own Communities: Working Toward Structural, Sustainable Changes When We Are Part of the Problem, Process, and Solution." Peace Division Program Summary Sheet, Div 48, APA Annual Convention, Washington, DC, August 3–7. http://www.peacepsych. org/images/APAofficialconventionprogrammingAug2011.pdf.

The City of New York. 2011. "Mayor Bloomberg Launches One NYC One Nation—A Multi-pronged Civic Engagement Initiative for Immigrant New Yorkers to Kick Off Immigrant Heritage Week." News release, April 11. http://www.nyc.gov/cgi-bin/ misc/pfprinter.cgi?action=print&sitename=OM&p=1364591423000.

DeAngelis, T. 2011. "Forging Bonds, Overcoming Stereotypes." *Monitor on Psychology* 42, no. 7, 86.

Dolnick, S. 2011. "Helping Immigrants Navigate Government." *New York Times,* April 10. http://www.nytimes.com/2011/04/11/nyregion/11civic.html?ref=nyregion&_ r=0.

Minnesota Idea Open (MN Idea Open). 2012a. "Competition News: Challenge III—Working Together Across Cultures and Faiths." http://www.mnideaopen. org/challenge3.

———. 2012b. "The Story." http://www.mnideaopen.org/thestory.

One Chicago One Nation (OCON). 2012. About us. http://onechicago-onenation. org/about/us/.

One Nation. 2012. http://www.onenationfoundation.org.

Quinn, D. 2009. "Interfaith Comedy Show at Urban Grace to Benefit Habitat for Humanity." *Tacoma Weekly,* June 3. http://www.tacomaweekly.com/citylife/view/ interfaith_comedy_show_at_urban_grace_to_benefit_habitat_for_humanity/.

The San Francisco Foundation. 2012. "Special Programs and Funds: One Nation Bay Area." http://www.sff.org/programs/special-programs-and-funds/one-nation-bay-area/.

Silicon Valley Community Foundation. 2012. "Bay Area Funders and Community Leaders Address Anti-Muslim Bias." Press release, March 1. http://www.silicon-valleycf.org/content/press-release-march-1-2012.

Part III

Community (and Change) Comes in All Shapes and Sizes

12

Growing Your Own

Stories About Mobilizing Philanthropic Leaders in Small Cities and Rural Communities

Nancy Van Milligen
Community Foundation of Greater Dubuque

In the 10 years between 2002 and 2012, the Community Foundation of Greater Dubuque (CFGD) grew from a big-picture concept, sketched on a fresh page of a writing pad, into a $32 million philanthropic leader with four rural affiliates (CFGD 2012a). This rapid growth, as evidenced by 362 funds and 3,079 active and recent donors, was due in large part to CFGD's formula for mobilizing philanthropic leaders in small cities and rural communities of Northeast Iowa. This chapter tells of six different ways in which this combination of empowerment and engagement was used to build charitable impact. The stories hold these common themes: (1) how incentives (whether time, friendship, creative energy, inspiration, dollars, or tax credits) sparked donor engagement; (2) how foundation-tested communication tools, including everything from professional marketing materials to templates for news releases and meeting notices, helped engage philanthropic workers; and (3) how personal relationships, based on a spoken and shared passion for the hard work of community building, supported and sustained the engagement.

How Community Visioning Efforts Energized Philanthropic Soldiers

In 2005, the Community Foundation of Greater Dubuque was still in the early stages of defining itself. Assets had grown to $4.5 million and the staff was comprised of President and CEO Nancy Van Milligen. The foundation clearly had an uphill climb to achieve name recognition and understanding of its unique role in the community. To achieve some modicum of understanding of the foundation's role, Van Milligen introduced the Dubuque Area Chamber of Commerce to the idea of *community visioning* to shape the community's future. It was readily received.

"Where do we go from here?" That question was at the heart of Envision 2010, the community visioning process designed to generate a list of 10 great ideas—ideas that could be put into action in the community by 2010.

Envision 2010 was a grassroots effort that invited community citizens to gather together to *envision* the future. The effort kicked off in July 2005, when the Community Foundation and the Chamber together asked community members to gather a group, brainstorm and submit their best ideas to move greater Dubuque forward and make it an even greater community.

Many partners came together to make it all happen, including donors, the media, local businesses and the local colleges—and those partners continue to work with the foundation today. But, most important, thousands of Dubuque citizens gathered in groups and submitted close to 3,000 ideas that changed the shape of the community.

The mission of Envision 2010 was to engage tristate-area citizens in a community visioning process: an open, all-inclusive discussion to develop a variety of ideas for the future of Greater Dubuque. The goal was to ensure that everyone had an opportunity to be involved in the process of determining the community's unique assets, needs, and goals and discussing what key community projects should be a part of its future.

The process was open and inclusive—all ideas were welcomed. Encouraging the connection of citizens to their community was critical, along with providing an opportunity for all to be involved on the ground floor of futuristic planning.

To ensure that every citizen knew what Envision was and had a chance to participate, organizers put great efforts into marketing and outreach to all citizens, especially those who might not be the first to volunteer. This was also an opportunity to educate many citizens about the unique role of the Community Foundation of Greater Dubuque. The Envision team took advantage of various forms of media, from what became a highly sought-after media kit with the new Envision logo, to radio, newspaper, a newsletter, a website, banners, invitations, billboards, and emails—not to mention the occasional balloon drop and press conference. (Looking back, it's interesting how little social media was used—how times change!)

Once citizens were aware of Envision, the rest was easy. A kickoff breakfast drew 420 community members from all over the community. Our efforts to intentionally and aggressively reach out to under-represented populations by connecting with their trusted allies and by getting information out in less traditional ways—the church pulpit, neighborhood associations, the NAACP, and labor unions—were successful. Participation was double what we had expected. Organizers took it in stride, brewing more coffee, cutting more bagels, and handing out more toolkits.

The idea collection process was simple: Gather a group, then brainstorm and submit your group's ideas. Citizens gathered on house decks, in church basements and in backyards. There were group meetings in bars, bowling alleys, and at slumber parties. Throughout the process we asked ourselves who we were not reaching and how we might be more effective. We hosted a "Night of Ideas," where we staffed public spaces such as neighborhood centers, diners, schools, and churches for folks who might not have a group or didn't feel comfortable facilitating a group to submit their ideas. Groups both large and small gathered and submitted ideas—more than 2,300 in all.

The idea selection process, however, was a bit more complex. In October, the Envision team formed a volunteer selection committee through a blind application process. A matrix that looked at age, gender, race, zip code, socio-economic status, and interest area was used in sorting through the applications to assure the selection committee was representative of the community. Over 70 citizens applied and 21 people were chosen from all walks of life. The group met two nights a week for over two months, thoughtfully discussing and narrowing the list from more than 2,300 ideas to just a hundred. With community input, they further narrowed the list to 30 and finally from 30 to the 10 great ideas announced to the community.

The process had a festive air to it. When the idea list was winnowed down to 100 ideas, community members were invited to a series of town meetings. In an atmosphere akin to a game show, they used electronic keypads to vote for their favorites, reducing the number to 30. Organizers also conducted a telephone survey of residents to help the 21-member steering committee pare the list down further.

Envision started with a flood of ideas and then used a very transparent process to narrow that list to just 10 ideas. The selection committee developed the following criteria to guide their decisions: "Big ideas with broad acceptance, which will have a long-term positive impact on the growth and quality of life of the greater Dubuque community" (Van Milligen 2005).

The 10 "Big Ideas" were unveiled at a lively community event. Young students dressed as "newsies" raced down the aisles with oversized newspapers shouting, "Extra! Extra! Read all about it!" One by one, the final ideas were announced, and they were ambitious to say the least: a Mississippi river project, a community health center, a major library renovation, an indoor-outdoor performing arts center, and improvements to the city's trail system.

The same day that the ideas were announced, a donor called the CFGD to give a $1.3 million endowment to launch the community health center.

Once the 10 ideas were unveiled, it was time for the community to take over—and they did an amazing job. Individual citizens, groups, organizations, businesses, and potential investors stepped forward to take ownership of one or more of the ideas. Committees with over 160 volunteers researched, fundraised, wrote grants, collaborated, planned, built, and implemented in an effort to turn the 10 ideas into a reality.

Today, the 10 ideas have all moved forward and many are completed. The CFDG was able to empower and connect people to commit to the community—and now those enthusiastic and creative volunteers are engaged as leaders in the community and are foundation donors and friends. Seven of the 10 ideas have even created endowment funds at the foundation.

Envision facilitated a number of partnerships that strengthened the community. It made a name for the Community Foundation of Greater Dubuque and gave the organization a place at leadership tables. Public engagement was key, and volunteers played important roles throughout the process. Beyond the 10 ideas, Envision gave people the sense that it is possible to have a voice in the community—that there is a role for everyone and a way to engage with others who share a bright and bold vision for what is to come.

A Passionately Led Giving Circle Creates a Space to Sample Philanthropy for the First Time

As the twentieth century drew to a close, women saw a substantial increase in the amount of money and education they had compared to previous generations. Because of this, they now had capacity and resources like never before. They gained control over their finances—and, consequently, their philanthropy. They recognized the daunting needs of ordinary people living with hunger, homelessness, abuse, and addiction. These were struggles of people everywhere and visible in their own communities, as well. Often the task of alleviating these burdens appeared insurmountable. Where and how do we start to make a difference and to have an impact? From this quandary emerged the idea of *women's giving circles*. Across the country, women gathered to discuss how they could make their communities better through collective philanthropy.

Such was the case when five women gathered in Dubuque to talk about the possibilities. "Should we have an investment club? . . . That gives to the community? We didn't want many meetings, yet we wanted to do something important, with passion," said Jeanne Lauritsen (2009), founding member and leader of the Women's Giving Circle of the Community Foundation of Greater Dubuque. "We hosted luncheons to brainstorm what this gathering of women would look like. How can women impact the community? By pooling money, ideas, and talent, we can have a bigger impact together than being out there by ourselves."

This conversation among women, which started in 2006, focused on the collective impact of giving and growing in their philanthropy. This group decided to learn about all the different ways they could help in Dubuque, how they could bring more women into the circle, and best ways to share the passion of giving with females of all ages. Here's their story:

> The Community Foundation of Greater Dubuque created its Women's Giving Circle (WGC) in 2007. Since then, it has grown more than 100 women strong with an endowment of over $130,000. It is comprised of women of all ages, incomes, and backgrounds connected by a common commitment to improve their community by giving back. The ladies from the country club are joined by religious sisters, college students, and community activists. The focus is on sharing the joy of giving, passing on the tradition of living generously, and working together to meet the needs of women and children in the community.
>
> Studies show that donors who participate in giving circles give more strategically and are more knowledgeable about their communities. . . . The Community Foundation's Women's Giving Circle is no exception. Members gather twice a year to learn about community challenges and area nonprofits. At these meetings, they learn by listening to a passionate director of a nonprofit or touring a nonprofit organization's facility. They then use this knowledge to inform their grant-giving decisions. Grant proposals are perused and individually scored prior to an active discussion of passions and programs. A consensus is then reached on which grants will be awarded. (CFGD 2012a)

Through the Women's Giving Circle's grantmaking process, WGC members are committed to removing barriers to opportunity and creating bridges to self-sufficiency with an emphasis on the needs of women and children. Over the past five years, the WGC has given $24,000 to 13 unique programs that have been involved in providing funds to help seniors get around town, to help women move from homelessness to self-sufficiency, to provide mentors for youth, to give abuse victims a voice through art, and many other great initiatives.

WGC members also give their time and support to special causes throughout the year. Circle members have provided and served meals for the Community Circles Initiative, supplied furniture to a family in Dubuque's Green and Healthy Homes Initiative, and given hats, gloves, and other winter gear to residents of the Elm Street Residential Corrections Facility. At the annual gifts and grants celebration in August 2011, the WGC awards grants and offers gifts of supplies and materials to nonprofits who make a request through the Women's Giving Circle.

These women believe in serving individuals and the community by creating opportunities and providing resources that lead to self-sufficiency. Together, they share the joy of giving, pass on the tradition of living generously to future generations and help members learn about and reach the most important needs in our community.

Affiliate Foundations Leverage Capacity to Extend the Reach of a Regional Host Foundation

The Community Foundation of Greater Dubuque started reaching out to rural Northeast Iowa in 2004. The state legislature had funded Endow Iowa, a "program created to enhance the quality of life for the citizens of this state through increased philanthropic activity by encouraging new investments to existing community foundations and facilitating the creation of new community foundations" (Dethlefs-Trettin 2012). The major component of Endow Iowa is a state tax credit equal to 25 percent of a qualifying gift to a community foundation. The gift must be to an endowment fund within the qualified foundation or community affiliate organization. Individuals, businesses, or financial institutions can claim the tax credits. The most recent legislation provides for more than $3 million in tax credits each year administered by the Iowa Economic Development Authority.

As President and CEO, I set about contacting leaders in neighboring Allamakee, Clayton, and Delaware counties. Working to establish affiliate foundations by engaging leaders living within the geographic boundary of a county would present both challenges and opportunities. The communities and leaders within the counties weren't used to cooperating. Over the past century in rural Iowa, high school sports have spawned intense rivalries between communities located 20 miles apart but still within the same county. Nonetheless, they were all facing decreasing populations due to the shrinking number of farm and farm-related jobs.

Doing good became the cause that would pull together these disparate factions. The community foundation model, which provided a platform for building individual philanthropic funds to support schools, churches, community development, health care, museums, and cemeteries, caught on as part of the mission of doing good, together.

Affiliate foundation board member Keith Garms is a native of his county and an active bank president. He has also served on the affiliate foundation board for eight years. "When we were approached by the Community Foundation of Greater Dubuque, we just knew this was something that was needed," he said. "We also believed there would be people willing to support it if someone would just do the leg work to get it started" (interview with Van Milligen 2012a).

The question of just who would do the leg work was answered when I started engaging the county economic development leaders. The county economic development board and staff signed on to the idea of building what they viewed as a platform for "savings accounts" to support the nonprofits. (*Savings account* was a more familiar term than *endowment*; for a while, the funds were even called *buckets,* based on the phrase "pass the bucket.") The host foundation then equipped the economic development staffers with all the tools for engagement, like this news release template:

> The newly formed affiliate Community Foundation will host a series of informational meetings around the county to introduce local residents and organizations to the newly formed Community Foundation, its grant administration process and the application procedures.

As the host foundation president, I found and shared incentives with the organizers. I engaged regional retailer Jim Theisen, who provided a matching grant to incentivize the affiliate leaders to raise their own start-up funds. The Iowa Council of Foundations also provided $25,000 matching grants to motivate and reward the county affiliates. According to board member Garms, there was a distinct turning point in the start-up phase. "People knew this was really going to happen when we raised the first $25,000, which also allowed us to capture a similar match from the state" (interview with Van Milligen 2012a).

Garms was one of the people who shared coffee and conversation with potential donors. Calling on attorneys, doctors, and retirees, his advocacy led to community foundation endowments for the historical society, opera house, and hospital. Annual grants from the endowment payout helped underwrite a summer intern for the museum.

Looking back, he said, "I am really proud of all our separate funds and all the talks I continue to have with people who want to do more" (interview with Van Milligen 2012b).

Affiliate foundation board member Roger Halvorson became involved in a more personal way. Halvorson was a retired real estate and insurance agent and had served in the Iowa legislature. He and his wife, Connie, asked, "What if the empty buildings on Iowa's Main Streets could be filled with new businesses?" In particular, they dreamed of businesses that represented a new creative economy, like locally grown arts, gifts, food, and wine (Van Milligen 2012c).

The affiliate foundation provided a vehicle for the Halvorsons to answer that question. The couple used their annual IRA distributions to begin an endowed fund that supported entrepreneurship training for new business owners. Through a partnership with the economic development group and the University of Northern Iowa, the six-month regional training program reached 42 new businesses the first year and 55 the second time it was offered. Following the group classes, consultants met with individuals to troubleshoot their unique problems. Even after the program ended, participants continued to share experiences and support through a website. Distributions from the Halvorsons' fund made it possible for entrepreneurs to create their own coffee shop in the county seat of Elkader.

Talking about the dark and empty corner stores and the needs of budding Iowa entrepreneurs was just the first step in engaging the Halvorsons, who continue to use their IRA to build the fund. Looking back, Roger Halvorson said, "It is amazing to see what can be done if people put aside only a part of what they have for their community" (interview with Van Milligen 2012c).

Engaging friends to work together in building a culture of givers is another strategy that strengthened the affiliates and leveraged the capacity of the Community Foundation of Greater Dubuque as a host foundation. In some cases, affiliate board members, even those from rival school districts, became friends. Such was the case with Matt Erickson and Brian Houlihan. Erickson is an attorney in Postville and Houlihan owns a manufacturing business in a town a half hour away, but they come together to advocate for and lead the county through their service on an affiliate foundation board. Both had taken turns in the president's chair, overseeing the annual grantmaking program, and both had served on the board of directors for TASC, an agency that serves individuals with developmental disabilities. Erickson and Houlihan made personal gifts to begin an agency endowment for TASC. Their shared philanthropic leadership sparked gifts from other board members, and the fund reached the payout threshold immediately. TASC executive director Mary Ament said, "Our community foundation endowment is a nice cushion for operations, a funding source for grant match, and a spark for signature projects within our program and facility" (interview with Van Milligen 2012d).

Thanks to the leadership of Erickson, Houlihan, and their other friends, who share a unique and satisfying community leadership experience as foundation board members, their affiliate foundation now hosts 16 endowments.

Equipping professional financial advisors with knowledge about community foundation endowments is another engagement strategy that has supported affiliate growth:

> Like most leaders, Dave Schroeder wears a couple of hats in his hometown community. He has been a volunteer board member of the affiliate foundation for five years, serving as treasurer. At the board table, Schroeder

explains the fine print of financial statements and IRS forms in everyday terms. It comes from years of experience as a professional financial advisor. Whether he's working with individuals and couples at tax time or advising business owners about giving back to the community, Schroeder is familiar with the advantages of Endow Iowa. For clients interested in philanthropy through endowments, the 25 percent state tax credit is really attractive. According to Schroeder, "Most people are not aware of the tax benefits and want to learn more about Endow Iowa." (CFGD 2012c)

Helping professional financial advisors translate Endow Iowa legislation to those they serve, often by engaging the tax advisors in board stewardship, has been an intentional focus within the affiliate foundations. Communities in the region have become stronger as knowledgeable advisors talk with clients about community foundations and Endow Iowa. For donors, the decision to give back often starts by speaking with a trusted advisor who can translate the Endow Iowa legislation; once donors understand the power of endowments, nonprofits and the individuals they serve benefit immensely. According to Schroeder, who also leads endowment-building efforts at the local hospital and school, "The partnership of the local nonprofits with the community foundation has been most beneficial, as it has provided structure and stability for endowment building" (CFGD 2012c).

By leveraging its capacity, the Community Foundation of Greater Dubuque has built affiliate foundations with strong boards that engage community leaders, professional advisors, and donors. The result is far-reaching philanthropy that brings together rural community members to strengthen nonprofits, meet local needs, and build funds for the future.

How the Endow Iowa Tax Credit Program Incentivizes and Rewards Generosity

Endow Iowa tax credits are state tax credits provided to individuals or businesses that donate to permanent endowment funds at qualified community foundations or community affiliate organizations serving the communities of Iowa. The Iowa Code (15E.305(2)) authorizes $2.7 million, plus a very small percentage (less than one-tenth of 1 percent) of state gambling revenues, for annual Endow Iowa tax credits (Iowa Community Foundations 2011, 1).

In 2010, the last reporting year, approximately $3.1 million in Endow Iowa tax credits were awarded statewide. According to tax credit applications: approximately $12.9 million in charitable giving was leveraged by the credits; the donations went to at least 71 different community foundations and/or community affiliate organizations; and the $12.9 million in donations was comprised of more than 1,723 separate donations. Of the total, 116 were from business establishments (corporations) or from financial institutions. The remaining 1,607 donations were from individual donors (Iowa Community Foundations 2012c).

Since inception of the Endow Iowa program, Iowa community foundations have leveraged more than $75 million in permanent endowment fund gifts. The contributions were made through more than 7,493 donations.

As a host foundation, the Community Foundation of Greater Dubuque has been especially successful in using the Endow Iowa 25 percent state tax credit to build philanthropy. Each year the foundation sets a goal of capturing the most Endow Iowa tax credits per capita annually and has achieved the benchmark in multiple years. Endow Iowa's story follows:

> For Mary Jo Tangeman, Endow Iowa was a terrific incentive to do business with the community foundation. Together with her family and in memory of her late husband, Rod, she made four significant endowment gifts to her hometown. Mary Jo made gifts to: the Guttenberg Library to support it as a leading source for literacy in the community; the Guttenberg Rotary to support those projects most important to Guttenberg's progress; the Guttenberg Fire Department for fire protection in the area; and the Guttenberg Emergency Medical Association to support the training and service needs of the volunteer members.
>
> The four endowments, which are growing now with Mary Jo's generous gifts of $50,000 each, are held by the Clayton County Foundation for the Future (2012). These funds are open to accept gifts from other donors who want to support these nonprofits and also take advantage of the 25 percent Endow Iowa state tax credit.
>
> Mary Jo and Rod owned the Security State Bank until 2008. Mary Jo made the endowment gifts after consulting with her tax advisor and estate planner. "Endowments were a way for me to give back to the community where we did business, remove assets from my estate, and really enjoy seeing the gifts at work in Guttenberg," she says. (CFGD 2012b)

The Community Foundation of Greater Dubuque, together with foundations throughout Iowa, has experienced strong growth thanks in part to Endow Iowa. Keeping in mind that even charitable souls love a bargain, the community foundation engages donors with a simple message: "You can give 25 percent more to your favorite endowment thanks to the Endow Iowa 25 percent state tax credit."

The Historic "Transfer of Wealth" Story Inspires Donors in Iowa to Make a Difference Now

Following the Great Depression and World War II, the United States entered a golden age of business growth and personal prosperity. Americans have created, invested, and multiplied unprecedented private wealth. Over the next 50 years, this capital—conservatively estimated at $53 trillion—will change hands. Most will certainly go to heirs (and taxes), but a portion may be preserved as a legacy for the future of Iowa.

Retaining a slice of that wealth for philanthropy as it transfers generations is a historic opportunity to strengthen our communities. That's why community foundations across Iowa have worked to secure planned gifts and bequests for endowment funds that will ensure a stronger future, forever.

Transfer of wealth research estimates the portion of wealth transfer likely to happen in each individual county in Iowa. Between the years 2000 and 2049, Iowa can expect to see $531.7 billion transfer from one generation to the next through probate estates. In 2010 through 2019 alone, $74.43 billion is expected to pass on to heirs.

With these opportunities and assets in mind, the Community Foundation of Greater Dubuque realized now was the time to educate leaders in rural Northeast Iowa about leveraging this phenomenon and using it to reinvigorate hope and stem the flight of capital from rural communities. Educating caring Iowans about the transfer of wealth and the importance of current and legacy gifts to their beloved communities is a strategy that has fueled countless endowed gifts, including one from Neil Webster, a retired cable television executive who established the Webster Fine Arts Scholarship Endowment.

At a time when many schools were slashing art and music budgets, the Websters recognized the value in promoting education in the arts and created one of the most generous scholarship funds in the history of the local high school. Former recipients of the award are now building the scholarship endowment fund. Parents, friends, as well as other people who value the arts participated as well.

According to one former recipient, who is now a physician's assistant living two hours away from her hometown, "I was honored to help organize this effort to engage past scholarship recipients in building the endowment in part because it was a chance to thank the Websters for the many generous gifts they have given our community, their scholarship being only one of many. I also wanted to be a part of this because I feel that it is impossible to overstate the importance that the arts have in our lives. I strongly believe any level of involvement in the arts is encouraged by the scholarship and can have a ripple effect in benefiting our communities."

Neil Webster has also provided for a legacy gift to be made to his endowment, a gift that will directly change the transfer of wealth equation for the benefit of his community.

Endowment Building Tools Equip Nonprofit Stakeholders to Sustain Their Future

The Community Foundation of Greater Dubuque has intentionally built a culture of giving in its service region by engaging donors of all means. One strategy to engage and involve legions of individuals who serve nonprofits was the Endowment Building Toolkit.

This toolkit was created to train affiliate board members as well as nonprofit board members and leaders about endowment building. The toolkit includes the purpose, strategies, and steps necessary to see success in building endowments and capturing the transfer of wealth within rural Iowa. This project, completed in partnership with the Iowa Council of Foundations, created a one-stop shop for endowment building programs. The materials help board members and volunteer leaders articulate, explain, and understand the role and opportunity of endowment building in rural communities.

Ewalu, a bible camp served by an affiliate foundation, has an endowment initiated by two couples with long histories of supporting the ministry. The friends had challenged each other to begin an endowment in Ewalu's name and to raise it to the $10,000 level, a goal that they reached in less than two years.

Dale Goodman, executive director at Ewalu, was interested in building the endowment and learned about the toolkit from the Community Foundation of Greater Dubuque. During the training, the 17 attendees, including board members, endowment committee members, and friends of the ministry, learned how to make visits to potential donors. Each attendee picked three to five names of people they felt comfortable visiting. In just three months, Ewalu's endowment fund at the Community Foundation of Greater Dubuque grew from $10,000 to $75,000.

So, what made it work? Fundraising is all about relationships—the relationship of the potential donor to the cause or mission of the nonprofit and the relationship of the donor visitor to the potential donor. In the case of Ewalu, both the donor visitors and the potential donors already felt good about the cause. And because the donor visitors made their own choices about whom they would visit, for the most part, they chose people they already knew.

According to Goodman, "The training was excellent. Virtually no one came to the training without some level of anxiety about 'asking for money,' but fundraising—and the anxiety about fundraising—changes completely when you get away from the idea that you are in some way begging and you embrace the idea that you are offering people an opportunity to support what they believe in. The training accomplished that. We had good practice sessions and everyone's comfort levels rose. Oh sure, there was still plenty of anxiety but ultimately the actual visits boiled down to friends talking to friends about something that they both cared about—and it all worked very, very well" (Ewalu Camp & Retreat Center 2012).

Both the Community Foundation and Ewalu followed up with thank-you notes, and the state of Iowa followed up with vouchers for the tax credits. A few people even asked, "Can I do this every year?"

The Endowment Building Toolkit is a model for training and engaging nonprofit board members and leaders in building a lasting legacy for their causes.

Conclusion

These six stories of empowerment and engagement at the Community Foundation of Greater Dubuque are among countless examples of foundation staffers, board members, and nonprofit leaders sharing a passion for community building with others. It starts with a shared belief that our gifts are precious and truly do matter.

Each charitable act started with a sentence, spoken or written, that invited the individual to join a culture of givers, breathe in the air of living generously, and join an assembly of community members who chose to be boldly optimistic about Northeast Iowa's future.

Bibliography

Clayton County, Northeast IA. 2012. Clayton County Foundation for the Future (CCFF). http://www.claytoncountyiowa.com/economicdevelopment/foundation-forthefuture.htm.

Community Foundation of Greater Dubuque (CFGD). 2012a. *Dubuque Works: A Workforce Initiative.* 2012 Annual Report. Dubuque, IA: CFGD. http://www.greaterdubuque.org/downloads/DubuqueWorks_Annual%20Report2012.pdf.

———. 2012b. "Success Stories: Clayton County Foundation for the Future." http://www.dbqfoundation.org/story/clayton-county-foundation-future.

———. 2012c. "Success Stories: Dyersville Area Community Foundation." http://www.dbqfoundation.org/story/dyersville-area-community-foundation.

———. 2012d. "Success Stories: Women's Giving Circle." http://www.dbqfoundation.org/story/womens-giving-circle.

———. 2012e. http://www.dbqfoundation.org.

———. 2012f. "Women's Giving Circle: Overview." http://www.dbqfoundation.org/what-we-do/initiatives/womens-giving-circle.

Dethlefs-Trettin, A. 2012. Former Executive Director of Iowa Council of Foundations speaking at Connect Conference for Iowa Council of Foundations, Des Moines, IA, March 6.

Ewalu Camp & Retreat Center. 2012. http://www.ewalu.org.

Forum of Regional Associations of Grantmakers. 2009. *The Impact of Giving Together.* May. http://www.givingforum.org/s_forum/bin.asp?CID=611&DID=25089.

Iowa Community Foundations. 2012a. "Endow Iowa." http://www.iowacommunity-foundations.org/endow-iowa.aspx.

———. 2012b. "Endow Iowa FAQs." http://www.iowacommunityfoundations.org/faq.aspx.

———. 2012c. "Endow Iowa Tax Credits." http://www.iowacommunityfoundations.org/endow-iowa-tax-credits.aspx.

———. 2011. *2010 Report to Legislature and Governor on Endow Iowa & County Endowment Fund Programs.* http://www.iowacommunityfoundations.org/files-images/PDFs/2010%20Endow%20IA%20CEFP%20Report%20to%20the%20Legislature%20and%20Governor_FINAL.pdf.

Lauritsen, J. 2009. "Women's Giving Circle." Annual Meeting, October 28.

Van Milligen, N. 2012a. One-on-one stakeholder interview. Guttenberg, IA. March 22.

———. 2012b. One-on-one stakeholder interview. Guttenberg, IA. April 19.

———. 2012c. Stakeholder interview at Clayton County Foundation for the Future Annual Celebration. Marquette, IA. April 19.

———. 2012d. Stakeholder interview at TASC board meeting with Community Foundation of Greater Dubuque staffers. Waukon, IA. March 28.

———. 2005. Envision 2010 Kick-Off Breakfast. Speech, July 8.

13

Connecting to Community Themes, Changing Community Values

Brian Payne
Central Indiana Community Foundation

It started out as a simple but ambitious idea. Let's take a lane away from cars to create a new kind of bicycle and pedestrian trail in downtown Indianapolis. It will connect the cultural districts and create badly needed momentum for this new concept of turning struggling historic retail villages into dynamic cultural destinations. This was the beginning of our case statement. Like many ambitious ideas, especially ones that propose to change the urban landscape, the Cultural Trail grew in complexity. It also grew in miles, in name, and in vision. Along the way, the Indianapolis Cultural Trail: A Legacy of Gene & Marilyn Glick aspired to change the way the rest of the country and the world perceived Indianapolis. It also aspired to change the way Indianapolis residents saw themselves and their city. Ultimately, the Cultural Trail became about changing what Indianapolis values.

The Indianapolis Cultural Trail: A Legacy of Gene & Marilyn Glick (Cultural Trail for short) is a $63 million, eight-mile, urban pedestrian and bicycle trail in the heart of downtown Indianapolis. Physically, it is a curbed, buffered, beautifully paved, richly landscaped, and artfully lighted trail that features over $4 million of public art. The idea grew from connecting the six cultural districts to becoming the downtown hub for the entire Marion County greenway trail and bike lane system to a uniquely world-class multimodal amenity that connects to every significant arts, cultural, heritage, sports, and entertainment venue in downtown Indianapolis. A guiding principle of the trail design was to create a journey throughout our downtown that would be as inspiring and beautiful as the many wonderful destinations. Ultimately, the Central Indiana Community Foundation, the Cultural Trail team, and its partners and donors wanted to create an urban bike and pedestrian trail that was bigger, bolder, and more beautiful than any in the world.

As the subcontractors install the final pavers on the last few blocks under construction, the response to and reviews of the Indianapolis Cultural

Trail—locally, nationally, and to some extent internationally—have been extremely positive. Civic leaders and urban planners from as far away as Cologne, Germany, and Calgary, Canada, as well as from cities throughout the United States have come to Indianapolis to tour and study the Cultural Trail.[1] Project for Public Spaces, the international consulting firm and place-making think tank, featured the Indianapolis Cultural Trail as its best North American example of "Bold Moves and Brave Actions" that make cities better places to live, work, and play (Project for Public Spaces 2008). The other cities highlighted were Melbourne, Australia; Zurich, Switzerland; Bogota, Colombia; and Hong Kong, China.

Dozens of reporters from daily newspapers and magazines have high-lighted the Cultural Trail's innovative qualities. *Dwell*, a San Francisco-based modern living magazine, called the Cultural Trail in a major feature article "an idea so radical as far as civic transportation goes that it sounds a little crazy" (Sullivan 2006). Some publications focused on flattering comparisons. "And score one for Indianapolis, which is embarking upon the biggest idea since Carl Fisher turned a Westside pasture into an automobile racetrack," exclaimed Bill Brooks, a columnist and publisher of the local newspaper *Urban Times* (Brooks 2006). *Metropolis*, the national magazine on art, design, and architecture, introduced its article on the Cultural Trail this way: "Bilbao, The Eiffel Tower, . . . and the Indianapolis Cultural Trail?" (The Indianapolis Cultural Trail 2012a; Arvidson 2008). Now, even the Cultural Trail team was a bit bemused by these possibly premature associations to global icons, but we did find it helpful in creating fundraising momentum.

As the Central Indiana Community Foundation (CICF) and I, as its president and CEO, got deeper into the leadership and community process of the Indianapolis Cultural Trail, and as the CICF has become, due to the success of the trail, a "go to" organization for people with big dreams for our community, the question of who has the ability to realize transformative, collaborative, cross-sector community projects keeps presenting itself to us in persistent and exciting ways. It has been our hope that the Cultural Trail would be an example to individuals and organizations, that it would inspire social and cultural entrepreneurs and corporate and civic leaders to dream big and make more transformative projects happen in our city. We even hoped the Cultural Trail would show that anybody with a great idea and the passion to see it through could accomplish big and bold change. Was that naive?

What kind of leadership does it take in American cities in the twenty-first century to create transformative cross-sector change? Is this different than in the past, and is it different from city to city? What are the skill sets and what kind of special status or influence is needed, if any? And finally, do community foundations have any special ability or standing to lead transformational projects in their communities? A deeper understanding of the case history of the Indianapolis Cultural Trail can lead to some insight on these questions for Indianapolis, and I believe, for other cities as well. Of course to understand where a city can go, and how it can grow, one needs to understand the culture of that city—and culture begins with history.

The Emergence of Indianapolis

A unique feature of Indianapolis is that it was not established by settlers but by proclamation. When Indiana was granted statehood in 1816, the U.S. Congress set aside four sections of public land for a possible site of the state's capital. In 1820, the Indiana State Legislature located the capital city on a site that was as close as possible in the exact center of the state and named it Indianapolis.

Other than the Indianapolis Motor Speedway and its Indianapolis 500, both of which celebrated their one-hundredth anniversaries in the past few years, not much differentiated Indianapolis from other midwestern cities in the early and mid-twentieth century. In fact, even in the 1970s and 1980s, Indianapolis was still being tagged with the nicknames of "Indiananoplace" and "Naptown." A string of strong mayors, starting with Richard Lugar in 1968, and some passionate corporate and civic leaders decided that Indianapolis needed to change. Lugar successfully fought for "Unigov," which merged Indianapolis with most of the rest of Marion County and significantly increased Indianapolis's population, tax base, and stature. What started out as a somewhat random stab at getting major sporting events to the city evolved into a full-fledged economic development strategy that made Indianapolis the amateur sports capitol of the country. A group of young professionals from business, law, and government created a loose network called the City Committee, and with the financial and moral support of Jim Morris, who was a former chief of staff to Mayor Lugar and the president of Indianapolis's Lilly Endowment, Inc. (one of the largest private foundations in America), the sports strategy reached new heights in the 1980s. Indianapolis drew national and international attention as a sports city in 1987, hosting that year's World Indoor Track and Field Championships and the Pan American Games.

The sports strategy continues to succeed in Indianapolis. In 1999, Indianapolis lured the National Collegiate Athletic Association (NCAA) headquarters to town. This has meant hosting a consistent rotation of "final four" men's and women's basketball championships and NCAA national conventions. The city is also home to major professional sports franchises: the Indianapolis Colts football team and the Indiana Pacers basketball team. Both are housed in state-of-the art facilities. The construction of a new football stadium, largely financed with public dollars, enabled Indianapolis to host the Super Bowl in February of 2012. Once again, Indianapolis played to its strength as the host of a major sports event and completely and successfully reinvented the two-week Super Bowl experience. In previous years, the Super Bowl had largely been a private party for major corporate executives. The local Super Bowl Steering Committee and the Indianapolis community (through 8,000 volunteers) transformed it into a celebration of football and community and everyday fans. The City and Steering Committee built a Super-Bowl Village in the heart of downtown, extended the NFL-produced NFL Experience to over two weekends and had a series of rock and country bands and other festival-like events (including a zip line) in the heart of downtown Indianapolis that were open to everyone. The City also created a major community renovation component known as the Super Bowl Legacy Project that inspired over $150 million of investment into a challenged urban neighborhood. The NFL now expects its future host cities to provide a Super Bowl Village experience and a major community philanthropic project. The 2012 Super Bowl was India-napolis at its innovative and community-focused best.

Beyond Sports and Corporate Leadership

Although the sports strategy has been undeniably successful and has played a big part in the development of downtown and in building pride in the com-munity, many residents and civic leaders believe the city needs to diversify its overall image beyond being a sports capitol if it is to expand a growing professional economy and retain the dynamic, entrepreneurial talent such an economy requires. Even though the sports strategy was significantly sup-ported by a charitable foundation (Lilly Endowment, Inc.), the movement's identity has been associated with the corporate sector. Put another way, civic leadership was, from early on, synonymous with corporate leadership. A cul-ture of corporate philanthropy and corporate responsibility was established and nurtured. This created a very efficient and effective, if not very diverse, leadership structure in the city. That combined with strong mayors and "good ol' Hoosier hospitality" and niceness created a strong and enduring culture of public-private partnerships.

This culture of public-private partnerships is still very strong, and civic leaders believe that no city does partnerships better than Indianapolis. How-ever, the private in public-private has changed significantly. Indianapolis, like many cities in America, began to lose its corporate headquarters in the 1980s. It started with the banks and continued with the out-of-town acquisitions of many of its insurance companies. Next, the local utilities moved out and the family-owned daily newspaper was sold to the national public media company

Gannett. The headquarters that stayed local had newly defined needs such as running growing global operations and fighting deep global recessions. Local CEOs had less time to spend on local initiatives. Indianapolis is lucky to still have corporate leaders like John Lechleiter, CEO of Eli Lilly, Dayton Molendorp, CEO of One America, and Mark Miles, CEO of Central Indiana Corporate Partnership. In fact, Miles and Lechleiter both played leading roles in bringing the Super Bowl to Indianapolis. Still, corporate leadership in the civic realm has changed and weakened and, like so many other things in twenty-first-century America, it seems naïve to believe it is going to change back to the way it was in Indianapolis or in most American cities. We at CICF believe that we have the skill set, resources, and even the duty to help fill this new gap in civic leadership.

Origin of the Indianapolis Cultural Trail

As previously stated, the idea for the Cultural Trail was a simple one. As the new foundation president and former arts leader in the community, I was appointed as a founding member of Indianapolis Cultural Development Commission in 2001 by Mayor Bart Peterson. The goal of this initiative was to elevate Indianapolis's cultural reputation and make the city a cultural desti-nation, in addition to being a sports leader. Financially, it was a five-year, $10 million effort that was funded equally by Lilly Endowment and the City of Indianapolis through its quasi-government agency, the Capital Improvement Board (CIB). At the very first meeting, commissioners were presented with the possible idea of transforming a half-dozen older, troubled, inner-city retail areas into dynamic cultural districts through product development, building-facade improvements, marketing, and ongoing management. The concept was vague, but I thought it had real promise because every cultural district would be inherently distinct from the others and unique among arts districts or artsy neighborhoods in other cities. If Indianapolis was going to become a regional cultural destination, I felt strongly that it needed to offer something different from what people could find in their own communities.

   With the bright-eyed enthusiasm of a new grantmaker, I immediately went to my board with the idea that our foundation should add funds and help define and craft a cultural district plan. When that was met with a thud, I went to some of our donors to solicit them. I received an equally unenthusiastic response. I was told that the district idea would fail because the potential districts were too far away and too disconnected from our downtown. In reality, one of the potential districts was just a few blocks away from the heart of our downtown and the farthest retail area that was identified, Fountain Square, was only a mile and a half away, but I admitted they felt far away, and the journey to these areas was an unpleasant one. One of those early donor conversations was with Myrta Pulliam, a civic leader and philanthropist. She didn't like the cultural district concept either but thought the least the city could do was paint a bike lane to Fountain Square.

Within days after my meeting with Ms. Pulliam, I was bicycling the Monon Trail, the city's very popular greenway rail trail, through Broad Ripple Village. It was one of those wondrous spring fever days in late April and it seemed like ten thousand people were having the time of their lives walking, jogging, and biking on this trail and stopping at boutiques, ice cream shops, and pubs. And the simple idea came to me. If the problem with the district concept is that they are disconnected, let's connect them with an urban version of the Monon Trail. Of course, a downtown trail would need to be more highly designed and should have lights to match a 24/7 urban lifestyle. We would need to take a lane away from cars, which could be controversial. Then I remembered a conversation I had with one of Mayor Goldsmith's senior staff members when I first arrived in Indianapolis in 1993 to be the managing director of the Indiana Repertory Theatre. I was told that one of the big reasons that Indianapolis was not especially vibrant after 5:00 p.m. was that it was way too easy for downtown workers to get on one of the five-lane, one-way thoroughfares and speed out of town at 50 miles per hour. The extra-wide, one-way streets, I learned, worked against the success of downtown. Great, I thought. We can take an easily disposable extra lane away from cars and give it to the people. So the original formula was to create a beautiful urban version of an incredibly popular trail amenity on a surplus traffic lane and connect newly designated cultural districts so they could be developed and become a lynchpin to the cultural destination strategy. What could be easier? I figured this project should, at the most, take five years.

Connecting the Dots

Looking back more than a decade later with the Cultural Trail almost complete, this was the first time I felt that I, as a community foundation leader, connected the dots in a significant and meaningful way. We at the Central Indiana Community Foundation believe that "connecting the dots" is job number one, and we would propose that community foundations are the best positioned organization or entity in any community to play this very important role—for example, taking information from one conversation with a social service grantee, a data point from a report on educational achievement, and a donor's passionate interests in helping clients of a specific community center and putting them all together in an action plan. Community foundations can easily connect a not-for-profit to a donor, a not-for-profit to another not-for-profit (in the same or different field), a donor to a donor, a donor to a city government leader, and a not-for-profit to a city government leader. The list of combinations can go on and on, and in our work at CICF, the list includes connecting others to national foundations such as the Annie E. Casey Foundation and local private foundations.

Who else in the community consistently has these kinds of broad and varied conversations and learning opportunities and the human capital to act on them? Corporate leaders used to. When I first moved to Indianapolis, I was impressed at how each bank, utility, and headquartered insurance company had a bevy of middle managers who seemed to have the job of being on community boards and participating in community leadership. Those jobs, however, started to drift away even before the financial downturn of 2001, let alone the Great Recession of 2008. Corporations no longer devote the human or capital resources to be able to connect the dots in the community. Activist private foundations certainly can play a major leadership role if they have a broad enough scope and a strong enough commitment to leadership. However, they are missing the deep relationships with individual donors and donor families commonly cultivated by community foundations. The Central Indiana Community Foundation celebrates the fact that it not only can impart information and expertise to its donors and fundholders but celebrates even more when it brings its donors' expertise to the community table as part of a greater community solution.

The United Way certainly has impressive connectivity in the social service sector, but their focus on this sector limited them from finding broader, cross-sector innovations. I was on the United Way of Central Indiana Board a number of years ago when new approaches to afterschool child care and afterschool education programs were seriously explored. Since CICF is a major arts funder, I suggested that arts organizations could partner with social service organizations and together they could create very effective afterschool programs. I was told that the United Way couldn't support any non–United Way agencies in a partnership like that. CICF is also a big funder of the United Way of Central Indiana and is pleased that the United Way is broadening its community leadership approach and recently announced a new partnership with the Arts Council of Indianapolis. The United Way is now creating deeper relationships once limited by their past singular focus on workplace fundraising. Still, even with these changes, the United Way is not nearly as well positioned to connect the dots across all sectors and with the broad range of community stakeholders as are community foundations. The rest of the not-for-profit sector is mostly focused on individual programmatic areas and does not have the mission, the relationships, nor the resources to look outside its own field of interest and connect the dots across sectors in new and innovative ways.

Building Community Support

Although the Indianapolis Cultural Trail began as an idea to support the concept of transforming tired, urban retail areas into citywide and regional cultural destinations, the Cultural Trail took on a life of its own and the case for support broadened and deepened almost immediately. Still new to the community foundation and needing to broaden my own understanding of the community beyond the arts and community leadership sectors, I was taking meetings with dozens of not-for-profit leaders. After learning about their organization's programs, passions, and needs, I'd reserve 15 minutes of the meeting to get their take on the Cultural Trail concept. I got great ideas and constructive critical feedback. My own ideas on the concept sharpened, and I became the archivist of other people's creative ideas for the trail. I was told that the trail would absolutely need to connect with Indiana University–Purdue University Indianapolis (IUPUI), the city's important and growing public urban university, and its dominant medical complex. Beautiful landscaping would be key if it was going to be truly differentiated from other urban trails, someone else emphasized. The ideas kept coming, from others and from me. My own ability to articulate the value of the concept was also transformed by these sessions.

These one-on-one meetings not only were the right approach for my own personal learning and thinking style but they protected the idea until it was ready for prime time and restricted it from groupthink, group dynamics, and neighborhood groups. Throughout my career, I have been wary of the way group dynamics can derail a perfectly good idea. One loud person or strong personality can turn the tide on an idea that everyone else supports but won't vocally fight for in that specific environment. So for the first full year of progress, the communication was strictly one-on-one.

By the end of 2001, I had met with senior members of Mayor Peterson's staff. First was Keira Amstutz, a key staffer with a wide range of responsibilities including being the mayor's point person for the arts. Amstutz liked the idea and led me to Melina Kennedy, the city's director of economic development. She was enthusiastic. The next step would be to meet with Jane Heneger, a deputy mayor. Pitching this to the mayor himself was still in the future. I just needed to know that I would have support among some of the city staff before I spent the time and energy to raise money for the concept. But Heneger became a champion for the project and was able to place a design and engineering feasibility study for the trail into an existing city contract.

The project was now armed with a study sponsored by the city that said the trail was possible from a city planning perspective. When I began to try to raise financial support, I relied on my new foundation relationships with

CICF's donors and fundholders and private foundation colleagues. I now had the pitch down. The Cultural Trail would be so bold and innovative that it would transform the way people from around the country would view Indianapolis and its progressive quality of life. A dynamic reputation is important if a city wants to attract the best executives, entrepreneurs, and new businesses. The trail would be a huge economic development tool for the city. It would lead to more conventions and leisure travelers. The trail would bolster both downtown commercial and residential development. It would greatly enhance the success of the six newly designated cultural districts. It would create a physical environment where the arts could thrive. In fact, the very name of the trail would introduce the positives of a "cultural" experience for people who never think about culture and lead to a more supportive arts and cultural marketplace. A trail this beautiful and centrally located would inspire people in our community to get exercise and take their health more seriously. The Cultural Trail would be such a safe and inspiring bicycle amenity it would create a bicycle culture in the city that hasn't had one since Henry Ford rolled out the Model T.

Four significant funders committed to the project based on this pitch and an accompanying color copy of a rendering of what the trail could look like. Two major CICF donors and board members, Lori Efroymson-Aguilera and Myrta Pulliam, committed a million dollars each. (Ms. Efroymson-Aguilera would contribute an additional million dollars later in the process.) Two locally headquartered private foundations, Lumina and the Nina Mason Pulliam Charitable Trust, each committed $500,000 through a competitive proposal process. These early commitments were so important because they gave the project credibility and signaled to others that maybe, just maybe, this idea might be viable. Indianapolis was in better shape financially than many cities, but budgets were very tight and I knew that asking for the city to contribute financially from its own budget would be a financial and political dead end. However, it did seem possible for the city to direct some of its federal transportation allotment to the Cultural Trail and raise additional federal transportation dollars for the project.

As fundraising continued, we finally took the concept to the public. The city organized two major public forums, each attracting approximately 200 people. It was becoming evident that the Cultural Trail concept was the right idea at the right time. People responded very positively, and the only major complaint was that it wasn't connecting to their neighborhood. City planners were shocked that no one was organizing against it or even expressing negative opinions because they were used to someone being against everything. With early fundraising success, a positive feasibility study, the advocacy of the mayor's top staff, and community support, Heneger and I were now ready to present the Cultural Trail idea to Mayor Peterson. The meeting went well and he was open to it, but, at that moment, he was less enthusiastic than most of the people we had pitched. In retrospect, I think we presented too many benefits of the trail instead of focusing on the most important benefits to the mayor. In fact, whenever I failed in our fundraising presentations in the first few years this was the mistake I made. I would learn to listen and better assess the most important elements for the individual prospect and dive deep into those. The mayor asked for time to consider the idea but encouraged us to keep developing support.

A few months later he called me to his office to tell me that he wasn't killing the project but that he needed to postpone a decision. He was trying to convince the state legislature that for the fiscal future of the City of Indianapolis and Marion County, the legislature needed to consolidate the county's nine township governments and the poor relief and fire departments under the city's management. He felt that his opponents would use a highly visible multimillion-dollar downtown trail project against him and his argument that the city was facing financial hardship. Even though the city would not have money invested, he was concerned his opponents could exploit the trail to their advantage. This was 2003. After the legislative session in 2004, one in which Mayor Peterson won a few hard-fought concessions to his plan, he had Deputy Mayor Heneger call me and set up a lunch appointment. That morning I traced back the nearly four years of work I had put into this dream and knew that within hours I would know whether it all had been a useless exercise or whether this grand vision would have, at least, a chance to be realized. When Heneger told me that the mayor had approved the project to move forward, I felt a wide and complex range of emotions. My life would change. The foundation might change. The city had a great opportunity to change. I also felt that this project had some mysterious spiritual force behind it that was bigger than any one of us who would work on it.

I also stopped to think that there would surely be many days in which I would regret ever having this idea. A project this complicated would certainly face monumental challenges. At that moment, I pegged the number of very bad days at 10 and therefore have felt blessed that I have only experienced six. These days of regret included the day in 2006 when the designers told us that the cost of the project really would be $50 million, not the $35 million that was estimated earlier. At that moment I tried not to panic. Ultimately, we just decided we would raise more money. The cost went up again to $63 million two years later, but somehow I was more emotionally prepared. Another day of regret occurred when a town hall meeting on a proposed public art installation turned ugly and abusive, complete with allegations that I and others on our team were racist. That story someday will make for a very interesting chapter in another book.

Internal Challenges

Up to this point, the Cultural Trail seemed more like my personal hobby than an official initiative of the Central Indiana Community Foundation. My bosses, the trustees of the foundation board, as a whole were not that enthusiastic. The Cultural Trail did not match their priorities, which were traditionally centered on providing basic needs to the disadvantaged. They also worried about the opportunity costs of such an endeavor. Every hour that I, as the foundation's president, spent on this trail was an hour I wasn't spending helping our community find breakthroughs that would help fight homelessness or hunger. Also, the trail seemed very risky to many trustees. What if we only raised enough money to build a mile or two of the trail? What if we were successful in building it, but it didn't deliver on the promised outcomes? The foundation would look like a failure. As a relatively new hire, I was highly attuned to these concerns and did most of my trail work in the evenings and on weekends. In those early years, I didn't involve my staff. I was concerned about being criticized for redirecting the foundation's efforts and resources toward a personal passion and away from the work that the board felt needed to be done.

This changed after Mayor Peterson gave a green light to move forward with the project. Officially partnering with the city and the mayor made the project seem legitimate in the eyes of the board. The culture of the foundation's board was also changing as we recruited a number of highly successful entrepreneurs. This was done with great purpose as I felt that the organization had the need and opportunity to move into a more proactive, entrepreneurial role in the community. Inspired by the Cultural Trail and work that our foundation was leading in helping families reach economic self-sufficiency, my staff and I found a new way to frame our foundation's work around community leadership and talent. This also legitimized our work on the Cultural Trail. We at our foundation believe that for central Indiana to thrive in the twenty-first century, it must do a superior job of developing, attracting, and retaining highly educated, creative, and community-minded people. Our Family Success and College Readiness and Success programs focus on talent development, while our Inspiring Places initiative focuses on talent attraction and retention. Although it is the most visible, the Cultural Trail is only one of a number of Inspiring Places projects in which we have committed our leadership. Still, this new way of looking at the foundation's vision for Indianapolis made the Cultural Trail project relevant for the foundation's board.

Building the Team

After receiving the mayor's approval, it was also time to build a team that could make the project a reality. I was lucky to convince corporate and civic leader Andre Lacy to help me create a blue-ribbon fundraising committee and to cochair it with me. We then signed on 15 major not-for-profit organizations, including the Greater Indianapolis Chamber of Commerce, the Indianapolis Convention and Visitors' Association, the Arts Council of Indianapolis, and the Indianapolis Urban League as Community Partners. Their role was to advise and advocate for the project within the community. They gave us additional community credibility and momentum.

Then Heneger, Amstutz, and a few other city employees and I went through a very exciting and competitive national RFP process for a trail designer and project manager. The project managers we hired, Melody Park and Mark Zwoyer of RW Armstrong, would be responsible for the myriad engineering and construction challenges on what some city engineers called one of the most complex construction projects in the history of the city due to the scale and linear nature of the construction and its certainty in interrupting daily traffic and commerce. The design firm we hired, Rundell Ernstberger, and its principals, Kevin Osburn and Eric Ernstberger, helped us further articulate the trail's guiding principles and vision and translated it all into a beautiful design. Over the previous few years, we had learned that the trail connected to an existing but stalled pedestrian master plan. We also learned that the Cultural Trail could be the downtown hub that connected other trails to form a dynamic countywide system of connectivity. Additionally, we discovered that by adding some routes and changing others, the Cultural Trail could connect to every significant arts, cultural, heritage, sports, and entertainment venue in downtown Indianapolis. What had started out as an amenity to simply connect the cultural districts had now became the physical and symbolic connector for our city.

At this point we were able to create a first-rate management team. This would be the group that would make the daily decisions—some small, some monumental—on how the trail would get realized. The team consisted of Heneger and then Amstutz representing the city and mayor as well as Osburn, Park, and Zwoyer. We also added Lori Miser, who represented the Department of Public Works (now the director of the department), Mindy-Taylor Ross as director of public art for the trail, and Gail Swanstrom as director of fundraising and community outreach. Everyone on the team saw this project as a special opportunity in their career and life. The team jelled and became family. The city, from Mayor Peterson to Heneger to Amstutz to Miser, kept exploring and winning millions of dollars in federal transportation grants for the trail. I stored my growing bike collection in my office and bought two Segway personal transporters. Swanstrom and I gave hundreds of bike and Segway tours of the proposed trail route. There is no better way to raise money than trapping a major prospect on a Segway for two hours. The joke was that we taught potential donors how to get on and ride a Segway but didn't teach them how to get off.

The Cultural Trail grew from its original five and a half miles to almost eight miles. Its budget grew from the conceptual $20.5 million to $35 million, and during those days of regret, to $50 million and then to the final $63 million. Of course, the Cultural Trail management team likes to point out that this includes a $6 million maintenance endowment, $2 million for public art, and almost $20 million in city infrastructure improvements under and parallel to the trail, none of which was in the original $20.5 million concept figure.

The process continued to take many twists and turns. When we needed a big fundraising boost, Gene and Marilyn Glick, major philanthropists in Indianapolis, provided it with a $15 million lead gift. This enabled us to announce the project, the final phase of fundraising, and the lead gift from the Glicks with great public fanfare and front-page news coverage. Mayor Peterson was now a very enthusiastic and effective advocate. "This is so big it's a little hard to figure out what words to use," Peterson said at the news conference. "The Cultural Trail, I believe, will really set Indianapolis apart" (Penner 2006). Two years later, Mayor Peterson unexpectedly lost an election to a third term and a relatively unknown candidate, Greg Ballard, took office. This was a very vulnerable time for the Cultural Trail. We had only one mile constructed and needed to raise a lot more money and keep the excitement going. The new mayor's policy philosophies were generally unknown, and on election night one of his biggest supporters, the sitting county prosecutor, announced that stupid efforts like trails would no longer get attention or resources. Fortunately, just the opposite occurred: I can't tell you how pleased our team has been that Mayor Ballard has become a good friend of bicycling, trails, and connectivity of all kinds. In fact, he is a visionary in this part of community life.

The Great Recession of 2008 completely stalled our fundraising efforts with $20.5 million to go, but the federal stimulus package opened the door to a solution. We competed with 1,400 other transportation-related projects from all 50 states, with combined requests totaling $58 billion from an available $1.5 billion merit-based grant pool. When Congressman Andre Carson, an advocate of our proposal, called me, I knew once again that in a moment my life would either change significantly for better or worse. When the congressman told me we were one of 51 projects funded and that we received our full $20.5 million request, I yelled so loud that our entire team came running out from an adjacent meeting room. Receiving this grant had the added benefit of signaling to the rest of the country that the Cultural Trail was a truly significant project and that Indianapolis was emerging in bold and innovative ways. Our Cultural Trail management team produced a video on the trail and its merits.

One of the members of the team posted the video on the Internet and it quickly went "viral," adding to the national visibility of the trail. Gail Swanstrom was the executive producer of this video and coauthored the grant proposal with management team members Miser, Park, and me. Gail and I became friends working on the Cultural Trail and then became husband and wife. The Cultural Trail's powers of connectivity are not to be underestimated.

Community Transformation in the Twenty-First Century

Who can lead innovative and transformative projects in American cities in the twenty-first century? We at the Central Indiana Community Foundation believe that the example of the Indianapolis Cultural Trail shows that community foundations are extremely well positioned to lead complicated, long-term, multisector transformation projects. Community foundations have the ability to bring together individual philanthropists, foundations, corporate leaders, all sectors of the not-for-profit field, and government officials. Deep and dynamic partnerships are the key. Positive change also requires capital. Community foundations, at least ones in large and midsized cities, are well-positioned to provide and acquire the human, financial, and influence capital that's needed to see transformation to completion. A community foundation's own financial wherewithal may be the least important of the three. CICF and its affiliate, the Indianapolis Foundation, only contributed $500,000 out of the total $63 million Cultural Trail budget, and that was given in grants of $50,000 to $100,000 each over seven years. It was the human capital in CICF's contribution of staff time and leadership and CICF's ability to influence others that inspired community leaders to take a hard look and ultimately get behind what many believed, at first, to be an overly ambitious idea.

The fact that community foundations, mayors, and visionary individuals can transform cities is a wonderful cause for optimism. When it comes to innovation and entrepreneurial vision and energy, there are no set rules—with the possible exception that no one person or one entity can do it alone. In Indianapolis, as I suspect in all cities, you can only accomplish truly meaningful change by partnering with others.

The Cultural Trail is delivering on the ambitions envisioned and promises made. The trail is alive with cyclists, pedestrians, and runners. It is being used by people of all ages and people who represent all aspects of our diverse community. New apartment developments, restaurants, and retails shops are springing up along the trail in the revitalized cultural districts and throughout downtown. New trails are being planned to connect more neighborhoods to the Cultural Trail and downtown economic and cultural opportunities. Indianapolis's convention bureau and the economic development corporation both prominently feature the Cultural Trail in their promotions and publications. Four major not-for-profits have located on the trail to enhance their visibility and engagement with the community. There's a new world-class bike hub with lockers and bike storage and a YMCA on the trail. Bike commuting is up and three bike shops exist downtown; none were there before the Cultural Trail. There are new community health programs that utilize the trail. The Trail's environmental design features are being copied in other parts of the city. Interest in public art is at an all-time high. The community cares about multimodal transportation options. Indianapolis is a different city from when the Cultural Trail began.

Note

1. The American cities cited here include Albuquerque, NM; Oklahoma City, OK; Grand Rapids, MI; Lexington, KY; Louisville, KY; and Jacksonville, FL.

Bibliography

Arvidson, A.R. 2008. "Winning Lap: Indianapolis Hopes to Make Its Cultural Mark with a Bike-and-Pedestrian Path That Loops Through the Heart of Town." *Metropolis*, April. http://www.metropolismag.com/story/20080415/winning-lap.

Brooks, B. 2006. "A Downtown Dream Comes True." *Urban Times,* November. http://www.brookspublications.com/files/CULTURALTRAIL_sept07.pdf.

Central Indiana Community Foundation (CICF). 2012. http://www.cicf.org.

———. 2007. *2006: Moving from "Good to Great" and Picking Up Speed.* CICF Annual Report, October. Indianapolis, IN: CICF.

Dalton, W.D. 1994. "City Committee." In *The Encyclopedia of Indianapolis,* ed. David J. Bodenhamer and Robert G. Barrows, 428. Bloomington: Indiana University Press.

The Indianapolis Cultural Trail: A Legacy of Gene & Marilyn Glick. 2012a. "Bilbao, The Eiffel Tower, . . . and the Indianapolis Cultural Trail?" http://www.indyculturaltrail.org/120.html.

———. 2012b. Testimonials. http://www.indyculturaltrail.org/testimonials.html.

———. 2012c. http://www.indyculturaltrail.org.

Lieber, T. 2007. "Payne Paved Way for Indianapolis Cultural Trail Project." *Indiana Business Journal,* November 5. http://www.indianaeconomicdigest.net/main.asp?SectionID=31&SubSectionID=62&ArticleID=37555.

Penner, D. 2006. "The Indianapolis Cultural Trail: $15M Gift Paves Way for Trail." *Indianapolis Star,* news release, October 13. http://www.hearthview.com/documents/newsattachment/Indy_Star_Cultural_Trail_101206.pdf.

Project for Public Spaces. 2008. "Bold Moves and Brave Actions: Indianapolis, USA." http://www.pps.org/reference/boldmovesandbraveactions/#indianapolis. Originally publisher in the March 1, 2008, e-newsletter.

Schimmel, K.S. 2001. "Sport Matters: Urban Regime Theory and Urban Regeneration in the Late-Capitalist Era." In *Sport in the City: The Role of Sport in Economic and Social Regeneration,* ed. Chris Gratton and Ian Henry, 259–277. New York: Routledge.

Sullivan, R. 2006. "Perpetual Motion, Volume Three." *Dwell* 7, no. 1, 189–207.

14

What Is the Appropriate Role of Today's Community Foundation?

Our Conclusion: Take on the Tough Issues, Create Public Space, Democratize Philanthropy, and Lead

Antonia Hernández
The California Community Foundation

Eight years ago, I was given the privilege to lead the California Community Foundation (CCF) in Los Angeles County. As a long-time public policy advocate, I jumped at the chance. My work at the Mexican American Legal Defense & Educational Fund had provided me a platform to advance the Latino Community at the national level through litigation, advocacy, and education. I now had the chance to apply what I had learned in a place I loved: Los Angeles. To me, the work would not be much different, but I would have additional resources to apply locally.

New to philanthropy, I saw the field through different lenses. My prior experiences had taught me that advocacy, community engagement, and public policy were effective vehicles for addressing the root causes of our most difficult societal issues. This background also allowed me to retool this community foundation with a different approach to issues. Our revised strategy would add new dimensions to our existing toolbox.

As we prepare to celebrate the one-hundredth anniversary of community foundations, and CCF's own centennial in 2015, we must step back, reflect, and assess our role going forward. Today's society faces many of the age-old problems of poverty and fragmentation that have confronted us in the past. But if these issues are to be solved, we must rethink past approaches and apply new, different solutions. Simply stated, if community foundations are to be relevant, we must lead, embrace change, and create new paths to accomplish the work that we have before us.

Chinese poet Lu Xun wrote, "Hope is like a path in the countryside: originally there was no path—yet, as people are walking all the time in the same spot, a way appears" (quoted in Kristof 1990). This short poem succinctly articulates the route that community foundations must take. We must be willing to rethink the application of the resources at our disposal and, at the same time, be the cheerleaders and champions for a more just, equitable, and compassionate society.

Taking on the Tough Issues: Community Foundations as Local Leaders and Placed-Based Philanthropy

Community foundations have a unique position from which to lead social change. As place-based institutions, our success rests in an ability to know and understand the places we call home. Well-positioned community foundations are independent, resourceful, permanent, locally focused, and—perhaps most important—understand the needs of the communities they serve.

Understanding the unique challenges and opportunities of the community we serve is critical if we are to succeed. The Los Angeles County experience is illustrative. Demographically, Los Angeles County today is larger than 14 states in this country. Its population is one of the most diverse in the world. Within its boundaries reside the largest concentration of immigrants and transplants from every state in the nation and virtually every country in the world. Significantly, Los Angeles County is the fifteenth largest economy in the world. But our economic engine is different. It is largely composed of small and midsize businesses that span a vast geographic region. Moreover, Los Angeles is a fast-changing, evolving cosmopolitan place where the entrepreneurial immigrant spirit is one of the major driving forces for growth.

Los Angeles has some of the greatest contrasts of wealth and poverty in the United States. The disparity between the rich and the poor is growing. The county is also home to the largest number of households with zero net worth and income below the poverty line. Yet, over the next 30 years, the county will undergo the largest transfer of wealth in the United States and possibly around the globe (CFF 2011). Within this context, CCF serves the largest population among U.S.-based community foundations.

The challenges and the opportunities are enormous. In the process of redefining our goals, we have determined that tackling the economic and social gulfs between rich and poor in our community is a high priority. As we began redefining our goals to meet this challenge, we recognized that the unique situation of our community foundation allows us to take on this issue. Through engaged leadership, direct participation, and genuine consideration of the views of community residents, we believe that we can make a difference in effecting comprehensive change.

A case in point is our recent initiative in Bell, one of Los Angeles County's 88 cities. A major corruption scandal involving the misappropriation of public funds in Bell (Gottlieb, Leonard, and Vives 2010) made national news and put CCF's values to the test. Our response to this local municipal crisis was to develop a civic engagement initiative in this largely immigrant and predominately low-income city. CCF brought the affected city residents together to find solutions. With community input, data, and research to guide us, we partnered with the public and private sectors and academia to develop a civic education and leadership development program that allows residents to better engage in the civic life of their city. For this model program, CCF partnered with a local Latino civic organization, the largest Spanish-language television network, and a major university to develop targeted curriculum and education materials. We hosted nonpartisan forums to explain how local government works and provided a platform for local candidates to share their views and explain their positions during the local elections conducted in the aftermath of this political crisis.

From that experience, we learned that the challenges faced by the residents of Bell are not unique. We therefore expanded the program to cover seven other surrounding cities. Eight community leaders from each city are enrolled in the program. The curriculum's focus is civic engagement, and we now have graduated the first class. The long-term goals of this initiative are to empower residents, strengthen democracy, and inspire the emergence of leadership for local elective office.

Addressing Poverty in the Twenty-First Century: Focusing on Place-Based Efforts

In much of the country we find today what is termed "the suburbanization of poverty" (Garr and Kneebone 2010).[1] In 2006, CCF embarked on one of the most ambitious endeavors in its history: developing a program to address this trend in Los Angeles County. In planning for this effort, we decided to amplify our impact and create a learning opportunity for other areas by concentrating our philanthropic resources in a single locale, engaging the entire community, and investing for the long term. Our aim is to create a model for sustainable change.

After an extensive assessment of several communities, CCF chose to devote our concentrated resources in the City of El Monte, 13 miles from downtown Los Angeles. El Monte reflects the socioeconomic and ethnic diversity of Los Angeles County, but evidences lower educational attainment and household income. Matriculation rates are just above 50 percent for graduating seniors in some neighborhoods. More than one-third of El Monte children are obese. But parents in El Monte are optimistic and see a good education and good health as vital to better lives for their children.

Now in its sixth year, our Community Building Initiative (CBI) is a 10-year program for which we have pledged $10 million, thereby providing the funds and the time to allow the program to take root in the community of El Monte (CFF 2012a). Besides the dedicated funds directed to the CBI initiative, additional funding is provided from our ongoing program priorities. The initiative is governed by a community advisory committee that includes robust local input and leadership participation. From the outset, the goals and objectives were identified through a community participation process geared to generate educational and health success through child and family empowerment. CCF supports the CBI through grantmaking, convening, and committed staff. Local residents have participated in leadership programs and generated a community-wide strategic plan that guides this program and other initiatives in El Monte.

As the initiative has evolved over the past few years, we have seen it go beyond the traditional approaches of funders' collaboratives, public-private partnerships, or multistakeholder initiatives. It has become a textbook model of sustainable "collective impact" initiatives, involving cooperative approaches built around "a centralized infrastructure, a dedicated staff, and a structured process that leads to a common agenda, shared measurements, continuous communication, and mutually reinforcing activities among all participants" (Kania and Kramer 2011).

Through the El Monte Community Building Initiative, CCF is leveraging resources from public agencies and social networks to help ensure that children and youth in El Monte grow healthier and are better prepared for school, college, a vocation and career. For instance, we have partnered with the U.S. Soccer Federation to build soccer fields. Los Angeles First 5, which focuses on programs for children under 5 years of age, is investing in the community to address school readiness. Other foundations have pitched in and are investing in reducing youth obesity.

Another example of the CBI's synergy is the El Monte Pledge, which is an agreement between the El Monte Union High School District (EMUHSD), Rio Hondo College, the University of California, Irvine, and Cal State University, Los Angeles, to provide participating students and their families with academic support leading students to college enrollment (Rodriguez 2010). The first cohort of El Monte Pledge students who graduated from high school in June 2011 yielded 409 fall enrollees at Rio Hondo College. Of these, 268 (65 percent) are from the highest-need neighborhoods. Eighty-three percent of El Monte Pledge students re-enrolled for spring 2012, a proportion that is higher than the collegewide return rate of 74 percent for first-time college students (Rio Hondo College 2012). This "Pledge" has expanded into the "El Monte Promise" to include academic and community-based support from pre-school through college and the promise of a scholarship—from funds raised by the local community—for El Monte students who sign and complete the El Monte Pledge.

To date, CCF has invested more than $5 million, and we continue to gain local and national funding partnerships for the initiative. Besides the benefits that it brings to El Monte, the CBI provides a learning opportunity for CCF and other funders to understand how to build resident and nonprofit capacity in suburban communities outside the inner city.

Advocates for the Public Good

To bring about positive change, community foundations must build their own public policy and advocacy capacities while investing in the nonprofit sector (Reed 1996). At CCF, we are not hesitant to support public policy work and encourage others to do so. Such efforts are necessary in order to effect change, especially when they are directed at assisting the most marginalized. In short, a community foundation that seeks to implant systemic change must provide policy leadership and foster debate and deliberation.

We have found that confronting the constantly shifting needs of our community requires continual rethinking of economic, educational, health, and environmental policies. However, change can only take hold if our communities themselves are engaged in the policy process. Thus, CCF grantmaking includes efforts to fortify community leadership and strengthen the public policy capacity of the nonprofit sector. Public policy and advocacy work that addresses the root causes of issues currently represents 20 percent of CCF's grantmaking.

Building the Capacity of the Nonprofit

For a community foundation to play a leadership role in its community, it must have a vibrant, effective, and well-connected not-for-profit sector. As grantmakers, we are enablers. The effectiveness of our work rests on the strength of the not-for-profit organizations in our respective communities. Therefore, one of CCF's major goals is to strengthen the infrastructure of Los Angeles County not-for-profits. However, this task is not always easy when dealing with 88 separate cities in a diverse Los Angeles County with a weak management service infrastructure.

UCLA's Annual State of the Sector Report, *Stressed and Stretched: The Recession, Poverty, and Human Services Nonprofits in Los Angeles* (Hasenfeld et al. 2011), pointed out that approximately 40 percent of organizations experienced a recent decline in revenues. Smaller organizations with revenues of $500,000 or less experienced a 57 percent decline. This drop in revenue from the traditional sources of foundation and government grants, coupled with the sharp increase in demand for services, has put Los Angeles nonprofits in very tenuous positions with regard to finances and organizational stability. Nonprofit intermediaries have not been immune to the stresses of the nonprofit funding environment. In a county with more than 19,000 active nonprofits and local management-support organizations employing just over 60 fulltime employees, it is easy to see that the management-support network in Los Angeles is just as fragile as the nonprofit sector that it seeks to strengthen.

Our response to this challenge was to change our grantmaking process, which, for the most part, is multiyear. We have streamlined the application and reporting process. At the same time, we have also worked to bring new organizations to Los Angeles. For instance, through the collective efforts of several local foundations, we brought in the Nonprofit Finance Fund (NFF) to provide a series of workshops for nonprofits to update their business models and adapt to changes in the economy and growing demand for services. Based on the success of these workshops, a group of local funders worked to bring NFF permanently to Los Angeles.

Further, in April 2012, CCF, along with the Weingart Foundation and Ralph M. Parsons Foundation, cohosted a convening on strategic restructuring for nonprofits. Estimated attendance was around 200 people, but registration soon ballooned to 700 participants representing more than 300 organizations (CCF 2012c, 7). As a result of this strong interest in strategic restructuring among local nonprofits, CCF and these two funders launched the Nonprofit Sustainability Initiative, which has 44 participant organizations undergoing a series of assessments and facilitated explorations of strategic restructuring ranging from sharing of back office services to full mergers between two or more organizations. Interest and activity in technical assistance and resources for strategic restructuring is expected to grow, and CCF will explore a second phase of this work with its funder partners.

Our efforts to strengthen the not-for-profit sector are also driven by the significant wealth transfer that is starting to take place and will continue over the next 30 years in Los Angeles County. We want our not-for-profits to take advantage of this incredible opportunity. Therefore, one of our aims is to assist these organizations to become more effective fundraisers and thus expand and amplify resources for positive change.

To this end, CCF commissioned a study from a group of wealth experts to analyze the magnitude of this transfer. We learned that Los Angeles County residents will transfer almost $114 billion in assets between generations in the next three decades. By 2060, the figure is projected to reach $1.4 trillion (CFF 2011). We believe this credible wealth can and must be tapped and channeled to improve society. For this reason, CCF has developed a program that provides planned-giving training workshops, tool kits, and other resources to enable the not-for-profit sector to capitalize on this immense wealth transfer.

The Power of Convening and the Role of Collaboration

Going forward, it is essential that community foundations provide communal meeting space. Many community foundations have recognized the importance of convening and have moved to facilities that provide meeting space. A few have taken a further step and purchased their own property, thus creating a communally focused space.

Responding to this trend and the vast size of our region is one of the emerging core competencies at CCF. Gathering people face-to-face as a means to strengthen advocacy-bolstering opportunities for learning and build bridges between and among communities and sectors is one of the best tools to develop trust among competing interests and foster greater civic engagement. We see our role as helping to foster relationships, identify barriers, provide leadership to resolve conflicts, and move the dialog forward with a unified agenda to produce positive change. As illustrated by the Bell and El Monte initiatives, we find that fully utilizing the power of convening to bring people together creates greater good.

Over the past several years, we have dramatically increased both our convening capabilities and the frequency of CCF-hosted events. We host and sponsor more partnership meetings, peer learning sessions, funder/donor briefings, events, and seminars than ever. In addition, CCF staff currently supports many outside civic task forces, advisory boards, and committees.

Bringing people together requires dedicated staff and physical space. To meet this need, CCF built a 6,000-square-foot meeting facility within our downtown Los Angeles headquarters. The facility includes catering/dining facilities and is richly decorated with artwork from local artists representing the rich mosaic of our area's ethnic and cultural diversity. It is designed to be a comfortable and highly functional space for the community.

Besides the power of convening, researchers emphasize that establishing strong networks is more important to an outcome than the actual size of the investment (Wei-Skillern and Marciano 2008). Collaboration plays a key role in our arsenal as we seek to leverage resources. While CCF is considered a large community foundation, we are relatively small in terms of dollars when compared with other philanthropies in our area. Notwithstanding, we believe that our robust networking and collaborative efforts allow CCF to have greater impact.

My job as a community foundation CEO is to be a collaborative civic leader, a patient optimist, and a promoter for diverse network-building and cooperative efforts. In Los Angeles County, we recognize that the challenges facing our region dwarf our limited resources. We understand that to achieve significant impacts we must employ multiple strategies that go beyond grant-making. For this reason, almost every initiative and program at the CCF is partially supported by other local and national funders. Working with other philanthropies is essential to our success. We not only collaborate with and rely on our funding colleagues in the region, but we work nationally to establish funding partnerships on issues that link us to social innovation occurring beyond Los Angeles County.

Fortunately, Los Angeles County is home to some of the most innovative and collaborative foundations in the country. The heads of the 12 largest foundations in the region convene three times a year. These meetings provide a forum to discuss common concerns, promote new programs, and seek support for new initiatives. As the CEO of a community foundation, I view my role as a connector among and between the local foundations. The University of Southern California manages this collaboration and provides academic depth and leadership. Now in its tenth year, it is supported by a small annual grant from each of these foundations.

Serving and Engaging Donors

The relationship between community foundations and donors is more than the stewardship of funds. We do not expect to be "Fidelities," that is, commercial gift funds. Community foundations of the future must embody the aspirations and hopes of the community while also serving the individual donors' passions. Donors are enriched by the knowledge and experience that a community foundation brings to issues affecting the community in which they live.

Our added value for donors is knowledge of the needs and proposed solutions to the issues faced by distinct communities. Creating connections for our donors to Los Angeles-based needs and responding to our donors' demands must be of equal importance. CCF's donors are vital partners in our work. While embracing donor's interests, our intent is to share the foundation's strategies, initiatives, and long-term goals.

For example, the recent economic recession has significantly raised the demand for food to be distributed by local food banks. CCF redirected funds to address this emergency. Thereafter, a donor indicated an interest in funding this need. We connected him to the food bank. As a result, an additional 40,000 families received direct assistance. Equally important, we brought a new donor to the food bank.

Often we are approached by donors with requests to fund new or existing programs outside our service region or areas of expertise. In such cases, we analyze the request and ask ourselves pertinent questions such as whether we can add value or expand philanthropy to an emerging issue affecting a significant segment of the population. As local stewards of philanthropy, we must be willing to be flexible and to venture into unchartered territory.

One initiative that exemplifies this approach is our Iraq Afghanistan Deployment Impact Fund (IADIF) (CFF 2012b). Shortly after I arrived at CCF, a donor who had contributed to my prior employer came to us with grave concerns about the needs of military men, women, and families affected by deployment to Iraq and Afghanistan. He sought to establish a donor-advised fund (DAF) concerning this issue. This request required outside-the-box thinking. We had not undertaken anything like this before. Would it require a redirection of our resources? We definitely wanted to be responsive but did not want this effort to divert our focus. It was not easy, but we came up with a solution that worked. We hired an outside consultant with experience in the field to take the lead.[2]

With an initial budget of $105 million to be spent over a one-year period, the IADIF was intended to support direct service programs for returning soldiers and their families around the country. The initial efforts yielded extremely impressive results and generated high enthusiasm. Based on this success, the donor enhanced his commitment, and we extended the project for another three years with a budget that eventually topped $289 million. CCF became the largest philanthropic foundation addressing the needs of military veterans and their families. We worked with the donor in developing the initiative to include funding research, advocacy, and public policy, a public awareness campaign, and formal collaborations with government agencies (Williamson 2009). As a related positive takeaway, we were able to involve other community foundations and grantees with whom we had not worked before.

This innovative, multilayered effort resulted in positive systemic changes for returning veterans and their families. Research conducted under the IADIF demonstrated that returning veterans in certain regions of the country were more impacted than others due to differing deployments, military bases, and medical treatment facilities. Applying our philosophy that locally based institutions are better suited to respond to local needs, CCF sought to establish local grantmaking partners in various affected regions of the country. CCF awarded $15 million to three community foundations in Texas to re-grant to local organizations. The San Antonio Area Foundation, the Dallas Foundation, and the Permian Basin Area Foundation in Midland worked together in a cohesive regional response to this issue. We used the same approach in Florida with the Gulf Coast Community Foundation.

We employed our convening strategy as part of the IADIF program and brought together grantees from around the country to form a coalition to advocate for fundamental systemic changes to improve support and care for the veterans of Iraq and Afghanistan returning from overseas deployments. We continued to apply our local strategies by providing resources to improve the organizational capacity of the not-for-profit groups that work with veterans. We commissioned the RAND Corporation to undertake a study that yielded a groundbreaking report entitled *Invisible Wounds of War* (Tanielian and Jaycox 2008). The first of its kind, the RAND report has received widespread recognition. Our efforts and this report earned accolades from retired Joint Chief of Staff chairman, Admiral Mike Mullen, who twice visited with us to discuss and laud the success of the program.

Our goal was to change the military's response to veterans' needs. Understanding how difficult this task would be, we conducted public polling and focus groups. The results of the polling strongly indicated that the public wanted our government to address the needs of returning soldiers.

This was a large undertaking. Some might contend that a community foundation had no business venturing into this arena. My response is that community foundations must find ways to respond to donors' interests even if they are outside their region or expertise. While undertaking this project, CCF did not deviate from its core mission. In the end, we served our donor; learned a great deal about an issue that affects virtually every community throughout the country; and validated that our strategies of convening, organizing, advocacy, and public policy are effective tools both at the local and national levels.

The Importance of an Engaged Board

Our board of directors is an essential partner with staff and donors in realizing CCF's mission. The starting point for an engaged board is assembling dynamic, active members and ensuring that they are representative of the demographics and multisectors of the community. It is important to seek members who are actually involved in the community (not just recognizable), have a perspective and point of view, and create an environment where respectful debate is encouraged and differences of opinion valued.

One of the key roles of the CEO is to ensure that the board understands and fully supports the foundation's goals and strategies. A rule that I adopted for communicating with board members is what I call the "three bites of the apple." It specifies that all issues requiring the members' vote must be vetted by the board three times. The first introduces the subject and gathers input. The second presents board members with the edited draft, which hopefully incorporates their input and solicits even more input. The final presentation is the actual vote. Most important, the CEO creates a culture in which staff members understand and value the active input of the board. An effective community foundation does not have a "rubber stamp board."

The CEO must also take the necessary steps to obtain board buy-in when introducing a new idea. For instance, when I arrived at CCF, the foundation did not fund public policy and advocacy. My past experience had shown that these two strategies are effective at addressing systemic issues. But I also knew it was imperative to find a way to present the use of these strategies in an understandable and practical way for board members. Such an opportunity arose when I learned of a situation requiring immediate action concerning a potential cutoff of funds for low-income housing in Los Angeles—a program priority at CCF. Several years ago, it came to light that the City of Los Angeles had failed to comply with federal regulations concerning Section 8 housing funds. As a result, the federal government announced that it was withdrawing $100 million intended for low-income housing. Neither the state, county, nor city had the resources to fill this huge loss. I took a request to our board for a $50,000 grant to fund a consortium of housing not-for-profit organizations to work with the City of Los Angeles to recoup the funds. The city and the consortium traveled to Washington, D.C., together to try to recoup the potentially lost funds. Fortunately, they were successful. This offered the board a concrete example of leveraging our assets through advocacy. Gradually, the board felt more comfortable funding advocacy organizations.

We now devote over 20 percent of our funds toward advocacy. The lesson: We must make our actions real, connect the dots, and demonstrate the direct impacts of the application of grant dollars to our boards, donors, and funders. Certainly, we want our boards to be comfortable and actively engaged as we evolve and confront new challenges. This requires clear and transparent communication and personal attention on an ongoing basis.

Conclusion

It is a challenging and exciting time to lead a community foundation. With the one-hundredth anniversary of community foundations upon us, we must celebrate past accomplishments, while continuing to refine and improve our existing business models to address the needs of twenty-first-century America. In doing so, we will strengthen our connections with donors, enhance our ability to advocate on behalf of the communities we serve, and provide tools and resources necessary for success.

Notes

1. According to a study by the Brookings Institution, by 2008, suburbs were home to the largest and fastest-growing poor populations in the country. Between 2000 and 2008, suburbs in the country's largest metro areas experienced a 25 percent growth in their poor populations—almost five times faster than larger cities.

2. CCF hired veteran's expert Nancy Berglass to serve as CCF's director of this initiative. For more insight on the policy and reintegration needs of the U.S. military and their families, see her report (Berglass and Harrell 2012).

Bibliography

Berglass, N., and M.C. Harrell. 2012. *Well After Service: Veteran Reintegration and American Communities.* Report, April. Washington, DC: Center for a New American Security. http://www.cnas.org/files/documents/publications/CNAS_WellAfterService_BerglassHarrell.pdf.

The California Community Foundation (CFF). 2012a. "El Monte Community Building Initiative: Empowering Children and Families for Success." https://www.calfund.org/page.aspx?pid=684.

———. 2012b. "Iraq Afghanistan Deployment Impact Fund (IADIF)." https://www.calfund.org/page.aspx?pid=706.

———. 2012c. *Strengthening Our Community: A Collective Response for Los Angeles.* 2012 Annual Report. Los Angeles, CA: CCF. http://my.calfund.org/2012-annual-report/.

———. 2012d. https://www.calfund.org.

———. 2011. *The Future of Philanthropy in Los Angeles: A Wealth of Opportunity.* Report, December. Los Angeles, CA: CCF. https://www.calfund.org/document.doc?id=503.

Garr, E., and E. Kneebone. 2010. *The Suburbanization of Poverty: Trends in Metropolitan America, 2000 to 2008.* Metropolitan Opportunity Series Paper, January, pp. 4–6. Washington, DC: Brookings Institution.

Gottlieb, J., J. Leonard, and R. Vives. 2010. "L.A. County Grand Jury Serves Subpoenas Seeking Thousands of Documents from Bell." *Los Angeles Times,* August 9. http://articles.latimes.com/2010/aug/09/local/la-me-08-09-bell-investigation-20100810.

Hasenfeld, Zeke, Hyeon Jong Kil, Mindy Chen, and Bill Parent. 2011. *Stressed and Stretched: The Recession, Poverty, and Human Services Nonprofits in Los Angeles. The Annual State of the Sector Report, 2002–2012.* Los Angeles, CA: UCLA Center for Civil Society. http://164.67.121.27/files/Downloads/StateNonProfSector_2012_forweb.pdf.

Kania, J., and M. Kramer. 2011. "Collective Impact." *Stanford Social Innovation Review* 9, no. 1.

Kristof, N.D. 1990. "China's Greatest Dissident Writer: Dead but Still Dangerous." *New York Times Book Review,* August 19, sec. 7, p. 15. http://www.nytimes.com/books/97/05/11/reviews/21513.html.

La Piana Consulting. 2012. "Nonprofit Sustainability Initiative Prepares Nonprofits for Partnership." Blog post, October 11. http://www.lapiana.org/about/la-piana-blog/2012/10/nonprofit-sustainability-initiative-prepares-nonprofits-for-partnership/.

Reed, Trudie Kibbe. 1996. "A New Understanding of 'Followers' as Leaders: Emerging Theory of Civic Leadership." *Journal of Leadership & Organizational Studies* 3, no. 1, 95–104.

Rio Hondo College. 2012. Data prepared by James Sass, Office of Institutional Research and Planning, August 30, from Banner/Cognos.

Rodriguez, L. 2010. "Schools Agree to Pact." *El Paisano,* September 10. http://www.elpaisanonewspaper.com/schools-agree-to-pact-1.2485512#.UTUPETeYJlg.

Tanielian, T., and L.H. Jaycox, eds. 2008. *Invisible Wounds of War: Psychological and Cognitive Injuries, Their Consequences, and Services to Assist Recovery.* RAND Corporation Monograph Series MG-720. Santa Monica, CA: RAND Corporation. http://www.rand.org/content/dam/rand/pubs/monographs/2008/RAND_MG720.pdf.

Wei-Skillern, J., and S. Marciano. 2008. "The Networked Nonprofit." *Stanford Social Innovation Review* 6, no. 2, 38–43.

Williamson, V. 2009. *Supporting Our Troops, Veterans, and Their Families: Lessons Learned and Future Opportunities for Philanthropy.* Report on the Iraq Afghanistan Deployment Impact Fund (IADIF) of the California Community Foundation (CFF), November. Los Angeles, CA: CCF. https://www.calfund.org/document.doc?id=215.

15

Investing in Human Capital to Transform Rural Communities

Paul Major
Telluride Foundation

Rural communities need dramatic and permanent change to survive and, hopefully, thrive in the second century. As Adam Smith noted in *An Inquiry into the Nature and Causes of the Wealth of Nations* (1776/1976), the "invisible hand of the markets" will determine the strength and future of an economy. This is especially true for rural communities. Unless rural communities intentionally focus on mobilizing their own human capital, creating a community culture of civic engagement, service, and leadership to shape their future, their prosperity will be shaped by forces beyond their control.

Rural and small communities are founded around three basic anchor institutions—local government (including school, library, emergency services, and fire districts), churches, and an economic base. The traditional anchor economic base of rural communities—exploiting natural resources, agriculture, small manufacturing, bedroom communities, and tourism—are under threat or have become highly transitory due to competition, globalization, and commodity pricing. The future may not be the old versus new economy, but no economy at all. The traditional characteristics of small and rural communities, such as independence, isolation, trust in one's neighbors, and a sense of place and history will not be immune to a fundamental change as a community's economic base diminishes or disappears. The second century for small and rural communities will be shaped by their ability to adapt to this external change and supplement or replace this fragile anchor that represents their economic base with new forms of capital.

The Naturita Library story illustrates a rural community in transition from a heavy reliance on traditional anchors and natural resource extraction to a community anchored in its human capital. It is also a story of how a resource-challenged rural area built a new library that was within four years named the Best Small Library in America and one of three libraries in the nation honored for its service by the U.S. Congress in 2012 (Berry 2011).

Naturita is a small town in the Paradox Mineral Basin, a 3,200-square-mile area located in southwest Colorado, defined by its natural resources and impacted by the boom and bust of resource extraction. Covering an area equivalent to Yellowstone National Park, and bigger than Delaware and Rhode Island combined, the Paradox Basin averages less than three persons per square mile. The communities of the Paradox Basin share a common geography, history, and economic base. The economy of this area remains depressed, having never fully recovered from the decline of mining, the chief source of income until the 1980s. Closure of the mines in 1984, due to new mineral discoveries in other parts of the world and a shift in the country's nuclear arms program, had a devastating effect on the economy. The area lost 40 percent of its population and become the nation's largest superfund[1] site (Hessler 2010; Johnson 2010).

While many Paradox residents had earned incomes from working in mining and agriculture, most of the wealth created went to the corporations that owned the underlying assets. The local workers had jobs, often irregular, but no wealth creation. Left behind was a low-wealth community with a diminished economic and human capital base. Such a pattern of development—one that creates income and wealth disparities—existed in the Paradox Basin and much of rural America for over a century. As this region continues to experience economic contraction, out-migration, and demographic shifts, it faces an enormous loss of built-up local generational wealth. When current generations retire or pass on their assets, however small, most of it flows outside of the rural area where that wealth was created.

The Paradox Basin, with its boom-bust cycle of resource extraction, is currently facing a time of great change with the revival of uranium mining and the resurgence in oil and gas development due to advances in extraction technology, including horizontal drilling and hydraulic fracturing. While many in the Paradox Valley are hopeful that uranium mining and the mill will bring another economic boom to the area, others realize the importance of securing a more sustainable and stable economy. They are looking to diversify types of economic development with renewable energy projects, small-scale niche agriculture, and tourism.

Concerned about the social fabric, community culture, and economic deterioration of their community, a group of citizens from Naturita envisioned a new library as a community gathering place in which residents could learn, gather, and discuss ideas, including revitalizing the local community. The old library, located in a dilapidated 500-square-foot shack from the mining era, was at its best neglected and at its worst a public health threat. The tight spaces, lack of adequate ventilation, lack of light, high levels of mold, and unsafe book stacks made the simple act of searching for a book a dangerous undertaking. Naturita is not known as an amenity-rich place; the town "has unpaved streets, a per capita income just over half the state average and a resource-dependent economy that has cycled through booms and busts" (Berry 2011). Fifteen percent of Naturita residents don't have telephone service in their homes. The commitment of a significant capital grant from the Telluride Foundation, conditioned upon the passage of a local tax and local fundraising, helped mobilize Naturita's residents. To build the library, funds from grants and donations were matched by area residents through a property tax increase approved by 80 percent of Naturita voters. It was the first self-imposed tax increase passed by the community in over 15 years.

The combination of funding sources resulted in the construction of the new Naturita Library. With the library, the community added the second structural core straw-bale library in the nation, including a geo-exchange system that taps into the earth's consistent temperature in order to heat or cool the building. However the new Naturita Library demonstrated more than just new architecture and new sustainability technology: It also demonstrated the power of community in a rural area that did not possess substantial fiscal resources. It demonstrated the power of human capital, exemplified in an intentional evolving community culture, civic engagement, and leadership, and nourished by limited but highly effective rural community philanthropy.

Moving beyond the particulars of the Naturita case, rural communities are defined by and anchored in the natural resources and geography of their location, whether farmland in the Midwest or the mines and timberlands of the rural West. The traditional commercial activities based on the natural resources of rural communities such as mining and ranching are their anchors. Small town manufacturing, agriculture, and resource extraction have long been a vital, yet challenging, part of the rural economy. Commercial activities based upon natural resources, the weather, pricing, and other factors beyond local control are susceptible to boom-and-bust economic cycles. The boom cycle quickly generates great wealth, while the bust cycle can mire communities in unemployment and the attendant social upheaval. Global forces, such as mineral or beef prices in foreign countries, directly influence rural economies and can destabilize them as an anchor to the community, often setting them adrift.

The following statistical snapshot of rural communities shows them to be both a complex and important continuing part of American society. Rural America contains the lion's share of the nation's sustainability infrastructure, supplying the food, energy, and other natural materials to support the country. But here the complexities start. While rural America contains 75 percent of the nation's land, it is home to only 17 percent of America's population. Rural America can be poor: 20 percent of rural children are considered to be poor;

32 percent of the population resides in low-employment counties; and over 20 percent of agriculture-based households have an income of less than $15,000 annually. Rural America can be very isolated. Overall Internet access in rural communities is 15 percent lower than user counterparts in metropolitan areas. Rural children begin kindergarten and first grade with lower reading and math scores than their peers (Gibbs 2004) and the number of children living in poverty in rural communities is on the rise (Mattingly, Bean, and Schaefer 2012). Rural citizens generally have a more troubled health status, live shorter lives, have lower educational attainment and lower incomes; yet these same people living in rural communities provide, as indicated earlier, most of our natural resources such as timber, water, minerals, oil, natural gas, food, and fiber.

Community foundations have not been a local common institution in rural communities, and even nonprofits can be extremely scarce due to the lack of communal wealth and individual income in rural areas. However, community giving has always been present. Some of the biggest foundations in the country, the Guggenheim and Rockefeller foundations among them, were formed from wealth extracted from rural communities that mined, drilled, and cut for their absentee owners. The act of giving has always been a strong and binding feature of rural community life. Taking the time to help neighbors build their home, fix their fence, conduct the fall round-up, or give money in small increments when possible for the causes that are local and matter to them have always been part of life in rural communities. This informal community giving of time, resources, and money, while rarely institutionalized into a community foundation, permeated rural communities and remains a strong example of their "community philanthropy."

Put another way, rural communities offer various forms of local capital. Recent research describes *rural capital* in the form of physical, financial, human, intellectual, natural, social, political, and cultural capital (Pender, Marré, and Reeder 2012, iii). While all these forms of capital may exist in a rural community at various levels, the development and expansion of *human capital*—and its subsets—is particularly important. Human capital is the base capital that a community can deploy and leverage to prosper and to utilize the other forms of capital. In order to expand this base resource in new ways, small and rural communities will need to change from relying on historic natural resources and systems, and instead invest and refocus on new forms of capital. It will require more than under-resourced local government, schools, and faith-based entities to thrive in the foreseeable future; it will require the entire citizenry fully engaged as human capital to serve to enhance their community. In the past, traditional rural human capital was tied to traditional, extractive, local economic anchors. As the strength of these economic anchors has diminished or even been eliminated, new relationships have been required. These emerging, reformed, or repositioned institutions, driven by the community's human capital, represent new anchors for communities. The strength, depth, and prosperity of these communities will be limited only by the reluctance or resistance of their traditional institutions to change, adapt, or even expire. Emerging and adapting institutions can provide opportunities for local citizens, including even the nontraditional uses of its natural resources. New economic bases are vital to prosperity. Strategies such as promoting entrepreneurship and innovation, establishing industry clusters, and attracting the creative class will initiate a comparative advantage in today's knowledge-based economy (Pender, Marré, and Reeder 2012, iii). These strategies rely first and foremost on the development of the human capital I have discussed here. Community foundations in rural areas that stimulate and advance the opportunities generated by this new human capital will help rural places navigate into the second century.

Philanthropy, in the form of community giving or recruiting outside community investment, will provide the financial seed capital to create new and engaged forms of local human capital. Financial capital facilitates the development of human capital to drive opportunities and change within a community. Few if any examples exist of low-wealth/low-income communities "pulling themselves up by their bootstraps" and making change without some level of financial capital that leverages the human engagement.

One building or project cannot fix everything; however, it can stimulate the generation of new human capital and serve as a new community anchor of change and success. In the Naturita case, it was the human capital—an intentional commitment to change the community culture, civic engagement, and leadership—combined with local philanthropy—community financial capital—that resulted in a local success.

Gone are the days when rural communities could control their economies or economic future. Rural economies as anchors are changing dramatically. Community giving—in all its forms—will enable the development of human capital. An intentional investment in and sustaining of people and their capabilities to lead and create will generate the conditions needed for small and rural communities to diversify and expand their economies leading to prosperity. In turn, the intentional development of human capital will form the new anchor of prosperity for rural communities in the second century.

Note

1. "*Superfund* is the name given to the environmental program established to address abandoned hazardous waste sites." See http://www.epa.gov/superfund/about.htm.

Bibliography

Berry, John N., III. 2011. "Labor of Love: Best Small Library in America, 2011—Naturita Community Library, CO." *Library Journal,* February 1. http://www.libraryjournal.com/lj/home/888540–264/labor_of_love_best_small.html.csp.

Dervarics, C. 2005. "Rural Children Lag in Early Childhood Educational Skills." January. Washington, DC: Population Reference Bureau. http://www.prb.org/articles/2005/ruralchildrenlaginearlychildhoodeducationalskills.aspx?p=1.

Gibbs, R., ed. 2004. *Rural Education at a Glance.* Rural Development Research Report No. RDRR-98, January. Washington, DC: U.S. Department of Agriculture.

Hessler, P. 2010. "The Uranium Widows: Why Would a Community Want to Return to Milling a Radioactive Element?" *New Yorker,* September 3.

Johnson, K. 2010. "A Battle over Uranium Bodes Ill for U.S. Debate." *New York Times,* December 26. http://www.nytimes.com/2010/12/27/science/earth/27uranium.html?pagewanted=all&_r=0.

Mattingly, M.J., J.A. Bean, and A. Schaefer. 2012. *Over Sixteen Million Children in Poverty in 2011.* Carsey Institute Issue Brief No. 54, Fall. http://scholars.unh.edu/carsey/176/.

Pender, J., A. Marré, and R. Reeder. 2012. *Rural Wealth Creation: Concepts, Strategies, and Measures.* Economic Research Report No. 131, March. Washington, DC: U.S. Department of Agriculture. http://www.rurdev.usda.gov/Reports/rd-ERR131.pdf.

Smith, Adam. 1776/1976. *An Inquiry into the Nature and Causes of the Wealth of Nations.* London, UK: Stratton & Cadell. Repr., Chicago, IL: University of Chicago Press.

Telluride Foundation. 2012. http://www.telluridefoundation.org.

16

Gulf Coast Community Foundation

From Conversion to Transformation

Teri A Hansen
Gulf Coast Community Foundation

Mark S. Pritchett
Gulf Coast Community Foundation

There is a saying in our field that "to know one community foundation is to know one community foundation." The unique character of each community foundation can be attributed to the distinct identity of the communities we serve and to our individual origins. The Gulf Coast Community Foundation began as a "hospital conversion" foundation that has developed into a creative and innovative anchor institution in our region. The best path to tell our story starts with our origins, when our DNA was transmitted through the controversial sale of a regional nonprofit hospital into a community foundation formed with that sale's proceeds. We will describe our contentious birth, because knowing who our "parents" were will provide some insight into how we think and why we have taken the actions we have. We will then journey through a course of challenges and changes. These will illustrate how a hospital-conversion community foundation that began with a big endowment and simple grantmaking functions matured over more than a decade and a half into a transformative foundation that is seen by many as an anchor institution for our region. Finally, we will examine impending issues that we think will alter the future of community foundations in exponential ways.

Stage 1: The Conversion

Gulf Coast Community Foundation is located in Venice, Florida, a little over an hour's drive south of Tampa. The city of Venice was established in 1925 by Cleveland's Brotherhood of Locomotive Engineers—not the last influence that Cleveland would have on this community. Our residents are mostly retired Caucasian midwesterners with an average age of 68. Our regional economy is primarily supported by a winter tourist season, retirement communities, and the health care industry. Construction and real estate were economic drivers until the Great Recession hit in 2007. Our region was one of the first into the recession and will be one of the last out.

One might assume that a community rich in good weather and wealthy snowbirds would be void of controversy (save for the occasional country club or condominium association spat) and fertile ground to grow a community foundation. In late 1995, Gulf Coast Community Foundation (first named the Venice Foundation) was created in a swirl of disagreement and quiet financial maneuvers surrounding the sale of the hospital. The big controversial issues centered on the reasons for selling the hospital, how it should be priced, and how the community should be involved in the transaction (Sirica 1999, 1–2). The decision to sell the regional nonprofit hospital revealed a divided community that struggled with how to let go of the past and how to embrace a new future in philanthropy.

The new foundation's transition board crafted an expansive programmatic mission that focused on "being a catalyst for positive community change in the areas of Education, Health and Human Services, Civic Affairs, and Arts and Culture" (Sirica 1999, 4). The Venice Foundation opened its doors as a community foundation on September 1, 1995, with $92 million in net profit from the sale of Venice's 342-bed community hospital and its related assets (The Venice Foundation 1995). The sale of the hospital created an instant community foundation.

The birth of the Venice Foundation with such a large endowment proved to be a blessing and a hindrance in the early years. The endowment was a blessing in that it gave the foundation time to mature, to cover its expenses, and to make grants without the sense of urgency to attract new donors. The region also had an affluent population of potential future donors from which to build relationships and donations. The economic times were stable. Poverty and unemployment rates were low. Arts and cultural offerings were plentiful. And there were other major foundations in the region, including several community foundations, to address community needs.

The endowment was an obstacle to future maturation because most board decisions regarding grants, investments, and operations were subject to intense community scrutiny. The leaders thought there was enough money to make grants and cover operations; they saw no urgent need to attract new donors. After six years of responsive grantmaking and little progress to draw in new donors, the Venice Foundation prepared for a new stage of growth and began a national search for a new leader.

Stage 2: Linear Growth

In the fall of 2001, shortly after the 9/11 tragedy, an executive search firm contacted Teri Hansen to gauge her interest in taking on a new challenge in Venice, Florida. Hansen, at the time, was employed as vice president for Gift Planning and Donor Relations at the Cleveland Foundation. Prior to that, she had built a community foundation from the ground up in central Indiana.

The board of the Venice Foundation was looking for someone with Hansen's experience to build a robust donor effort, strengthen their governance function, and expand grantmaking and initiatives. Hansen took the reins of the Venice Foundation in early 2002. She met with community leaders and former board members to begin crafting a strategy of second-stage growth. The first priorities focused on three areas: building strong governance practices among board members, creating a strategic plan, and rebuilding the donor-development function. The board instantly recognized the benefits of strong governance practices—a clear sense of accountability, more effective meetings, and alignment with the organization's strategy. A newly crafted mission simply stated, "To improve the quality of life in the communities we serve."

Knowing that controversy was in the DNA of the Venice Foundation, Hansen encountered her first major community dispute after her first year on the job. There was a general feeling among the board that the Venice Foundation's name did not fully represent its past or its potential future. Board members from surrounding communities desired a name change because the "Venice" brand did not properly recognize their contributions to the founding hospital (The Venice Foundation 2003a). As early as 2000, two years before Hansen's arrival, the board considered a name change to Gulf Coast Community Foundation. The term "Gulf Area" was represented in the parent company of the hospital, and "Gulf Coast" reflected the regional approach of the hospital serving patients from beyond Venice (Sirica 1999). The board decided to change the name of the Venice Foundation to Gulf Coast Community Foundation in spite of the demands from a small group of community detractors. To show the community the board was listening to the opposition, though concerned it would not quell all controversy, the board added "of Venice" to the name three months after the initial change (The Venice Foundation 2003b).

Gulf Coast Community Foundation of Venice (Gulf Coast) pursued its strategy of building "a culture of philanthropy" in the region through leadership and social capital. The foundation was invited to be part of a Harvard University study on social capital in the region in the summer of 2002. The results of that study were presented at a community luncheon, painting a picture of the region's civic health and showing where it could improve building social capital, including philanthropy. This initiative and further work to strengthen social capital that grew from it raised Gulf Coast's leadership stature. Staff and board members served in leadership positions throughout the community—chambers of commerce, economic development organizations, civic groups, and policymaking organizations. Gulf Coast also launched and funded a comprehensive regional health initiative—the Community Health Improvement Partnership—which continues to live today under the umbrella of the Sarasota County Health Department. Gulf Coast set new standards for leadership and building an underpinning for strong community philanthropy.

In 2004, the region was devastated by Hurricane Charley. The day the hurricane hit, Gulf Coast launched on its website a vehicle for the community to come together and contribute to the recovery efforts. The foundation matched the gifts, and the community began to see the need for philanthropic dollars beyond those of the original endowment. Immediately following, Gulf Coast commissioned a four-county study of how the community responded to such a widespread disaster. Key findings were that relationships across county lines aided in evacuation, response, and recovery. The white paper became the template and catalyst for more intracounty (public and private) coordination (Gulf Coast Community Foundation of Venice 2004).

The foundation also pursued its strategy of building a culture of philanthropy by fortifying the governance of nonprofits. An initiative called Building Better Boards assessed current board governance and then prescribed a customized governance-improvement program that would strengthen the nonprofit's leadership. This initiative has subsequently evolved into a more sophisticated nonprofit assessment called Invest in Incredible that helps build stronger governance as well as staff, organizational, and financial stability.

Gulf Coast Community Foundation of Venice was developing into an anchor institution in the region. Leadership on key regional issues quickly differentiated Gulf Coast from other foundations in the area. For example, in 2005, at the height of Florida's real estate boom and rising home prices, Gulf Coast saw a need to build affordable workforce housing. Hardworking nurses, teachers, and other middle-income workers could not afford to buy homes. The demand for workforce housing exceeded the supply. Families and individuals were forced to move miles from work or to rent substandard housing, straining social capital and making it difficult for employers to fill critical positions.

Simultaneously, Gulf Coast was interested in expanding its grantmaking tools to include mission-related investing. In 2005, Gulf Coast saw a mission-related investment opportunity: to fill this workforce housing deficit by designing and building an environmentally friendly, mixed-income, mixed-use neighborhood with homes for working families. The project was named the Bridges. Gulf Coast commissioned the conceptual design and then purchased land adjacent to a major interstate highway. Land permitting and building negotiations continued until the hot housing market began to cool and then buckled under the weight of bad mortgages, declining home prices, and the subsequent collapse of financial markets.

By 2008, it became clear that Florida and the rest of the country had entered an unprecedented economic downturn referred to as the Great Recession. The supply of affordable workforce housing was no longer an issue, as a surplus of foreclosures and falling home prices resulted in plenty of available housing. The Bridges project was placed on hold indefinitely. Gulf Coast had taken a risk to address a growing problem. The foundation's only failure was not seeing the approaching recession—but then, who did?

Now, Gulf Coast was positioned to take on even bigger challenges. The next stage of growth would be more dramatic than ever. Gulf Coast was about to launch itself into the realm of catalytic change through public policy action and major donor engagement.

Stage 3: Catalytic Change

By 2007, Gulf Coast Community Foundation had assets topping $260 million (Gulf Coast Community Foundation 2007, 55). The largest community foundation in Florida, it had a solid reputation as a grantmaker. Gulf Coast expanded its leadership role in the region by promoting better governance and taking on difficult issues. Yet something was missing that, in Hansen's mind, would keep Gulf Coast from becoming a top-tier community foundation. That missing piece was how to address systemic issues by leveraging philanthropic resources with public policy action.

So, in 2008, the board embarked on a search to grow Gulf Coast's ability to address systemic issues. Hansen recruited and hired a former association executive with research, policy, and lobbying experience. Her hope was that Gulf Coast would begin to get to root causes of some of the economic, social, and education issues in the region.

The strategy worked and coincided with Gulf Coast's invitation to participate in the California Community Foundation's Iraq Afghanistan Deployment Impact Fund (IADIF). Gulf Coast applied and received a $5-million, two-year grant to assist military personnel and their families in 25 counties in central and southwest Florida affected by the wars in Iraq and Afghanistan. This was the largest single gift ever entrusted to the foundation since the sale of the hospital in 1995. Gulf Coast issued a policy report two years later, and it was embraced by Florida's lieutenant governor (MacManus and Schuler 2011). It was a pivotal success, and moved Gulf Coast further toward becoming a fully articulated community foundation.

Also in 2008, Gulf Coast tested the policy arena through an unlikely set of circumstances. A local widower asked Gulf Coast to help him set up a foundation after his wife Denise Amber Lee was tragically abducted, raped, and murdered. It is argued that her life could have been spared if several 911 phone calls were not mishandled in a dispatch center. When Gulf Coast asked how he wanted to memorialize his wife, he simply said that he wanted improvements made to the training of 911 operators and dispatchers who might have saved her life. Gulf Coast listened to his request and went further. The staff recommended and the board approved a policy study of the emergency 911 system in the State of Florida to understand if this tragedy was an isolated occurrence or a systemic issue (Gulliver 2009). The results were shocking. There were no uniform standards for training in the 264 different call centers throughout Florida. The tax fee collected to maintain the 911 system was used primarily to buy equipment and rarely used for training. Gulf Coast took the results of that policy study and provided it to key policymakers. During the 2009 legislative session, a bill was passed into law requiring uniform training standards for 911 operators and dispatchers. Gulf Coast had successfully leveraged philanthropic dollars and addressed a systemic issue through policy change. The widower Nathan Lee now speaks about this policy success throughout the nation. Because of his story and our policy initiative, other states are improving their training laws and regulations.

Gulf Coast continues to focus on addressing systemic issues by leveraging its philanthropic dollars with funding from private foundations, corporations, and donors. In education, we have launched a catalytic campaign to improve our children's poor academic performance in science, technology, engineering, and math—the STEM subjects. Our catalytic STEM education initiative is branded as STEMsmart (2012). In the first year of the project's implementation, math test scores in two of the three participating high schools increased significantly. In full partnership with two school districts, we have transformed the methods by which teachers teach and the ways in which students learn (Semon 2012). We are engaging the wider community through a broad marketing campaign, collaborating with donors to help fund the initiative, and enlisting businesses to provide students with real-life experiences of how STEM is applied at work. STEMsmart is featured in Florida's statewide strategic plan for economic development as an innovative education program to spur job growth.

As an anchor institution in our region, Gulf Coast takes on the toughest issues. When regional unemployment skyrocketed to 13 percent during the Great Recession, Gulf Coast partnered with the John S. and James L. Knight Foundation, local governments, corporations, and training organizations to systemically address how to get people back to work. Gulf Coast adapted a national workforce model so it would succeed in our local market. In just two years of operation, this innovative workforce model known as CareerEdge (2012) has a remarkable track record. An impact analysis of its first year of operations revealed that more than 1,475 workers were trained during that period, all of whom either received promotions or wage increases or were placed in jobs. CareerEdge assisted 284 new hires, of which 139 workers had been out of work for as long as 24 months. Ninety percent of CareerEdge workers are moving up the educational ladder to improve their earning power. Gulf Coast also published a policy report titled *Will Work for Change* that will be used to promote a new demand-driven system for workforce development in Florida and the nation (Gulf Coast Community Foundation, 2012b).

Gulf Coast Community Foundation has made the most of its controversial and opportunistic beginnings as a hospital conversion. Starting with traditional grantmaking, Gulf Coast has become an anchor institution in our region, seeding leadership and attacking our most difficult issues. The key success factors in our journey were embracing our roots, developing regional leadership, thinking systemically, taking calculated risks, and acting catalytically. Now, we are focused on the future and asking ourselves which trends we should monitor and how we might stay ahead to maintain our relevance as a regional anchor institution and community foundation.

Exponential Change and Relevance

One question we ask every day is, How do we maintain our relevance as a community foundation? The exponential rate of change in technology definitely threatens that relevance if we maintain the status quo. Gulf Coast has embraced technology as a means to help build a culture of philanthropy in our region. We have created two technological tools that help us promote charitable giving and volunteerism to residents who might have never thought about giving back.

Gulf Coast Gives (2012) is a fun web portal that lets anyone become a philanthropist in just seconds. The beauty of Gulf Coast Gives is that every contribution counts, whether you can give $5 or $500. Community nonprofits, teachers, and civic groups post projects on GulfCoastGives.org and use social media to promote contributions. The website provides a platform for citizen philanthropists to help nonprofits close the distance between a dream and a dream fulfilled.

For those in our community who prefer to volunteer, Gulf Coast has created the "perfect" place where they can donate their talent. You'd Be Perfect for This.org (2012) allows nonprofits and civic clubs to post their volunteer opportunities in the clearest, most concise, and colorful way possible. Community members can browse the site for all sorts of opportunities to give their time to good causes. With just a few clicks, they can volunteer themselves, a friend, or their whole office for a day or an extended engagement. It doesn't get easier—or more fun—than this!

Even with these technological innovations, Gulf Coast wrestles with anticipating what the future role of technology will be for community foundations and whether we will be able to adapt. Salim Ismail of Singularity University revealed to community foundations attending the 2011 Fall Conference a glimpse of how technology will be a disruptive force. Ismail travels the world showing audiences driverless cars, 3D printers making new 3D printers, and labs manufacturing organs—all of which exist right now.

Ismail explains in an interview with Endeavor Global that the accelerating rate of change in technology will only get faster and faster (Endeavor Global 2012). These exponential growth trends affect our daily lives now, and our minds simply cannot comprehend this accelerating pace of change. Humans are trained to think in linear steps, but technology innovation is advancing exponentially. Salim Ismail reaffirmed earlier proclamations that if you are building a product or service using today's technologies, you may be out of date by the time you get to market.

How do we as community foundations stay relevant in a flurry of technological change? How will community foundations keep pace with those technological disruptions and continue to scale our solutions in our communities? Ismail suggests that community foundations move out of our comfort zones and collaborate with new partners that are outside of our profession—just like the learning atmosphere incubated at Singularity University.

A Nonprofit Free Market

Dan Pallotta, writing in his provocative book *Uncharitable,* asserts that the world of charity and nonprofits will never have enough money or marketing prowess to solve the planet's biggest problems. That's simply because "charity has been separated from the rest of the economic world, denied important economic rights, and forced to operate under a counterproductive set of rules" (Pallotta 2008, 41). Pallotta recommends removing the nonprofit restraints and embracing a free market system. He calls for a capitalistic free market for nonprofits, with stock markets, patient capital strategies, and higher pay, and he suggests that "if we allow charity to use free market practices, we will see an increase in the money being raised, more effective solutions, and a circular reinforcement that will further increase investment in solving the great problems of our time" (Pallotta 2008, 46). Pallotta concludes that if we really want to help the poor, if we really want to cure disease, then we need a set of free market rules that will promote big solutions to big problems. How would community foundations embrace this new ideology? What would happen if the charitable deduction were eliminated and a new free market were created? Would community foundations become the new Wall Street traders as part of a new free market system for solving the world's biggest problems?

Private Sector Rules

In his book *Saving the World at Work*, Tim Sanders implies that the for-profit private sector may beat philanthropy to the punch in creating a capitalistic system for doing good in our communities. Sanders believes that the upcoming generation of consumers will dictate that the current free market system of companies demand they do more good in the world (Sanders 2008). He says that companies that operate in the business of "doing good" are beginning to increase their market share and refers to this shift as the Responsibility Revolution (Sanders 2008, 4). While Sanders initially focuses on ways to save the environment, he provides a few examples of companies that are pioneers in doing good while making money: Medtronic (medical care), Timberland (manufacturing), Interface (carpeting), Whole Foods (supermarkets), SAS Institute (technology), and Lush (retail). The two essential questions a company in the future will ask are, "Is this good for the company?" and "Is this good for the world?" While Sanders's for-profit overthrow of today's philanthropic model may be at best a "weak signal" on the horizon, it is one that philanthropy and community foundations should monitor.

Crushing National Debt: How to Pay the Credit Card

Finally, the most current and looming issue might be the mounting federal debt. The Great Recession exposed the country's financial fragility and heightened the need to take action on the impending fiscal crisis. As revenue plummeted and spending soared, our national debt took on proportions that are difficult to comprehend. The rate of debt is moving from linear to exponential. The public debt recently surpassed $16 trillion, and there is no end in sight for dealing with this issue (Dinan 2012). That $16 trillion is approaching $50,000 for every person in the United States, about $130,000 per household (PolitiFact Virginia 2012). If taxes go up, then how will those who contribute to charity be affected? If the charitable deduction is placed on the chopping block, will it start a dramatic decline in charitable giving? If spending cuts are put into place, what will happen to the health and human service organizations we support? What new social issues will arise if these services are cut? Remember also that strapped governments at all levels are likely to walk away from current responsibilities. The role of community foundations may therefore become significantly larger. The consequences are grave if we do not address this issue for us and our future generations.

All of these issues and trends are in various stages of culmination. Technology will progress exponentially; that is a given. Whoever keeps up and executes wins. The nonprofit sector must continue to monitor free market principles. Look at how Kiva and DonorsChoose have successfully blended philanthropy and technology into fun charitable giving. Will community foundations be able to match or exceed that customer experience?

Community foundations should warily eye the for-profit sector's entry into philanthropy. Will community foundations clearly articulate why donors should choose us if Fidelity can process charitable giving faster, cheaper, and smarter? There is no way community foundations can compete with this transactional model. Also, community foundations will be criticized if they try to invest in technology as quickly and often as the for-profit sector. That raises the question, Will community foundations become an extinct "charitable middleman" in a new charitable free market? Have we reached the top limits of our market share? Or will the for-profit sector see "green" in doing good and simply buy us out?

Community foundations should embrace these trends and avoid the possibility of becoming irrelevant. Remember what happened to many nonprofit hospitals in the 1990s? Playing with future scenarios is fun unless you are forecasting your own demise.

This final section began with what issues or trends might affect the future relevance of community foundations. We can choose to passively watch what happens or actively move forward into the future. At Gulf Coast, we are fortunate to begin every day knowing we have the power to make a difference. These are responsibilities and privileges too important to relinquish. We intend to embrace the future and continue to innovate into the next 100 years.

Bibliography

CareerEdge. 2012. "What We Do: Training the Next Generation of Skilled Workers." http://www.careeredgefunders.org/what-we-do.html.

Dinan, S. 2012. "Federal Debt Tops $16 Trillion, Treasury Department Says." *Washington Times,* September 4. http://www.washingtontimes.com/blog/inside-politics/2012/sep/4/debt-tops-16-trillion/.

Endeavor Global. 2012. "Salim Ismail on Singularity University [Transcript]." February 16. http://www.endeavor.org/blog/salim-ismail-on-singularity-university-transcript.

Gulf Coast Community Foundation. 2012a. http://www.gulfcoastcf.org.

———. 2012b. *Will Work for Change: Demand-Driven Solutions for Florida's Future Workforce.* Report, June. Venice, FL: Gulf Coast Community Foundation.

————. 2007. *2007 Annual Report*. Venice, FL: Gulf Coast Community Foundation.

Gulf Coast Community Foundation of Venice. 2004. *Lessons Learned: A Review of Our Regional Disaster Response*. Report, December. Venice, FL: Gulf Coast Community Foundation of Venice.

Gulf Coast Gives. 2012. Website. https://www.gulfcoastgives.org.

Gulliver, D., ed. 2009. *Florida 911: The State of Emergency*. Report, August. Venice, FL: Gulf Coast Community Foundation.

MacManus, S.A., and S.C. Schuler. 2011. "Collateral Damage: Floridians Coping with the Aftermath of War." *Backgrounder,* no. 68 (February). Tallahassee, FL: The James Madison Institute. http://www.jamesmadison.org/pdf/materials/Backgrounder_Veterans_MacManusSchulerFeb11.pdf.

Pallotta, D. 2008. *Uncharitable: How Restraints on Nonprofits Undermine Their Potential*. Medford, MA: Tufts University Press.

PolitiFact Virginia. 2012. "The Truth-O-Meter Says: 'The National Debt Is Equal to $48,700 for Every American or $128,300 for Every U.S. Household. It Is Now Equivalent to the Size of Our Entire Economy.'" *PolitiFact,* Virginia edition, February 3. http://www.politifact.com/virginia/statements/2012/feb/03/randy-forbes/rep-randy-forbes-says-national-debt-comes-48700-pe.

Sanders, T. 2008. *Saving the World at Work: What Companies and Individuals Can Do to Go Beyond Making a Profit to Making a Difference*. New York: Doubleday.

Semon, N.J. 2012. "Preparing for the Future." *Harbor Style Magazine*, July. http://trendmag2.trendoffset.com/display_article.php?id=1087979.

Sirica, C. 1999. "The Venice Foundation." In *New Foundations in Health: Six Stories*, ed. Milbank Memorial Fund. Report, May. New York: Milbank Memorial Fund. http://www.milbank.org/uploads/documents/nf/venice.html.

STEMsmart. 2012. "STEMsmart, the Spark: Behind Every Great Movement Are Activists." http://www.stemsmart.org/about/who-we-are.

The Venice Foundation. 2003a. Board of Directors' meeting minutes, February and March.

————. 2003b. Board of Directors' meeting minutes, May 9.

————. 1995. Board of Directors' meeting minutes, September 21.

You'd Be Perfect for This. 2012. "We Want to Be Perfect for You. Here's a Little About Us." http://www.youdbeperfectforthis.org/pages/about.

Part IV

The Risks and Rewards of Strong Leadership

17

An Emerging Civic Leadership Model

A Community Foundation's Distinctive Value Proposition

Paul Grogan
The Boston Foundation

Since the founding of the first community foundation in 1914 by visionary Cleveland banker Frederick Goff, this once-novel class of institution has continued to grow and thrive. The original idea was to pool charitable resources to permit a focused effort on the underlying causes of urban problems, as opposed to charity as a mere palliative, dealing only with the symptoms of distress. In our case, the founders of the Boston Foundation were a couple of enlightened trust officers at the Boston Safe Deposit and Trust, which is now part of the Bank of New York Mellon. They were very articulate about the need to attack the underlying causes of urban distress, and that has been the mantra of the Boston Foundation. Community foundations have since developed a sterling reputation in grantmaking and stewardship, serving as the quiet, behind-the- scenes supporters of their communities.

What stands out from this narrative is the wide range of activities these young foundations engaged in to establish their standing in the community. A revelation in a recent reread of Waldemar A. Nielsen's perceptive 1985 history of the large American foundations, *The Golden Donors: A New Anatomy of the Great Foundations,* was the close resemblance between the early work of the first community foundation and what is viewed today as a new focus on civic leadership. Nielsen chronicles Goff's work to fulfill the "two greatest needs of the new foundation: public recognition and money" (Nielsen 1985, 245). Goff's successful plan included a series of reports and recommendations on pertinent Cleveland issues, including the welfare system, public education, and criminal justice. Reports were carried to the public through the newspapers, and major municipal reforms followed. These activities inspired trust in the community, and fundraising was so successful that by the mid-1920s the foundation decided to place a greater emphasis on traditional grantmaking and stewardship of philanthropic assets, and the research program was set aside. Other early community foundations followed a similar progression and, to varying degrees, the field has remained focused on these two important roles.

However, as the field comes into its second century, there has been a growing recognition that community foundations can be more than that. This volume chronicles the diverse and exhilarating set of opportunities for community foundations as reputable, place-based, anchor institutions. My colleagues have written about nurturing innovation, revitalizing fundraising, embracing technology, and more. Many are playing an engaged role as a leader and convener in their community. At the Boston Foundation, we found our opportunity to build a distinctive franchise in a progression from a quiet grantmaker to a vocal and visible civic leader.

Our transformation began as the Boston Foundation was contemplating the retirement of a distinguished president and CEO, Anna Faith Jones. During her tenure, Jones engineered dramatic structural change at the foundation: she broke the Trust and gave the Boston Foundation the ability to fully appoint its own board, enabling the creation of a larger, far more representative body. This new board, consisting of heads of nonprofit grantees, local philanthropists, college presidents, lawyers, financial and investment managers, and media and community leaders, has been indispensable. It has provided critical guidance and legitimacy for the foundation's work and engagement with tough issues. Additionally, when the board came to consider Anna Faith Jones's successor, it was from a position of deep community knowledge, influence, and the freedom to be innovative. They found that, despite a truly enviable track record in transformative grantmaking and an excellent reputation throughout Greater Boston, they were not satisfied. They were restless. They asked themselves that hard question: Is the Boston Foundation all it can be? And the answer came back a resounding "no."

Ira Jackson, chair of the program committee at this time, described the board's motivation this way:

> We tried to think creatively and critically, as only this sort of transition lets you do. . . . It was evident that we were treading water. We were too invisible, polite, too traditional and "that's the way it always has been." We were doing good work, but not great. (Jackson 2012)

A major theme in the board's deliberation was their perception of a precipitous decline in civic and business leadership in Boston, and the conviction that someone needed to fill that vacuum. The board of directors thought, Why not let the Boston Foundation take on part of the leadership role, functioning as a permanent, prestigious organization, with considerable resources, devoted to the welfare of the community? Why couldn't the Boston Foundation be, not necessarily the entire answer to declining leadership, but at least part of the answer?

At the transition, the first thing looked at was whether the foundation had the capacity and the people to do this kind of work; clearly, it did not. At this time, there was little in the way of public affairs capacity, just one individual responding to press inquiries, and a part-time writer who focused on the foundation's publications. The Boston Foundation needed to build an integrated public affairs unit that would drive the process of change. We were fortunate to be joined by an accomplished journalist and newspaper executive, Mary Jo Meisner, who was looking for her next move following a success-ful career in newspapers that included stints as city editor of the *Washington Post,* editor of the *Milwaukee Journal-Sentinel,* and editor and vice chair of a chain of community newspapers based here in Boston. Under her leader-ship, the Boston Foundation created a new department of Communications, Community Relations, and External Affairs. As this function has grown, so has the department, which now includes eight specialists in press, govern-ment relations, the web, social media, communications, and marketing, in addition to research staff.

Components of Civic Leadership at the Boston Foundation

This newly established communications capacity was used to begin a process of mapping out what this new externally oriented focus might mean for the Boston Foundation. It resulted in a radical repositioning of the foundation as a leadership institution that had taken on a fresh and distinct set of functions. Central to this new role was the foundation's pledge to help the community define and act upon the most pressing challenges and largest opportunities of the time.

The first component was research. While the Internet has allowed great strides in the distribution and communication of data and information, this overwhelming wealth of resources has made reliable aggregators and inter-preters even more valuable. In addition, information found on the Internet must come from somewhere, and when you are looking for research on local problems, the pool of sources becomes much smaller. The Boston Founda-tion now functions as a think tank joined to a foundation, and its internally generated data and research have allowed the region to partake in unusually rigorous and intelligent conversations; when everyone is looking at the same information, the conversation is more productive and ideological boundaries are less pronounced. Data and rigorous analysis have developed into a requirement in the city; New York City mayor Michael Bloomberg (2010) frequently notes, "In God we trust, everyone else bring data," and that is now the mentality in Boston. The Boston Foundation has become a "go-to" place for research, and that status has provided us with the legitimacy necessary to take public stances on controversial issues. Rather than stepping forward with a position out of the blue, the foundation can point to recent research justifying our interest; we can back up our views with reliable data.

Indeed, community foundations are so well suited to play a leadership role precisely because they are providers of data and research. Like newspapers, community foundations are place-based institutions, in tune to the unique needs, culture, and interests of the areas they serve. Community foundations are independent and nonpartisan, well positioned to conduct objective research and work with a diverse range of partners. The serious mission-based argument of community foundations was articulated with precision by Alberto Ibargüen, head of the Knight Foundation: "Community foundations were created to meet the core needs of communities. In a democracy, information is a core need" (Ibargüen 2008).

The Boston Foundation's entrance into the arenas of data, research, and civic leadership was based on the Boston Indicators Project, one of the first civic indicators projects in the country. This huge research effort was launched at the foundation in the 1990s, in partnership with the city's redevelopment agency and the Metropolitan Area Planning Council. The project collects data and information gathered by a wide variety of civic institutions, public agencies, academic think tanks, community-based organizations, and individuals. In addition to sharing the data, we synthesize and disseminate key findings and trends in reports, on the web, and through conferences and forums. The tremendous amount of information provided by the Boston Indicators Project was the impetus for the Boston Foundation's decision to play a more public role in the community.

The foundation also began to commission significant additional research, beyond the Boston Indicators Project, to extend our ability to look at in-depth at key issues and challenges. This was enabled by a recent development: the emergence within the last decade of a whole series of think tanks in Boston. Previously, there were certainly some individual professors at individual institutions who might have taken an interest in a local problem, but not the university-based teams focused primarily on local and regional issues that exist now. Universities are studying global phenomena, but they are also studying what is happening in the low-income neighborhoods of the city. Harvard University, Northeastern University, the University of Massachusetts, and others have stepped into this space. There is also an independent think tank,

MassINC, which is not university affiliated but does high-quality analytical work. And so, in addition to internal capacity, we could immediately begin to draw on the intellectual firepower of these think tanks to examine data on local and regional problems.

Spending on research from the Boston Indicators Project and through these outside institutions has increased from roughly $100,000 in fiscal year 2001 to $615,000 in fiscal year 2012, with discretionary grantmaking dollars serving as the key source for funds. In fiscal year 2012, research accounted for nearly 4 percent of all of the foundation's discretionary grants. And the shift was quite sudden; discretionary grants for data and research grew from less than 1 percent to approximately 3.5 percent from fiscal year 2001 to fiscal year 2002, the year we shifted our focus.[1]

Over the past decade, we've learned a great deal about how to use our research capacity most effectively. One of our earliest reports, a Greater Boston Housing Report Card, described housing production, trends in housing prices and rents, the preservation of affordable housing, and Massachusetts funding levels for subsidized housing. It was the first in a series of reports released annually since 2002, keeping the conversation about housing needs and challenges in the public view. The commitment to these measures allows the foundation to play the role of a watchdog or monitor, which has since been replicated with "report cards" in other areas like education and health.

On the issue of the cost of health care, the Boston Foundation has kept up an unrelenting and persistent stream of reports showing how the cost of municipal employees' health care has become unsustainable. The reports looked at tools available for municipal officials to moderate health care costs, at the benefits and limitations of moving municipal health care plans to the state-run Group Insurance Commission, and at the rising cost of municipal plans in relation to state and federal plans.

The most influential report, however, related the cost of municipal health care costs to education funding. *School Funding Reality: A Bargain Not Kept* (Moscovitch 2010) showed that new money the legislature had voted for education over a decade had been completely consumed, and then some, by rising health care premiums for teachers and other public employees. This led to major reform in municipal health care in Massachusetts just six months later, over the strenuous objections of organized labor. In Massachusetts, where unions have traditionally held significant sway in a very Democratic legislature, this is a considerable achievement; the Speaker of the House later confided that this report "settled the issue" for him. *School Funding Reality* also demonstrates another key element of our reports: creating statistics that capture the public's attention through innovative research or by making connections between issues. This tactic can lead to new conversations, a refreshed view of entrenched positions, or game-changing knowledge that brings key players to the table.

A fear was that our research and these reports would simply gather dust on readers' shelves, as so many reports do. We wanted them to be actionable, and for that we needed a distribution system. Reports released by the Boston Foundation are disseminated through an ongoing series of public forums, attended by public, private, and nonprofit sector leaders, under the umbrella concept "Understanding Boston" (The Boston Foundation 2012b). We host anywhere from 12 to 15 major forums at the Boston Foundation every year, and most of them are packed, spilling over into additional rooms with simulcasts of the program. From the start, it was important to us that these forums bring out the right people. Now, if the foundation hosts a forum on an educational topic, for example, we will be joined by people like the Boston Public Schools superintendent, the commissioner of education, and potentially the mayor or the governor.

One concern was whether these forums would be well received—and well attended. What if we throw a party and no one comes? It helped to have the virtue of being seen as a neutral convener. Of course, we are not entirely neutral on every issue, but a reliance on data and conversations that include a wide variety of opinions allow us to avoid, in most cases, the reputation of having an axe to grind. Additionally, when the Understanding Boston brand was first set up, there was much intrigue about what the foundation was up to; people were seeing a new Boston Foundation. Finally, and most important, there was an unmet need and real hunger in the community for access to this data and research and for these kinds of conversations.

Along with data and forums, the foundation has made a concerted effort to be very visible in the media and the community. When they first discussed the changes at the foundation, our board contemplated a common challenge of community foundations: "If we want to attract resources and we want to be influential, just exactly how does it help us that no one knows who we are or what we're doing?" (Jackson 2012).

Our board concluded that however attractive humility is as a personal quality, it does not make sense as a strategy for an institution seeking to exert influence and impact. Using data and research as a platform, we mounted a very active communications program nearly overnight. We went from being a foundation that, for its previous 90 years, had done everything it could to shun publicity to one that was actively seeking attention. It was a conscious decision to do this so quickly, as the behavior change itself attracted attention and curiosity.

One of the troubling trends in America is the decline in newspapers and the civic implications accompanying that decline. As of yet, there isn't anything in the new media that comes close to replacing the communal asset created by the leaders in a community reading a good metropolitan newspaper every day. Boston is very fortunate; most leaders in government, in business, and in the nonprofit world do in fact read our excellent metropolitan newspaper, the *Boston Globe,* each day. We also do not lack for other reliable media sources focused on local and regional issues, with a widely respected public radio station (WBUR), an excellent independent magazine (*CommonWealth Magazine*), and various other regular papers with a good following. The Boston Foundation has made it its business to cultivate strong relationships with these traditional media and to position itself as a knowledgeable independent source of data and insight on various public issues.

In addition to using these media outlets to advance our advocacy and leadership work, we have made a concerted effort to tell the story of the Boston Foundation. Joel Fleishman is eloquent on this issue in his book *The Foundation: A Great American Secret.* He describes foundations as "organizations that devote their efforts to changing society, yet rarely seek to measure, or even comprehend, the extent of the changes they actually produce" (Fleishman 2007, xiv). Beyond not having a clear understanding of their own accomplishments, foundations frequently do a poor job communicating the impact of their work to the public.

When I joined the Boston Foundation, I was familiar with its grantmaking and, having been involved in housing and community development, I was aware of the great accomplishments of the foundation in that area. However, I was naturally curious about successes in other realms. In my early days as president, I went around asking staff, board members, and people from the community for a David Letterman–style "Top Ten List" of the Boston Foundation's accomplishments. I asked, "If you had to defend our tax exemption in the next five minutes, what would you say?" It was disconcerting how few concrete examples were cited. One of the things we did to combat this lack of knowledge was to excavate our hidden and disconnected history. A consultant, Patricia Brady, an amateur historian and a great writer, traced our story back to the 1950s and brought forward, admittedly with 20/20 hindsight, the best investments the foundation had made. She uncovered a remarkable track record of prescient grants and often spectacular successes. It turns out that the Boston Foundation's grantmaking was responsible for many transformational events in the city over decades. These achievements were largely unknown even to the board and staff, and the Boston Foundation's role in them had been forgotten by the public.

This is a big problem in the foundation world. Foundations enjoy extraordinary privileges and have a commensurate public obligation to transmit both what they think they've accomplished and what they think they haven't.

Knowing more about the Boston Foundation has given the community new appreciation for our many contributions to the community over the years. And admitting to some failures has gained us credibility.

The final element of this civic leadership strategy was hands-on public policy work. Many foundations will keep their distance from the public sector to avoid what they see as the taint of politics, but we view it as absolutely essential to our mission. There is not a single large and important problem in society that can be solved without the public sector. To significantly improve K–12 education outcomes for Boston's students, we cannot ignore the time students are spending in school and that the public education system is run by the City of Boston. Similarly, the foundation lacks sufficient grantmaking dollars to take on challenges like decaying cultural facilities, high housing prices, soaring rates of obesity, and the increase in preventable diseases without pursuing systemic change or leveraging public dollars. Having established our desire to enlarge our impact leaves us no choice but to engage with state and local governments. We cultivate deep relationships with elected and appointed officials at all three levels of government, but particularly at the state level. We are helped in this by geography: Boston is the capital of Massachusetts. The State House is a 10-minute walk from our offices. It would be fundamentally different if the state capital were in Springfield. We are, of course, the Boston Foundation, but the policy levers that have the most impact on the issues we care about are at the State House.

Across the country, community foundations are increasingly engaged in this space. One of the most common ways to approach a growing role in policy work is by funding advocacy organizations working on issues of critical community importance. Over many decades, the Boston Foundation has not only funded advocacy but provided the start-up capital for many of the state's most important and influential advocacy organizations. Grantees have included the Massachusetts Immigrant and Refugee Advocacy Coalition (MIRA), an advocate for the state's one million foreign-born residents; Health Care for All, a key architect of the Commonwealth's health care reform, which served as the basis for the Affordable Care Act (also known as the Health Care for America Plan or ObamaCare); and the Massachusetts Association of Community Development Corporations. The implausible idea of cleaning up the Boston Harbor, then one of the most polluted harbors in the country, which ended up being a $4.4 billion-dollar environmental success story, was triggered by some zealous advocacy organizations, with the Boston Foundation's persistent support. These organizations pushed and prodded—and ultimately litigated (with litigation funded by the Boston Foundation)—to get state and federal authorities to own up to their responsibility, and the result was a clean harbor. The Boston Foundation has been an enthusiastic funder of advocacy groups for some time. However, it is a fundamentally different proposition for the foundation itself to play a major role working directly on public policy. That was the major shift.

We engage public officials in our decision-making processes and offer ourselves as a source of information and a conduit to the business and nonprofit community. Perhaps most important, the foundation is a partner willing to get in front of a controversial issue, providing political cover and additional policy options for elected officials. It is now part of the culture of the institution, and the expectation is that staff members throughout the organization, particularly our program officers and senior managers, will build relationships with all key elected and appointed officials in their sectors at city and state levels.

The Boston Foundation conducts public policy work in an aboveboard, rigorously nonpartisan and nonpolarizing way. A key component of this standard is basing recommendations and advocacy positions on data and rigorous research, which provide legitimacy for our presence in this arena and objectivity in our stances. The other essential feature is our continued focus on building coalitions of business and civic leaders to join us as we advocate for major policy changes. There is actually great receptivity on the part of business and civic leaders to participate in the public realm. Many are discouraged by the perceived level of effort and time required for getting involved, the perception that they will not be able to influence the system, and that perhaps the power of interest groups is too strong. At the Boston Foundation, an essential part of our role is to take on the burden of handling the details and logistics of these coalitions and build a group large and varied enough to make a real impact, but without asking anyone else to do too much. When it is easy to get involved, it is surprising how many are willing to contribute their time and influence. They just need to be asked—and organized.

Driven by numerous success stories, we developed the mentality that the foundation is at its best when using "all the tools in the toolbox" (The Boston Foundation 2012a, 26)—when grantmaking, organizing, research, forums, press, and public policy all work in concert. The things we are trying to do are difficult, and we do not always succeed, but the foundation has compiled a list of notable legislative achievements in workforce policies, the environment, affordable housing, arts and culture, criminal justice, home rule, education, and health care in just a few short years.

Conclusion

While this paper has emphasized the positive, there are potential downsides to the more visible role taken by the Boston Foundation. For instance, the institution can run afoul of powerful interests. Frankly, if you're doing it right, you definitely will. Nothing important in society changes for the better without conflict; as the legendary Boston mayor Kevin White used to say, "If no one is angry at you, you are not doing anything very important." Therefore, with this different role comes a very different level of risk management for a community foundation. If you are frequently in the press for positive reasons, when something goes wrong it could be in the papers as well. Some people will be unhappy with you. When we face these conflicts, we do so with robust coalitions of business and civic leaders helping us to shape the agenda and with the legitimizing force of data to back up our positions. But if the board of trustees of a community foundation has no tolerance for criticism or conflict, it would be very difficult to play this role.

There is also no question that a transition like this is a challenge. It certainly was for the Boston Foundation, despite significant advantages: a wealth of universities, location in a state capital, robust discretionary endowment, and strong support from the board. However, this is part of a major movement in the community foundation field and represents a significant opportunity for growth and impact.

Emmett D. Carson's call for community foundations to reevaluate and adapt is both urgent and imperative. The field faces unprecedented external pressures and competition, and it has not done a good enough job explaining the value of philanthropy and the nonprofit sector. What is the distinctive value proposition that we offer? What our communities are most in need of is enlightened civic leadership. Across the country, we are in need of civil, broad, data-driven conversations about our future. If community foundations can be central to bringing those exchanges into being, then we will be making a distinctive contribution to our community.

There is a common apprehension that playing this role might alienate existing or future donors. While certainly a concern, ultimately the Boston Foundation has found a great appreciation for its public policy leadership role among donors and prospects. It gives us a more distinctive identity in this competitive environment, and new donor-advised fund (DAF) customers often cite this as the reason they chose us.

Additionally, in our experience, this role can be turned into a revenue stream. When the foundation first contemplated this larger role, we did not have the necessary resources for all the additional work involved. The Board insisted that new revenue be identified. We decided to test whether our donors and board would help by making contributions to an annual fund called the Civic Leadership Fund. This was the first time the Boston Foundation asked for contributions to support its own operations. But it worked: The fund has grown from approximately $325,000 in its initial year in 2003 to over $1.4 million in 2012. A number of community foundations have now started their own version of the Civic Leadership Fund, and others are planning to adopt the model.

The Civic Leadership Fund has had several unforeseen benefits as well. It has succeeded in attracting support from a large number of the most prominent and respected citizens of Boston, many of whom were not previously donors to the Boston Foundation. Giving to the fund in small amounts is a soft introduction, in some cases leading to increased involvement such as opening a DAF or contributing to one of our programmatic initiatives. Support from admired citizens has also served as a kind of validation of the foundation's role.

Finally, these fundraising calls and engagement with business and civic leaders are an indispensable way for foundation leadership to engage and get feedback from the community. When I was appointed to the Boston Foundation, Creed Black, former head of the Knight Foundation, told me, "Watch out. When you become the head of a foundation, you have had your last bad meal and your last honest conversation" (cf. Neill 2011). This is an amusing way to convey a profound truth: that foundations have a lot of difficulty getting good information about how they are doing, and any institution that is deprived of this vital feedback has difficulty improving. The only solution is to proactively create situations where you will get candid feedback, and no one is as frank and outspoken as when you are asking them for money.

The days of quiet philanthropy are behind us. As a field, we will need to get over our fear of conflict and embrace healthy disagreement, and even rancor, when necessary. We will need to put our grantmaking dollars to work in supplying our community with relevant, accurate, and timely information to help our country make informed decisions. We will need to build a new network of independent leaders for every city and region. We will need to excite a new, vocal generation about philanthropy. In the new world of scarcity, all will be under pressure to sharpen their value proposition. The civic leadership model can do just that for community foundations.

Acknowledgments

This paper is an abridged version of a monograph prepared by Paul Grogan for publication by the Center for Strategic Philanthropy and Civil Society, Sanford School of Public Policy, Duke University. To see the unabridged version, go to http://cspcs.sanford.duke.edu/content/changing-game-civic-leadership-boston-foundation-2001-2012-paul-s-grogan.

Note

1. Numbers based on author's calculations.

Bibliography

Bloomberg, M.R. 2010. Remarks by Michael R. Bloomberg, '64. *Commencement Ceremony*, The Johns Hopkins University, May 27. http://web.jhu.edu/commencement/speeches/2010/bloomberg.html.
The Boston Foundation. 2012a. *2012 Annual Report.* Boston, MA: The Boston Foundation. http://www.tbf.org/~/media/TBFOrg/Files/Reports/TBF%20Annual%202012.pdf.
———. 2012b. "Understanding Boston." http://www.tbf.org/understanding-boston.
———. 2012c. http://www.tbf.org.
Fleishman, J.L. 2007. *The Foundation: A Great American Secret—How Private Wealth Is Changing the World.* New York: Public Affairs.
Ibargüen, A. 2008. "Knight Foundation's Media Innovation Strategy." Speech, June 10. http://www.knightfoundation.org/press-room/speech/knight-foundations-media-innovation-strategy/.
Jackson, I. 2012. Interview with Naomi Lee Parker, March 21.
Moscovitch, E. 2010. *School Funding Reality: A Bargain Not Kept.* Report prepared for the Boston Foundation and the Massachusetts Business Alliance for Education, December. Boston, MA: The Boston Foundation. http://www.tbf.org/impact/objectives-and-strategies/strategies/~/media/TBFOrg/Files/Reports/MBAE%20SchoolFinanceReport.pdf.
Neill, R. 2011. Remarks About Creed Black as Knight Foundation CFO. Speech, August 20. http://www.knightfoundation.org/press-room/speech/remarks-about-creed-black-kf-ceo/.
Nielsen, W.A. 1985. *The Golden Donors: A New Anatomy of the Great Foundations.* New York: Truman Talley Books.

18

The Courage to Lead

Worth the Risk?

Josie Heath
The Community Foundation
Serving Boulder County, Colorado

Moving from Transactional to Transformational Leadership

The history and experience of community philanthropy in Boulder, Colorado, is wrapped up in the development of the Community Foundation Serving Boulder County, Colorado. When we were just starting out, our story was similar to that of many small community foundations nationally. We had vision and high hopes, but few resources. And so our early years were spent primarily building donor-advised funds (DAFs) and trust within the funding and nonprofit communities. We focused on providing data and excellent donor service and convening important conversations.

But we became impatient. We saw the huge needs in our community that were going unaddressed. We wanted to tackle them, but did not yet have the necessary unrestricted assets.

In 1999, when we were only eight years old, everyone seemed worried about Y2K. We launched a campaign called the Millennium Trust (The Community Foundation Serving Boulder County, Colorado 2012d) as a symbolic gesture of hope for the next 1,000 years. We asked everyone in our county to contribute the last hour of their income in that millennium to seed an endowment for the next. We had no idea what to expect.

The campaign raised $1.8 million in four months. Thousands of people responded, including many children who sent their allowances. Today, this annual endowment grant tradition of supporting local nonprofits continues according to yearly guidelines set by 20 of the foundation's 6,178 original donors, whose names are picked randomly out of a fish bowl. The committee in 2008, for example, focused on building a nonprofit safety net infrastructure during the recession. Four years later, the volunteers turned their attention to community engagement.

You could say creating the Millennium Trust was our test flight, when we first tried incorporating community leadership into our otherwise donor- and grants-focused organizational model. Over the next eight years, we launched an annual awareness campaign focused on building a local Culture of Giving. We published a *TRENDS Report* on the social and economic health of our community. We launched an Entrepreneur's Foundation, which encourages founders of startups to give 1 percent of their company's equity to us for the betterment of their communities. We cultivated inclusive leadership for our county's public and private sectors through leadership initiatives. We launched Social Venture Partners (2012), started a health improvement collaborative, and built a fund to mark our fifteenth birthday. Called "15 Forever," the fund works by annually convening 15 young people—all of whom are 15 years old—to give away $15,000 to a cause that will have a positive impact on the lives of other 15-year-olds in their community.

We asked each of our trustees to spend at least one of their first years on the board on our grants committee. Increasingly, as newer board members came on and served on the grants committee, they noted how much more they had learned about the community's needs and how embarrassingly meager our grant amounts were in comparison to those needs. These board members were carefully selected and saw themselves as change agents. But were we really making change?

We also hosted "lunch and learns" for prominent community members so they and our trustees could learn about pressing community issues. They began to see that the needs were great and that our foundation could do much more.

We were building the case internally for becoming true community leaders who measured our impact based on real community outcomes. Yet, we continued to run into resistance about risk. Over and over, board meeting after board meeting, the same themes played:

- What will our donors think?
- Aren't we too new to take this on?
- Don't we have to wait for bequests to have unrestricted funds?
- Why aren't many of the other community foundations doing this?
- What do they know that we don't?

We recognized that we live in a culture that does not have the stomach for error, and criticism comes quickly if you are wrong, especially when you are young!

Finally, in 2008, our board decided that if we were serious about moving from transactional work to transformational work, we needed the power of information and the money to bring about that change. They agreed that if we were to do this, we needed to continue supporting our donors as they gifted through their DAFs, but we also had to grow our pitifully small unrestricted fund called the Community Trust.

We launched a four-year, $4 million campaign. We announced our intentions at our fall event on September 8, 2008. Finally, a courageous decision—and we were flying high.

Three weeks later, the stock market crashed.

The sense of doom across our country quickly seeped into Boulder County as well. We would need to do more to help folks realize that we could not back down on our efforts to make change.

Letting Data Lead

Before you can convince a county of 300,000 people to invest with you, you have to get them to believe you are on the right track. In our case, we spent 18 years building trust. The trust consisted of about 200 families who opened donor-advised funds through us and experienced what it was like to become part of something bigger than themselves in their philanthropic journeys.

Most of us get through daily life fairly well, and we seldom have the chance to be a major change agent. When we do not get out of our box, we usually feel comfortable, maybe even complacent, and we attribute our helplessness about taking on issues as just too much for any single one of us to tackle. Fortunately, though, some people invariably ask: But is this all?

We helped donors join us on our journey by exposing them to new information, helping them see everyday stories of people marginalized in our own community, recruiting their peers to this work, and showing them that we were willing to stake our reputation to take risks with them to address these issues. We have always believed that one of our greatest strengths is mobilizing human capital and connecting people back to their community.

Our donors expressed excitement about being a part of the solution. One of our earliest donors told me recently that starting her fund with us and then learning to fund "upstream issues"—not just putting her finger in the dike by only funding what she had always funded—had brought her a new sense of energy and engagement with the greater community. Our recent *Donor Perception Report* (CEP 2012) confirms this is a prevalent feeling among our donor base.

We built trust with our county's 400 nonprofit organizations by granting to them and providing them technical assistance and annual awards. The importance of building solid relationships with the nonprofit community, not only as grantees but also as problem solvers, cannot be underestimated.

A huge reservoir of trust was also built through the community volunteers who served on our unrestricted grantmaking committees. They got to see firsthand the great work of local nonprofits and the strong relationships we had developed with them.

We also got a lot of help from our local newspaper and a couple of excellent branding and marketing firms, all of which were headed by community foundation trustees.

Trust was a good start, but folks needed more than that. They needed data. Perhaps the cornerstone of the trust we built was our *Boulder County TRENDS Report,* a biennial magazine that synthesizes 100 indicators of our county's social and economic health. The report presents our community's strengths and areas for improvement with longitudinal data (The Community Foundation 2012b). Best of all, it's highly readable.

The data from our *TRENDS Report* revealed that the achievement gap between children growing up in poverty and their more well-off peers was larger in our county than almost anywhere else in the state. We weighed the prospect of adopting this as our issue against many other worthy local concerns; including youth risk behaviors and mental health.

Ultimately, our trustees decided the data were pointing us toward the achievement gap. Our emphasis would be on showing the impact of this gap on our local economy, individual life outcomes, and how this really was an issue of social justice. It didn't seem just that our county's income was the twelfth-highest in the country, and our local school district was one of the top three performers overall—the data clearly showed this to be the case, and yet the 23 percent of kids who were growing up in poverty had a statistically lower chance of graduating from high school than their peers not living in poverty.

As advocacy goes, this was a fairly mainstream and worthy issue, albeit not the passion area of everyone we work with and serve. Even so, we had to ask ourselves if we had the stomach for taking it another step, doing real advocacy, taking big risks. Were we willing to challenge this very well-educated and resource-laden community about why we had this "hidden underbelly" of poor educational performance right here in our front yard? What if some of the people who didn't want to acknowledge this were our very own donors? What if—heaven forbid—we decided that one of the solutions meant raising taxes on their property?

One of our former board chairs gave us an entire month, between jobs, charting who was doing what locally, statewide, and nationally in closing the achievement gap. She shared her findings with our board. Overwhelmingly, communities and school districts across the country were finding that the best way to bring up the academic performance of students in poverty was to invest in their early childhood education.

Based on these findings, our board established early childhood education as our top priority, committing $1 million of the $4 million we were raising to achieve the goal of closing the achievement gap through early learning.

Our trustees began by spending hours interviewing national groups working to close this achievement gap, especially through early childhood education. (And, in fact, the engagement of the trustees on this issue has been and continues to be outstanding.) This work resulted in the establishment of the School Readiness Initiative (The Community Foundation 2012a), chaired by two of our extraordinary former board chairs. It continues to actively engage trustees in fundraising, strategy formation, and coalition-building to promote school readiness throughout our community.

From the beginning, a key strategy of the School Readiness Initiative was to build financial capacity for institutions and nonprofits that served our target population of kids growing up in poverty during the preschool years. We sought to make leveraged investments that were transformational, countywide, sustainable, and whose impacts on student achievement were measurable.

Early on, we found an organization right in our own backyard that was doing nationally innovative work on a small scale to eradicate the gap. Providers Advancing School Outcomes (PASO) was using two very skilled Latina women to recruit informal day care providers in low-income neighborhoods for year-long training in early education practices. These were the people working with the families, friends, and neighbors who provide most of the care for low-income families in our community (United Way of Weld County 2012).

We showed our board a video we compiled of some parents whose children had benefited from the care of a PASO-trained provider. Here's how it began:

> Alberto Pantoja works long days as a landscaper in Longmont. His wife, Sonia De la Tore, works at McDonald's from 4:30 a.m. to 1:00 p.m. The couple, originally from Juarez, Mexico, has three children, all of whom were born here: a 15-year-old daughter; a 12-year-old son, and a 5-year-old girl.
>
> Neither Alberto nor Sonia has a high school diploma. They both speak far more fluently in their native Spanish than in English. Their older kids struggle fiercely in school, with their middle son only recently improving his scores on the Colorado Student Achievement Program (CSAP) tests to the 50th percentile.

Yet, Alberto and Sonia are evangelists for school readiness.

"Early education is the best thing that can happen," Alberto said. "It's the soul of a child's education."

Alberto and Sonia went on to talk about what a difference their youngest daughter had experienced in school, and how much better her educational journey had been after her day care provider received and implemented PASO training. Our board was moved by the presentation, and chose to act by granting $90,000 of the discretionary dollars we had raised in our Community Trust campaign to keep PASO up and running. (The Community Foundation 2012e)

It was the largest discretionary grant in our history. It helped PASO win a $629,000 grant from the state three months later, allowing the fledgling program to double in size. Today, PASO has, once again, doubled its capacity and coverage area, and our donors continue to invest in its innovative work.

Shaping Community Values

Strengthening a small organization is one thing. But we also realized we needed to build capacity on a larger scale in order to close the achievement gap significantly. That would involve wading into policy, and potentially even taxes.

Colorado's western, independent voters are part of the reason why we have the Taxpayer's Bill of Rights (TABOR), which prevents legislators from raising our taxes without it going to a full vote of the people. It is the most restrictive tax and spending limitation in the nation. That means that civic leaders concerned, for example, that Colorado spends 18 percent less per pupil than the national average and comparatively ranks very low in public education funding, must convince a majority of voters to raise their own taxes if they want any increase in tax-supported public education funding. In short, TABOR is great if you want to keep your taxes low (in Colorado, they are among the lowest in the country). But it's a huge obstacle if you want to create a new, sustainable public funding source for increasing the educational programming of children living in poverty (Center of Budget and Policy Priorities 2013). In the West, and perhaps to some degree everywhere in America right now, our community grapples with what is required to balance our passion for individual freedom with our stated desire to build and invest in community.

Another stumbling block for the foundation was the more general need to educate the entire community, not simply the board of trustees, on the notion of the achievement gap and how closing this gap among our children would be of benefit to all of us. Here in Boulder County, voters have repeatedly voted to tax themselves to buy open space and preserve our local environment and trails. And they have passed local taxes for other issues, but closing the achievement gap has not been among them.

We at the foundation realized that if we wanted to lead our community toward narrowing the achievement gap, we would have to step past our comfortable role as neutral convener. We would need to take risks and begin positioning ourselves as catalysts for change. We would need to begin to re-shape our community's values and practices to align with its greatest needs. To be successful in such a clearly different mode of community foundation goal setting and practice, however, meant that this could not simply be our agenda.

Before he was governor of Colorado, John Hickenlooper helped raise a tax as mayor of Denver that provided sliding-scale tuition for every four-year-old to attend preschool. We thought Denver had a model we could use in Boulder County. Therefore, enthusiastically, we asked the local Early Childhood Council of Boulder County to be our allies. They were not as enthusiastic. In fact they were quite critical—they felt it was not the right time, not the right idea. They wanted to wait until there could be a more comprehensive Early Childhood Framework that included early learning; family support and education; and social, emotional, and mental health support, as well as health coverage. Who could argue with that? We wanted that too, but the price tag for all of those programs was staggering, especially in a down economy. Furthermore, we discovered that many of the children most at risk in our county were never going to be in a formal child care setting: They were being cared for by family, friends, and neighbors. So as we embarked on this venture, we found ourselves without a key community ally.

Moving forward, we realized as we began to talk about this gap that many local thought leaders had children who were grown; consequently, they felt this was not "their issue." And yet, even as of this writing in 2013, more than 4,000 children under age five live in poverty in Boulder County. This means that their parents, together, bring home less than $24,000 per year. Most of the parents who can afford formal day care don't see the children from these families at their children's day care site. And their own kids won't meet many of our local children living in poverty until kindergarten, or in some cases, until first grade, because kindergarten isn't mandatory in Colorado, nor is it fully funded.

If parents weren't seeing the problem until it was too late, we realized, surely the broader general public was missing it, too. We were so curious about this that we actually sat behind a one-way mirror and watched as a national pollster quizzed a male focus group and a female focus group about early learning for at-risk kids. In our focus groups, their answers revealed that many women found the achievement gap morally wrong to the point where they are ready to take pains to close it, once they learned about it. Men, on the other hand, wanted to hear a business case before voting to change the status quo, especially if it meant raising taxes.

The Knight Foundation awarded us a Community Information Challenge Grant to help us see if we could cut through the chatter and convince our community to see the vital importance of early investments in children. We called this awareness campaign "ReadySetLearn." (ReadySetLearn-Early.org 2012). Its premise was that early learning is a matter of personal, economic, and national security.

Why use the "security" metaphor here? The answers became apparent rather quickly. We learned that personal security was important because prison planners told us that elementary-school reading scores for at-risk kids are one of the best predictors for how many beds they'll need 10 years down the line. We learned that economic security could be a key selling point in our part of Colorado because, without a strong educational foundation, students grow up to become tax consumers rather than tax generators. Finally, we found that national security could be an important reason for educational gap closing because today 75 percent of 17-to-24-year-olds do not meet the basic minimum standards required for military service.

Using such logic, we started a full countywide campaign. We ran newspaper ads. We bought bus billboards. We were on the radio. We staffed a booth at every festival we could think of. We flew in a national expert to drive home the point in front of 500 local business and community leaders.

Encouraging Community Investment

Awareness was very important, but it was only a start. Nearly everyone nodded affirmatively when asked if we should do more for our young children. We also recognized that wonderful people across the country have been working on this issue for years. But the data told us we needed to go past the talking stage and move to action. The challenge was to figure out how to go beyond the usual advocates to engage the entire community in addressing this issue. Could we put a stake in the ground, promising measurable progress and accountability? How could we do any of this without a sustainable source of funding in a TABOR state?

We did not take the decision to consider a ballot initiative lightly. Before we decided to launch our Community Trust campaign, our board had developed a position on public policy. We decided that for an issue to be formally considered by the Community Foundation, it must be relevant to the Community Foundation's mission and have a direct impact on the organizations the Community Foundation supports or the organizations' clients. Furthermore, we decided that a public policy issue may be brought forth for board consideration by any member of the staff or board, but for the board to formally approve or oppose a position there must be a majority of trustees in support of the action. Finally, we suggested that the board could also recommend financial support and relevant action steps.

We knew there were other important questions we should ask before embarking on the path to advocacy: What are we capable of doing? Who might be our key allies and supporters? What is a win for us? What would a loss mean for the foundation and our cause? What financial support would be required? Were we the only ones taking this on?

After much discussion (necessary because many of our trustees had never been politically engaged), the board decided that our preference would be to go for a countywide sales tax initiative on the 2010 November ballot to fund preschool for four-year-olds throughout the county.

Our trustees met with the county commissioners to make the request to put this on the ballot. While they were not met with dead silence, there was clearly no interest. Some thought it would be too much competition for the open space initiative that the commissioners wanted on the ballot. The commissioners also already had a tax increase to backfill state cuts to human services on the ballot. More tax increases on the upcoming ballot did not seem like a winning strategy. And they asked, "Why did the Early Childhood Council not support it?" The commissioners said no.

Fortunately, our awareness campaign had caught our school board's attention. They were already considering putting a mill levy override (property tax increase) on that November's ballot. The superintendent of Boulder Valley School District and the chairman of its board came to our board meeting and formally asked us to financially support and take a leadership role if they were to do a campaign. We were torn.

Our original goal had been to have a countywide funding mechanism, and we were reluctant to commit to only half of the county by working with only one of our two school districts. We negotiated, however, and they agreed that $5 million of the $22.5 million in new annual funding would be permanently earmarked for new preschool and kindergarten slots for low-income schools. That would at least take us part way to our goal.

It was the end of August 2010. Two of our senior staff would be gone most of September—one to get married; the other to have a baby—and our board chair was getting married! As a small community foundation, we were already feeling stretched. We still needed to finish our time-intensive certification process for National Standards. In the face of all this, our board still chose to drive forward, putting $80,000 toward the campaign and approving me as its co-chair.

Just a few days later, that Labor Day, we watched smoke rise over the mountains west of Boulder. The Fourmile Fire, in our backyard, was on its way to becoming the most destructive wildfire in Colorado history.

Putting Out Fires

As we returned to work from the holiday weekend, two local residents asked me for a meeting. One had lost his home in the fire. The other had been evacuated. They asked us to start a fund for fire victims. They didn't have any money. They hoped the foundation could find a way to fund it.

It was a compelling plea for help. The fire burned more than 6,000 acres and destroyed more than 160 homes.

"But wait," I thought. "We're 'all in' for a ballot tax initiative this November, we've got to do the National Standards now, and furthermore, we have key people who are out. There is no way we can take this on, too."

But we were also a community foundation. We live in a community that prides itself on entrepreneurism and a "can-do spirit." After quick calls to the area's nonprofit emergency assistance providers, it was clear that they did not have the capacity to take this on as a fire fund right now. They hoped that we would do it.

Our board agreed to open the Boulder Mountain Fire Relief Fund (The Community Foundation 2010).

At an emergency meeting, the board considered a possible process and resources we could tap to lead this effort. Within 24 hours we convened all the past chairs of the foundation, who would oversee a fire committee under the umbrella of the community foundation. We spent hours on the phone with community foundations in New Orleans, Baton Rouge, Washington, DC, New York, and Iowa, learning from their lessons with disasters.

A local radio station organized a benefit concert for the fund. The "Fourmile Canyon Revival" featured the jam bands Phish, String Cheese Incident, Leftover Salmon, and Big Head Todd and the Monsters. It sold out in two minutes and raised $350,000 for the fund. We wished they had secured a larger venue!

We were deluged with questions we had never considered before. How could we give to individuals? Which volunteer fire departments should receive funds, and how much should they receive? How would we give away 200 tickets allotted for volunteer firefighters and victims? And, of course, how could we deal with frustrated Phish fans who did not get tickets?

During these same days, this all became background for the parallel work of support for the tax initiative we were championing. We knew we needed to be flexible enough to support this emergency fund, while simultaneously ensuring that if we were in on the ballot initiative, we would be in it to win.

While demonstrating our flexibility to deal with a community emergency, we also had to help our donors understand why this was the right time to step up our advocacy for closing the achievement gap among our youngest learners. We worked on strategy for the campaign. We took to the streets with trustees holding campaign signs and materials. We garnered key endorsements from the local newspaper, the Boulder Chamber of Commerce, and a tax-weary public, mobilizing volunteers, pushing, pushing, pushing to tell the story of the need to take this big financial step now.

The ballot issue won on election night, with 61 percent in favor. It was the highest vote-getter on a full ballot. An annual $23 million, in perpetuity, would go to the schools. And $5 million of that would be permanently available for additional preschool and full-day kindergarten slots at the elementary schools serving our lowest-income populations.

That fall we also raised and distributed $800,000 to the fire departments, individuals and families most impacted by the Fourmile Fire.

Staying Accountable

Now comes the hard part. We traded on the public's trust in us to help the ballot issue pass. We told them why this was important and that we would help measure progress toward our goals.

The new funding is in place, and we are working with the Boulder Valley School District to measure and report its impact on our achievement gap. We will broadly share this progress with leaders in the business, civic, and faith realms and suggest ways that everyone can help us attain these goals. However, we are also painfully aware that even though it felt like a big campaign with a big payoff, $5 million more in a $250 million+ school system isn't a game-changer unless communitywide pressure stays up on the issue.

In 2012, we successfully completed our four-year, $4 million goal to build our unrestricted assets. The campaign has allowed us to double the fund's general support to local nonprofits, and it has built a modest cash fund that we will continue to use to invest in eradicating the achievement gap through early learning.

In the 2012 election, we successfully supported a school-funding ballot campaign in our county's other school district. Our board wanted to reduce fiscal pressure on the St. Vrain Valley School District, because it was doing more than most school districts in our state to invest in early learning and other approaches to closing the achievement gap. Also, two-thirds of our county's children in poverty are in the St. Vrain district, so this measure was key to building human capital within our most vulnerable population. The measure won handily, with 57 percent support in a part of our county that had previously struggled to approve school-funding measures (The Community Foundation 2012c).

But that's far from the end of this story. Our new vision is that the entire county will own the goal of closing the achievement gap through investing in early learning and school readiness, and that the gap will close significantly by 2017. We know that many people and organizations must be involved in order for this to happen. We will need to circle back to be sure that those who originally were not on board with the idea are heard and hopefully will join the effort.

We have hired a new director of School Readiness to help our foundation champion this initiative. His first tasks included (1) serving as a liaison for our successful ballot issue efforts with St. Vrain; (2) building buy-in for the vision with local business, civic, and faith leaders; (3) firming up our baseline information on the existing achievement gap; and (4) ensuring that all the collaborators on this issue have an eye toward the same vision and are holding each other accountable. In short, we are building the human capital to achieve success for the goal of closing the gap.

He will not be working alone. Our community foundation's board, volunteers, donors, and grantees will continue working to expand trust networks and visibility for this issue. Our hope is that five years from this writing, we can honestly say that our community has sustainably embraced this issue, that far more of our children are ready for school, and that our community foundation is ready to focus on whatever has emerged as the new, most important issue of communitywide concern.

We will also judge our success, in part, on the extent to which other communities look to us as a national model for how community foundations, large and small, can shape community values and take risks to effect transformational change.

The Case for Taking Risks

There is no doubt that in choosing to stand for something, we have connected in a deeper way with many of our donors who share our passion and now know who we are. Despite the excitement of our success, however, not all of our donors shared our enthusiasm for this undertaking. One said, "Are you just going to be the tax and spend foundation?" Another said we had waded much too far into the area of "stirring things up." As Wallace Stegner said, we in the West know "the fate of all leaders who go too far ahead" (1954, 307, 366–67), but I like to think that as avid hikers, we welcome the journey and the chance to bring companions along.

Fortunately, a recent *Donor Perception Report* (CEP 2012) conducted on our behalf by the Center for Effective Philanthropy found that most of our donors felt supportive: "Donors at The Community Foundation rate extremely positively on a number of measures. On many items through the report, including the likelihood that a donor would recommend The Community Foundation to a friend or colleague, The Community Foundation rated near the top of CEP's comparative dataset. In fact, for the clarity of the Foundation's communication of its own goals, The Community Foundation is the highest ranked Foundation in the dataset." Donors to our foundation were also more likely than at any other community foundation surveyed to say that working with us made them feel more connected to their community. Fortunately, we live in a community that mostly shares our progressive outlook, but as so many in the West, we have our fair share of folks who believe it is "everyone for himself."

Perhaps most important, more of our donors than those at a typical foundation said they plan to give additionally to unrestricted or field of interest funds in the next five to 10 years. "Donors are aware of and supportive of the Community Trust Initiative, the Foundation's initiative to close the educational achievement gap through an unrestricted grant-making endowment," the report's authors summarized (CEP 2012).

Conclusion

Despite our progress so far, we continue to grapple with trying to move from a transactional leadership model—based on pass-through grants from lead donors—to a transformational leadership model. We talk about that term, *transformational leadership,* quite a bit at the board level. We're currently trying to define exactly what it means for our organization.

I believe transformational leadership starts with a vision of what is possible. It is most successful when developed collectively by trusted leaders who have integrity and are willing to share ownership of the vision.

Some will see the possibilities immediately. Others will want to see the facts and the data and want to know who else is "on board." Transformational leaders know that forging a new path is not always a straight line. There will be twists and turns, disappointments and successes. Their role is that of listener, encourager, motivator, trusted partner, and authentic and passionate holder of the vision. They must know that the journey may be long and sometimes lonely. Most important, transformational leaders will continue to stand up and be counted.

Community foundations attract extraordinary people as trustees and staff, and they are uniquely positioned to address critical community issues. Our foundations can play the role that I think the residents of our communities long for right now: participating in civil conversations about difficult and complex issues and then taking action to address them in a just and thoughtful way. In an increasingly globalized, transient world, people still look for ways to feel connected and make a difference in their own community. Helping communities find the balance to create this civil society—respecting our fierce sense of individualism while building a community where there is opportunity for all—will be a key issue for community foundations and for the communities they serve, large and small.

When you enjoy a position of trust, it comes with responsibilities. Most community foundations have that prestige and trust, but it is not enough for us to just rest on our laurels. We need to put this prestige and trust to work for those we serve and muster the courage to take on the big issues facing our communities. Whether it is confronting injustice or speaking truth to power, it comes with the privilege and accountability of being an anchor institution in your community. That fact alone makes community foundations indispensable for our second century. Those with the courage to lead will find the positive transformation in their community definitely worth the risk.

Bibliography

Barge, Chris. 2013. "St. Vrain and Boulder Valley Expanding ECE." The Community Foundation blog post, March 4. http://www.commfound.org/content/st-vrain-and-boulder-valley-expanding-ece.

The Center for Effective Philanthropy (CEP). 2012. *Donor Perception Report Prepared for Community Foundation Serving Boulder County.* June. Cambridge, MA: CEP. http://www.commfound.org/fundholders/PostDonorPerceptionReport.pdf.

Center of Budget and Policy Priorities (CBPP). 2013. "Policy Basics: Taxpayer Bill of Rights (TABOR)." February 15. http://www.cbpp.org/cms/index.cfm?fa=view&id=2521.

The Community Foundation Serving Boulder County, Colorado. 2012a. "About the School Readiness Initiative." http://www.commfound.org/content/about-school-readiness-initiative.

———. 2012b. *Boulder County TRENDS Report 2011.* Boulder, CO: The Community Foundation. http://www.commfound.org/trendsmagazine.

———. 2012c. *The Community Trust Initiative: Catalyzing Transformational Change—Case for Support.* Report, May 10. Boulder, CO: The Community Trust. http://www.commfound.org/giving/CT_CaseForSupport.pdf.

———. 2012d. "Millennium Trust." http://www.commfound.org/nonprof/mt/.

———. 2012e. "School Readiness Initiative—Success Story: Alberto, Sonia, and Providers Advancing School Outcomes." http://www.commfound.org/communityleadership/eci/pantoja.php.

———. 2012f. http://www.commfound.org/home.php.

———. 2010. "Update on the Boulder Mountain Fire Relief Fund." New release, October 7. http://www.commfound.org/content/update-boulder-mountain-fire-relief-fund.

ReadySetLearn-Early.org. 2012. "The Facts: Who Would've Thunk It?" http://readysetlearn-early.org/facts.

Social Venture Partners Boulder County. 2012. http://www.svpbouldercounty.org.

Stegner, Wallace. 1954. "Beyond the Hundredth Meridian: John Wesley Powell and the Second Opening of the West." Boston, MA: Houghton Mifflin.

United Way of Weld County. 2012. "FFN PASO Program." http://www.unitedway-weld.org/promisesforchildren/paso-program.

19

From Hula-Hoops to Trusted Philanthropic Advisor

An Innovative Pathway of Public Value

Douglas F. Kridler
The Columbus Foundation

As the clock ticks down to the end of the first century of community foundations' existence, a century of the creation and proliferation of community foundations across America, we can peer across the bridge into the next century—a century of challenges unimagined 100 years ago—and wonder about the ability of this giving platform we call community foundations to serve and survive in the century ahead. We owe it to the multitude of people who have worked together to create and enhance this community resource of significance and staying power over the past hundred years—a resource that shares the values of openness and sharing so vivid in our time, but was born in another time entirely—to mark the advancements and lessons learned in the first century.

To do so, this chapter examines the regeneration of value and utility of the community foundation through a close look at one community foundation, the Columbus Foundation (TCF), which has been committed to the innovation of its business practices as well as the evolution of the community field throughout its history. It is hoped this examination may give some signal as to the ability of this field to continue to evolve in order to calibrate to society's and our community's needs, as well as to the changing landscape of philanthropy in America. The viability of our business model is a precondition to the viability of our future, and, while elsewhere in this volume others explore the ability of our current business model to be sustained, it is my hope that by shedding some light on the innovations the Columbus Foundation has undertaken, it can be established that there is ample reason to be optimistic about the ability of community foundations to adapt and thrive in the century of changes ahead.

It is remarkable to note that both the Cleveland and Columbus foundations were born during troubling and uncertain times of war—Cleveland in the same year that World War I began, and Columbus during the bleak days of World War II. It says a lot about the people of both communities that they had the strength of character and vision to think about how to lift up their communities at these times when fear and uncertainty was abundant, and optimism in short supply.

It is also worth noting that the Midwest was fertile ground not only for crops, but also for community foundations. Of the 26 community foundations established in the decade following 1914, half were located in the Midwest— and nearly a quarter of those were in Ohio.

The Columbus Foundation's roots were humble. The first unsolicited gift ($25) came from Olga Anna Jones (1888–1973), a former teacher, editor of the *Ohio Woman Voter,* and reporter for the *Columbus Citizen.* She had served on the Columbus City Council from 1923 to 1928, the first woman to do so. At the time the foundation was created, she was living in Washington, D.C., writing booklets for the war effort. When she heard about the new foundation, she was eager to show her support, and our founder, Harrison Sayre, who admired her "spunk and imagination," could not have been more pleased: "We shall be proud to have the Columbus Foundation known as one established by modest gifts from many benefactors" (quoted in Jensen 2013, 19).

Then along came Frederick B. Hill and his version of the Hula-Hoop, the sales of which helped spur an extraordinary expansion of the philanthropic toolkit in America.

Frederick B. Hill made plastic tubing for industrial use. He never imagined making a household toy—until one day he spotted children playing merrily with what later became known as the Hula-Hoop. Hill didn't invent the plastic ring that became known later as the Hula-Hoop—it actually replicates a toy that can be traced to ancient Greek times. Little did Hill know that his plastic version of this hoop not only would create countless opportunities for fun but also would fuel support for the fastest growing philanthropic vehicle in the twentieth century: the donor-advised fund (DAF).

Using proceeds from his Hula-Hoop, Hill worked with the founders of the Columbus Foundation in 1948 to set up one of America's first DAFs, thereby simplifying his giving while benefiting from the community wisdom engendered in the fund's enabling organization, the Columbus Foundation (2012b).

Just as the invention of the Hula-Hoop could be traced to others, so too could the origins of the donor-advised fund. Hill wasn't the first donor to think of and fund what became known as a DAF (the New York Community

Trust is actually credited with the creation of the first such fund in 1931). But his doing so at the Columbus Foundation helped a little-used giving vehicle take off in America.

Since the creation of the first DAFs in New York and the second in Columbus, Ohio, this giving vehicle has grown to staggering proportions, making it perhaps the most dynamic and fastest growing philanthropic vehicle in the history of philanthropy. In its report on DAFs released in July 2012, the Congressional Research Service estimated that, as of 2008, about 1,800 organizations reported having donor-advised funds. Collectively, these organizations held about 181,000 funds with total assets of about $29.5 billion. Donors contributed about $7.1 billion to DAFs, and grants from DAFs were approximately $7 billion, for an average payout of 13.1 percent (Sherlock and Gravelle 2012).

The establishment of Hill's donor-advised fund at the Columbus Foundation was actually the brainchild of founder Harrison M. Sayre, who also showed a determination to find innovative ways to advance the field of community foundations. That determination led to his playing a crucial role in the inauguration of another fieldwide innovation, co-created by the Columbus Foundation and a handful of other leaders—the Council on Foundations.

The National Committee on Foundations and Trusts for Community Welfare (the original name for what is now known as the Council on Foundations) was organized in 1949 under the leadership of Edward L. Ryerson of the Chicago Community Trust and funded by a small number of individual community foundations, the Columbus Foundation among them. Harrison Sayre continued his work with this group and was the chief proponent of its admitting private foundations as members in 1958 (something that Sayre grew to regret because he felt it led to dilution of focus on its original purpose, to serve the interests of community foundations).

Then, in 1960, according to the Council on Foundation's recorded history, "aided by a grant of $50,000 from the Ford Foundation to help the Council become 'a national institution,'" Columbus Foundation founder and director Sayre was named the Council's first president, with responsibility for presiding over the board of directors. The commitment to the Council's development was sustained when, years later, Richard Oman, Sayre's successor as the executive director of the Columbus Foundation, became the first chairman of the newly formed Committee of Community Foundations of the Council on Foundations.

The Columbus Foundation's record of innovations and field leadership did not stop with the development of the Council on Foundations. The Columbus Foundation was "one of the first community foundations to apply broad-based, fundraising principles, similar to those in practice at colleges and universities.

In 1983 the Foundation's first vice-president for development was hired. By 2000 there was a development staff of ten. Their dedication and expertise contributed to a more than tenfold increase in assets between 1982 and 2001: from nearly $59 million to $678 million" (Jensen 2013, 36–37).

This was significant, as it marked the beginning of the end of the time when community foundations recognized that banks could be relied upon to give sufficient attention to marketing and fund attraction for community foundations. The leaders of the Columbus Foundation felt it was time to chart a more self-reliant and innovative course of growth than the historic division of duties between the banks and community foundations provided.

The importance of this can hardly be overstated. On the one hand, it seems a simple move of self-evident merit; instead, it was seen in the community foundation field as risky and controversial, and some wondered whether the Columbus Foundation was betraying the origins of community foundations by adopting a more aggressive development approach, one modeled after university fundraising practices. What the move has led to instead was the strengthening of the viability of community foundations, the ability to become leaders in articulating the cause of community-based philanthropy, and the deepening of stewardship activities that strengthen relationships with current and prospective donors.

The commitment to broadening the scope of our development effort also included developing planned-giving expertise, the enhancement of which was overseen by James I. Luck, executive director of the Columbus Foundation. That has proven to be a most enlightened decision. It has led to the staffing of that department with professionals who hold the kind and quality of legal and technical expertise that has enabled the Columbus Foundation to earn the trust of top legal and financial advisors as well as donors themselves, all of whom are seeking expert advice of the highest quality available in their community.

The result? Over our history, over $1.5 billion in gifts to the Columbus Foundation has been dedicated to the advancement of Columbus's communities and causes, enabling more than $1 billion in grants to be made to strengthen and improve our community for the benefit of all our residents. At present, another $1.5 billion in charitable funds is registered in our foundation asset base, and a fund of almost a billion more dollars is projected in future planned-gift expectancies.

The next innovation brought forward by the Columbus Foundation for the benefit of the community foundation field was a natural outgrowth of its dedication to more robust donor service and development, and the emergence of a similar focus among an increasing number of community foundations across America.

In the 1980s, the community foundation movement was going strong, with rapid expansion of the number of foundations in areas urban and rural. The curiosity about how community foundations were growing led to the idea by Jim Luck, then director of the Columbus Foundation, to do an annual survey of the community foundation field. In 1989, the Columbus Survey was born.

Since that time, the Columbus Survey, now administered by CF Insights, has tracked the gifts, grants, and asset sizes of community foundations around the country. And, while some over the years have taken exception to the idea that by doing this annual survey somehow we are communicating to each other that these three things—gifts, grants, and asset size—are what matter most, the simple fact is that the Columbus Survey is a fascinating and unique source of historic and current data about key dimensions of the growth of community foundations.

The next significant innovation for community foundations came as the Columbus Foundation worked closely with the Greater Kansas City Community Foundation, a leader in the development of online research about nonprofits, to build a community database of detailed information about nonprofits in the region. Our efforts in this innovative area began in 2006 and took two years to get online, requiring new foundation staff and investment in a broad array of new online tools. When we finally were able to get up and running, we had transformed the way the foundation communicated with donors. Our donors now had 24/7 access to detailed information about the projects they were invested in. Today, we realize that having these services accessible online helps ensure that the information is available not only to our donors, but to researchers, other funders, and reporters who can access the information at any time. While to readers today it likely seems obvious that these services would ultimately be available online, the work to build out this web-based suite of services we call PowerPhilanthropy was anything but obvious at the time.

One of the key parts of the development of an online feature was a decision made right from the start to build it not only for our own donors but for the public as well. Up until then, donor services and new product features were built and offered to our donors exclusively, or, in the case of the Columbus Survey and the creation of the Council on Foundations, primarily for the field itself.

Rick Batyko, former marketing director for the Cleveland Foundation, once observed that the challenge for community foundations was how to take the public from "awareness to familiarity" about our work and our usefulness to them. Constrained by a limitation of marketing dollars to advance that understanding, the Columbus Foundation set out to meet the public where they were—online. As such, in order to create a buzz in the community about the launch of PowerPhilanthropy, the Columbus Foundation created the first large-scale online *match day* in 2008.

The notion of a match day was a generative strategy that would allow donors and the general public to make online gifts to the nonprofits of their choice via the new PowerPhilanthropy platform. This was a new initiative that generated not a little of worry to go along with the excitement it raised at the foundation. Therefore, the shift to pure staff joy was palpable when all $250,000 in funds offered to match each online gift dollar for dollar were exhausted in less than 44 minutes (TCF 2008). The notion of going online and the innovation of the match day were both well-received innovations at the Columbus Foundation. Since then, we have expanded the promotion of our match days even further through the use of social media. Our marketing team, led by veteran Carol Harmon, has developed tools to aid potential recipients in promoting the matching fund opportunity to their respective donors. This, too, was unprecedented in our field, and it enabled us to utilize viral marketing for a match day while spending almost nothing in promotion of the event. Our subsequent match days have generated millions of dollars in charitable giving since that first exciting, anxious day.

This was a huge, exciting, and publicly celebrated success for the Columbus Foundation and its donors and has inspired other community foundations all around the country to undertake match days of their own and expand on the model. It has even spawned the development of software products by companies such as Kimbia and Razoo that are dedicated to providing software to enable community foundations of any size to produce their own match day in their own community or even, in the case of the Saint Paul Foundation, statewide. Now the hundredth anniversary of the founding of the first community foundation is being celebrated in part with a national Day of Giving, modeled off of the Columbus Foundation's original match day concept.

As stimulating as match days have been for donor and public online giving, they have also led to community foundations being able to communicate in an efficient way with the thousands of donors who participate in these public giving events, a valuable online marketing opportunity for engaging new customers.

Another significant innovation came about when the Columbus Foundation created its Critical Need Alert product in 2004. These periodic signals to our donors are designed to share our community knowledge about areas of vivid need and opportunity and to provide neatly researched and packaged solutions for donors to invest in to solve significant and urgent problems in our community. Developed during my tenure as president and CEO of the Columbus Foundation, and leaning on the community knowledge of our Community Research and Grants Management staff led by Dr. Lisa Courtice, we felt that it was the peak of our responsibility to indicate our community's greatest needs to our donors and to create the best paths to respond to those needs.

The Columbus Foundation was reluctant to single out any need, for fear that it would alienate and aggravate the lay and professional leaders of nonprofits in areas not included in the proposed funding solution provided in the Critical Need Alert. My belief is that it is our job to find and lift up the greatest needs and best opportunities to our donors, and by doing so we distinguish ourselves from other giving vehicles such as commercial gift funds that are less dedicated to donor education.

The key driver for the creation of the Critical Need Alert at the Columbus Foundation was the observation that it is not enough to just *have* community knowledge; the key to fulfilling our potential is how effectively we *share* it. The courage to lift up a critical need and a specific strategic funding opportunity to act on that need, along with the creation and 24/7 availability of our online giving and information platform PowerPhilanthropy (TCF 2012e), empowers our donors. It ensures that existing donors and the public at large can benefit from the sharing of our community knowledge and use those online tools to inform their investment decisions and access their funds.

An example of how useful the Critical Need Alert activity and function became can be seen in the identification of an opportunity called the Benefit Bank. Working with the National Council of Churches and the leaders of the Ohio Association of Foodbanks, we tracked the significant growth in the challenges facing the poor in our state. In 2008, the Columbus Foundation created a Critical Need Alert to alert its donors to this opportunity, and from that garnered enough donations to fund the creation of the Ohio Benefit Bank network, an online program designed to make it easier for the poor in our state to determine their qualifications for support and the necessary filing required to receive that support. The success of this effort, which has spread statewide and continues to be funded primarily by the Columbus Foundation, is heightened by the fact that almost $1 billion in benefits have been identified and made accessible to the poor and working poor since our first grant to start the Ohio Benefit Bank in 2009 (TCF 2012d).

Having established an attractive array of giving vehicles like donor-advised funds, scholarship funds, field of interest funds, designated funds, and others that enable donors of a broad array of giving interests and timetables to invest in their community, we knew we truly were beginning to better realize our goal of increasing the amount of community wealth that is devoted to charitable giving. And that is a measure of our impact in the community. Our goal isn't to divert charitable capital from its destination of supporting the work of nonprofits in our community; rather, it is to be as inspiring, professional, and effective an organization as possible, with the goal of enlarging the amount of money devoted to charitable giving in our community. Our success is the community's success, and that is the motivation for the final innovation I will mention in this chapter: the creation of the first Strategy Map for the field of community foundations (see Figure 19.1).

Figure 19.1 **Our Strategy Map**

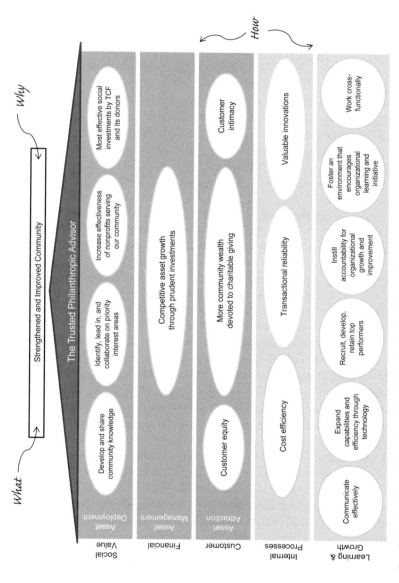

Source: The Columbus Foundation. Copyright © The Columbus Foundation. Used by permission.

Not long after I became president and CEO of the Columbus Foundation in 2002, we set out to clarify—for ourselves, our stakeholders, and ultimately the community in which we work—our success as a value-creating organization. How could we expect our value to donors, nonprofits, and other community improvement partners to be understood if we hadn't clarified for ourselves how we can harness, focus, and articulate a coherent, aligned, and consistent goal-attainment strategy from among the myriad great things a community foundation does?

With the guidance of Columbus Foundation governing committee member Len Schlesinger, aided significantly by contributions from Columbus Foundation staff member Sidney Hargro (now executive director of the Community Foundation of South Jersey), and with the active engagement of foundation staff, governing committee members, and other stakeholders, we articulated our aims, our goals, and our reason for being. We did this by tracing how the various activities of our community foundation relate to each other to create a value that we and our donors can understand. Using the Strategy Map format developed by Harvard professors Robert S. Kaplan and David P. Norton, we set out to capture, distill, and communicate the *what,* the *why,* and the *how* of our work.

By building out our Strategy Map, we defined our role in serving our donors as that of "Trusted Philanthropic Advisor." Trust is something earned, not declared, and our track record since 1943 of being a valuable part of both our community's progress and our donors' pursuit of the best in philanthropy is what earned their trust. Just as donors may consult on other matters with a legal or investment advisor, we too stand as professionals dedicated to advising them about how they might realize the most effective philanthropy possible.

Part of the trust in community philanthropy is derived from our ability to advise donors based on their personal goals and insights rather than focusing solely on the advancement of the community foundation itself. Financial and legal advisors throughout our region are our biggest advocates: They have seen how we work to help donors achieve their goals, not just sell them on the Columbus Foundation's view of what matters most. We pride ourselves in developing opportunities to inspire our donors to co-invest their funds alongside strategic allocations of unrestricted funds (i.e., our Critical Need Alerts), but we also value their life experiences, priorities, and paths in our collective philanthropic effort.

Community foundations face changes and challenges demanding innovative responses. How we respond will determine whether we go the way of newspapers, symphony orchestras, and other signs of community vitality in the past century that were under so much financial strain at the time of the writing of this book. It is clear that in their first century, community foundations have been a uniquely beneficial channel for our communities and our country—and that going into the next century, community foundations can continue to provide a channel through which the broad and changing interests of a community are served, while the inspirations of individual lives and contributions are marked and remembered. If we see ourselves not merely as a gifts and grants business but as a dynamic and innovative platform for community progress and for the building of valuable emotional bonds between residents and their community, we open our organizations and our communities to a bright future of possibilities.

Our first unsolicited gift of $25 came to us from a woman of humble means but great capacity for service during World War II, a time when no one would have been criticized had they thought more about survival and fear than vision and optimism. Now, as this first century of the existence of community foundations draws to a close, the Columbus Foundation, like other community foundations across America, is a platform of vibrant philanthropic possibilities for community improvement. Given the will and courage to continue to evolve that platform in unprecedented and thoughtful ways, we will continue to build on the impressive legacy earned in the community foundation's first century.

Bibliography

The Columbus Foundation (TCF). 2012a. "Critical Need Alert for Hunger." http://columbusfoundation.org/giving/critical-need-alert-for-hunger/.

———. 2012b. "History." http://columbusfoundation.org/about/history/.

———. 2012c. *It Is Here: The Columbus Foundation 2011 Annual Report.* Columbus, OH: The Columbus Foundation. http://columbusfoundation.org/wp-content/uploads/TCF_AR11_LoRes_Spreads.pdf.

———. 2012d. "Ohio Benefit Bank." http://columbusfoundation.org/central-ohio/transformative-grants/ohio-benefit-bank/.

———. 2012e. "PowerPhilanthropy." http://columbusfoundation.org/p2/.

———. 2012f. http://columbusfoundation.org.

———. 2009. *The Safety Net Fund: Critical Need Alert.* 2009 Investment Report to Donors. Columbus, OH: The Columbus Foundation; Cambridge, MA: Root Cause. http://rootcause.org/documents/ReportForDonors-TCF-Final.pdf.

———. 2008. *Community Pride Made Visible: 2007 Annual Report.* Columbus, OH: The Columbus Foundation. http://columbusfoundation.org/wp-content/uploads/tcf-2007-annual-report.pdf.

Jensen, E. 2013. *The Columbus Foundation: The First Fifty-Eight Years.* Columbus, OH: The Columbus Foundation.

Kaplan, R.S., and D.P. Norton. 2004. *Strategy Maps: Converting Intangible Assets into Tangible Outcomes.* Boston, MA: Harvard Business School Press.

Sherlock, M.F., and J.G. Gravelle. 2012. *An Analysis of Charitable Giving and Donor Advised Funds.* CRS Report for Congress R42595, July 11. https://www.fas.org/sgp/crs/misc/R42595.pdf.

20

Community Foundation Leadership in the Second Century

Adaptive and Agile

Kelly Ryan
Incourage Community Foundation

Judith L. Millesen
Incourage Community Foundation

> *You did then what you knew how to do, and*
> *when you knew better, you did better.*
> —Maya Angelou

Our story begins with this quote from Maya Angelou because the message is so simple and yet so powerful. Simple because its meaning is quite obvious: of course we do better when we know better; and powerful because in order to do better, we need to know better. To know better, we need to learn. We need to be inquisitive, to experience different ways of thinking and doing. To learn, we must open ourselves up to the contradictory feelings that emerge when we admit we don't have all the answers. Learning requires reflection, adaptation, and humility. To learn means we need to grow our minds, our hearts, and our behavior . . . then something different happens. This is a story about what our community has learned; how we have collectively grown our minds, our hearts, and our behavior. It is a story about how we have done better because we know better. It is a story in its infancy . . . for as we continue to learn, we believe the best is yet to come.

Who We Are and What We Knew

South Wood County—located in rural, central Wisconsin—is home to 45,000 people. An abundance of natural resources, including the Wisconsin River and plentiful timber, made it a natural choice to create and grow a paper industry. Consolidated Papers, Inc., a Fortune 500 company headquartered in south Wood County for nearly a century, had a sterling reputation in the industry, and the region became known as one of the finest papermaking communities in the world. Members of the Mead family led the company—first George W. Mead, then his son Stanton Mead, then Stanton's son, George Mead II. Multiple generations benefited from stable employment and the generosity of the firm's founding family. At its peak, Consolidated employed nearly one-half of the region's 12,000 workers, and the Meads played a defining role in civic leadership, philanthropic giving, and community development (Jones et al. 1923; League of Women Voters of Wisconsin Rapids Area n.d.).

In addition to papermaking, south Wood County is also home to a second major industry: cranberry growing and processing. Interestingly, Wisconsin actually grows more cranberries than any other state and today is home to the majority of Ocean Spray growers. Wisconsin Rapids was the birthplace of Northland Cranberries, Inc. The corporation was formed in 1987 by bringing together a few established growers in central Wisconsin. By the mid-1990s, Northland was the largest cranberry grower in the world with 25 marshes in Wisconsin, Massachusetts, and Canada. The company was also a pioneer of cranberry drinks that were 100 percent juice. Cranberry growing and processing supplemented papermaking to provide central Wisconsin with a strong economic base, one that for many years proved resilient to downturns in the national economy.

The community foundation was established as the South Wood County Community Foundation in 1994, during a time of real prosperity not only in the paper industry but also within a rapidly expanding cranberry industry. Virginia Brazeau, a visionary fourth-generation cranberry grower, was struck by the basic premise of a community foundation to serve as a permanent resource to meet the changing needs of the community while expanding and democratizing philanthropy. She and the Richard S. Brazeau Family Foundation established the community foundation with a $1 million matching challenge, eight years of administrative funding, professional advisor support, and technical assistance. This thoughtful start-up strategy was needed to help the new concept of a community foundation take root in a community that was fairly insular and resistant to change.

For years, our work reflected the traditional roles of a community foundation. We raised money from the community to do community-based work, including awarding scholarships, helping individuals accomplish their philanthropic goals through donor-advised funds (DAFs), and making reactive grants to community-based organizations seeking funding to improve or expand work. While this strategy provided what was needed to raise money from the community, our work was somewhat characteristic of the majority of the community foundation field; we were fundamentally a "charitable check-writing institution" focused on growing and managing assets. That is until we publicly shed that persona and began our transition to that of a community leader in response to emergent economic hardships that were facing our region at the turn of the twenty-first century.

What Happened: The Impetus for Change

The regional economy flipped upside down in the late 1990s, when the global papermaking industry underwent a dramatic restructuring and the cranberry industry experienced tremendous upheaval. Modern paper facilities were being constructed overseas in countries with a low wage scale, and demand dropped quite a bit as a result of the recession and shifts in the use of paper products. Consequently, in 1999, Consolidated announced that 700 jobs would be eliminated. One year later, the company sold to a large multinational firm, Stora Enso, based in Helsinki, Finland. The sale and additional cost-cutting measures resulted in the loss of another 1,300 jobs.

The cranberry industry grew tremendously as a result of increased consumer demand in the 1980s, driving the price per barrel from less than $20 in 1973 to about $60 in 1996. This led to a large expansion in the number of acres planted, which unfortunately produced a glut, driving the price per barrel down to less than $10 in 2000. Many cranberry farmers were driven out of business and some saw their personal wealth vanish. Northland Cranberries responded by selling one of its two lines of fruit juice in 2000, and in 2004 sold its flagship production facility in Wisconsin Rapids.

The sale of Consolidated Papers, Inc., along with the subsequent mill closures, reductions in staff, relocation of the corporate headquarters to Finland, and its effect on related businesses and suppliers, created significant challenges. Many residents found themselves unemployed; in middle age, they had their identities and self-esteem challenged because they no longer had a job, a stable income, or employment prospects on the horizon. Economic and social service impacts of unemployment and dislocation appeared and began to take root. Our community faced increased poverty, stressed safety net services, declining real estate markets, increased foreclosure rates, declining school age populations, and falling revenues as middle-class working families left to seek employment elsewhere. Homelessness became visible—perhaps for the first time ever.

Though the job loss was significant—nearly 40 percent of total employment was lost by 2005—the larger and deeper challenge was overcoming a culture that had evolved during a century of prosperity and insularity. Dependency, paternalism, risk aversion, and entitlement were accepted norms for many individuals and institutions. Additionally, a leadership vacuum occurred after most of the industry executives and management either left or were transferred to other areas. The cultural and economic challenges were compounded by human reaction to loss: fear, anger, grief, and conflict. The spirit of our community was suffering; residents felt powerless and saw no way out. During a site visit in 2007, Susan Berresford, then president of the Ford Foundation, captured the sentiment of our region in her address to residents when she said, "It's hard to see the future with tears in your eyes."

In short, our community had lost its way of life and, with it, its identity. We were forced to let go of who we were and what we knew. It was in this context that the community foundation began its own transformation—responding to what was viewed by staff and a majority of the board members as a moral imperative to act. Never before had the wisdom and vision of Virginia Brazeau been so relevant. If we were truly a permanent resource with a commitment to meet the changing needs of our community, then this would likely be the most significant change any of us were to see in our lifetimes. The "clarion call" from the community in 2002 was to create jobs, to provide leadership, to "do something." After much discussion, research, and dealing with our own internal conflict (related specifically to the "right" role of a community foundation), the board and staff agreed that the community foundation would play a significant role in not only rebuilding our community but also healing the spirit of our residents.

At the same time, the Chamber of Commerce had recently hired a new executive director, Connie Loden. Connie came to the community with a great deal of experience both domestically (at the local, state, and national level) and abroad in integrated community economic development. Under her leadership, the Chamber (which would be renamed Heart of Wisconsin Business and Economic Alliance) initiated a strategic planning process that identified the need for job creation and a diversified economy that would "find a new company that would replace lost jobs." Connie knew that the smokestack-chasing strategies of the past were no longer viable alternatives. She knew that progressive community economic development—the kind of development that requires a variety of programs focused on promoting entrepreneurial growth and empowering citizens—would have a synergistic effect and open new ways of thinking for people.

Together, Connie and Kelly Ryan recognized that what was needed was a way to put the area's economic future into the hands of the people who lived and worked there. The Community Progress Initiative (CPI) (2008), a joint partnership between the Community Foundation of South Wood County and the Heart of Wisconsin Business and Economic Alliance, was established to promote responsible, collaborative, and visionary citizenship to transform community culture and invigorate economic development. Launched in 2004, CPI was a bold three-year program in South Wood County and the Town of Rome; its focus was creating vibrant communities with prosperous local economies. The project aimed to:

- create a business-friendly environment and empower entrepreneurs;
- shape a shared vision for people throughout the region;
- stimulate new enterprises, resulting in additional job opportunities;
- build the area's endowed charitable assets to support sustainable community development;
- motivate emerging young leaders to drive positive change; and
- inspire community spirit and pride. (Future iQ Partners 2012)

CPI programming, created and executed by community foundation and chamber of commerce staff, focused on two primary areas: creating a business-friendly culture and building a strong and positive community. Rather than devote significant time explaining the various elements of the program (see Easterling 2010; Millesen 2008; Millesen, Strmiska, and Ahrendt 2007), we have chosen to focus our attention on how this initiative served as a platform for helping us to think differently about our work and inspired a culture change in our community.

Knowing Better: How We Learned

Interestingly, a commitment to "knowing better" does not always translate into knowing how or what exactly we are supposed to learn. We were certainly aware of Albert Einstein's definition of insanity and knew that continuing to do things the same way we had always done in the past was unlikely to produce a different outcome. So, we asked for help. We asked our peers in the field, including researchers and others with different knowledge than we possessed. We asked those engaged in community development work elsewhere. And, most importantly, we asked people from our own community. The help we received was transformative—from the process of engaging those with an interest and passion to offer what they knew, all the way through the implementation of the wisdom and advice that was offered, we learned so much about ourselves, our community, and the process of change. In this chapter, we share with you some of what we learned.

Learning from Our Peers

There were a number of important people who were doing interesting work and writing about the potential of community foundation leadership. The

Mott Foundation and Ford Foundation were hosting focus group discussions to learn more about the future of community foundations. The results of this work would inform a seminal publication for our field: *On the Brink of New Promise: The Future of U.S. Community Foundations* (Bernholz, Fulton, and Kasper 2005). The Nebraska Community Foundation was piloting its first "Transfer of Wealth" study as a tool to assist rural communities in retaining wealth. Chapin Hall Center for Children hosted four four-day meetings with a group of senior community foundation leaders who were asked to provide insights into the changing roles of community foundations, particularly as they related to addressing the needs of children and families living in distressed communities (Hamilton, Parzen, and Brown 2004).

Peter Pennekamp of the Humboldt Community Foundation would talk passionately during events hosted by the Coalition of Community Foundation for Youth (CCFY is now known as CF Leads) about the "inclusiveness of community foundations" and their unique ability to serve as a platform for building community. In fact, the Humboldt Area Foundation was one of the first community foundations to spearhead an effort to develop organizational and community leaders by creating the Cascadia Center for Leadership. The founding goal of the program was to develop effective communicators who would engage the community across the invisible divides among business, government, nonprofits, and educational organizations (Cascadia Center for Leadership 2004). Emmett D. Carson (2004) was speaking passionately about the promise of community foundations as change agents; most notable was his speech at the Community Foundation Symposium in Berlin, Germany. The Council on Foundations was assembling recognized community foundation leaders (Community Foundations Leadership Team, or CLFT), who were acting in partnership with local residents to strengthen communities through effective philanthropy.

We also had the opportunity to learn from others who were doing work that would become an important part of the transformation we were about to experience. For example, we listened to Katherine Tyler Scott and Irma Tyler Wood, partners in the leadership development firm KiThoughtbridge, talk about the basic concept of adaptive skills in a session at the 2002 Council on Foundations annual conference. Three years later, with help from the Ford Foundation and a visionary program officer, Linetta Gilbert, we invited Katherine and Irma to Wisconsin Rapids to develop the Advanced Leadership Institute (ALI).

ALI focuses explicitly on developing adaptive skills that allow participants to successfully grapple with complex challenges and changing conditions. The curriculum combines concepts about community stewardship focused on trust and relationships with a variety of pragmatic skills and tools that allow graduates to lead change, actively listen, manage conflict, identify common goals, and move groups toward concrete decisions and actions. In addition, participants learn a variety of problem-solving techniques that can be used in leadership situations, especially when conflict arises (for more information about ALI, see Easterling and Millesen 2012).

Learning from those engaged in community development work, Connie Loden's professional experience prior to becoming the executive director at the Chamber put her in touch with a number of different people who were thinking about community and economic development a bit differently than our community was expecting. She knew that a "buffalo hunt" for the next big manufacturing company was not likely to be successful. Connie invited her colleague David Beurle from Innovative Leadership Australia, an Australian-based company that specializes in innovative approaches to local and regional community economic development, to come to Wisconsin Rapids. David shared with us and with our community his ideas about entrepreneurial activity, leadership, and a "grow from within" strategy. In his address to the residents at the CPI launch in 2004, he advocated for a catalytic and holistic approach that, as he described, would ensure "all the critical elements in a community or region are working together to create a prosperous and vibrant future" (Beurle 2004).

With the support of the Ford Foundation, we also had the opportunity to bring speakers to the community to share innovative ideas and frame issues in new and understandable ways. C.Y. Allen, founder of Professional Communication Services and professor of communications at University of Wisconsin–Stevens Point, kicked off the series with a talk titled, *How to Drive Change in Your Community.* We also heard from Tom Thibodeau, associate professor and the director of Servant Leadership at Viterbo University, who shared with us his thoughts about faith and social justice in a presentation he delivered to the community called *Faith in Action—Living in a Just World.* John Powers, a nationally acclaimed speaker and playwright, used humor to inspire and challenge those in attendance to make our community a place to love in his presentation, *Loving Where You Live and What You Do.*

In 2006, we visited Maine and New Hampshire as part of a group that included representatives from the Community Foundation of Northern Ireland and the new Black Belt Community Foundation, located in Selma, Alabama. We observed community development strategies specifically at Coastal Enterprises in Maine and at the New Hampshire Community Loan Fund. We learned more about how the residents in Maine were developing job-creating natural resources and small business ventures in rural regions. In New Hampshire, we saw how the Community Loan Fund was using philanthropy to seed community loan funds, to make mission-related investments, to think differently about workforce training programs, and to invest in long-term community development strategies. Black Belt's motto, "Taking what we have to make what we need," seemed to embody all that we saw; and we talked at length about how this kind of asset-based strategy seemed to be vastly different from the work done by so many of our colleagues.

A group of 16 south Wood County residents also had the opportunity to visit the Republic of Ireland and Northern Ireland. Avilla Kilmurray, CEO of the Community Foundation of Northern Ireland, shared the important work that her organization was doing in a country with such a rich heritage, but also conflict and deep difference embedded in its culture. Emotions were high as she led us through the streets of Belfast, describing the years of conflict and bloodshed, and shared with us the programs that were showing the first glimmer of hope toward a peace agreement between the Protestants and the Catholics. Avilla explained the community foundation's role as much more than that of grantmaker; the foundation was deeply engaged in programmatic and leadership work focused on brokering peace and building social capital.

Groups also visited North Carolina to tour small communities that used art, heritage, and innovative technologies to revitalize areas recovering from loss of or reductions in textile manufacturing, furniture manufacturing, and tobacco farming. We traveled to Duluth-Superior to learn more about community civility and the *Speak Your Peace* project. And a group went to Australia to learn about entrepreneurial activity and the importance of shifting thinking and attitudes as a way to foster culture change. The power of shared learning and exposure to new thinking was nothing less than transformational for study tour participants.

Learning from Those Who Believed in Us and Our Community

The relationship we formed with two visionary descendants of the Consolidated Papers family produced overwhelmingly positive outcomes for all involved. Ruth Barker and Gilbert Mead, both grandchildren of George Mead I, grew up in Wisconsin Rapids and had a strong affinity for the community. Although Ruth and her husband, Hartley, had moved to Scottsdale, Arizona, and Gilbert and his wife, Jaylee, were living in Washington, D.C., both couples remembered a time when "there was a lot going on." Convinced that it was possible to revitalize the community, both families equally contributed a gift to establish the Barker Mead Fund at the community foundation.

The Barker Mead Fund, an administrative fund designated to build community capacity, allowed the community foundation to expand its staff; provided flexible discretionary funds to support community development opportunities as they arose; initiated a nonprofit endowment match opportunity; created small "seed" endowment challenges for each community within the region to encourage philanthropy and grantmaking among residents; and provided the needed administrative support that allowed the foundation to leverage additional funds not designated for operations. Additionally, the two couples collaborated in the purchase and renovation of an office building to assure the foundation had a permanent home. Both were staunch advocates for change, vision, and what Gilbert often referred to as "courageous" leadership.

Perhaps one of the most amazing things we have learned, beginning with our work with the Community Progress Initiative and continuing through the work we do today, is how important it is to offer a seat at the table to those with a stake in the outcome. We have hosted focus groups, convened stakeholders, held town hall meetings, conducted telephone interviews, and offered assistance to those interested in running for public office. Recently, we conducted the largest citizen survey in the history of the south Wood County area. We heard from over 4,500 residents and were able to advance a community-wide dialogue about the future.

At every step along the way, we have invited people in our community to share their hopes, their dreams, their ideas, and their talents so that together we could create a shared future. We invited people into our community to share their thoughts and ideas about how we could harness the passion of our residents to create a resilient economy and a vibrant future. What we have learned through the simple process of engagement continues to defy even our own expectations. It is nothing short of inspirational.

We have also learned that real engagement means not only providing a seat at the table and collecting information, it requires acting on what we have learned. With help from a cadre of consultants and national partners, we have contextualized the data and translated it into a useful format that can be shared with our community and others who are interested in learning from our experiences. As Christopher Goett, managing director of Community Foundation Services at the Council on Foundations, said during a recent visit, "I think the Incourage Community foundation is a place that we look to at the Council in terms of highlighting their innovative approach. . . . They're kind of putting the community back into community foundation" (quoted in Shunda 2012).

We were also fortunate to learn from governance consultants Sandra Hughes and Judith Millesen. At the time we first met Sandy in 2003, she was working with BoardSource and had been hired to lead us through a board assessment process. Sandy's candor in describing our board as one of the weakest she had seen in a community foundation—one that was insular and reflected a history of elitist decision making and behind-closed-doors deal making—was an important turning point in our history. With Sandy's guidance, we helped some board members move on, created a community nomination process that would identify new people to serve, reorganized how we did our work, and instituted processes that would make our decision making more transparent.

Judy Millesen began her work with the foundation and the board as we were transitioning out of CPI in 2008. The intense publicity and marketing around CPI blurred organizational identity for both the organizations engaged in the work and the initiative itself. Judy led the board through a two-day retreat focused on articulating a set of shared values and deciding a future direction that would build on the good work of CPI while at the same time forging a path for the community foundation that was distinct from the work that had been done over the past three years. Using core concepts from *On the Brink of New Promise* (Bernholz, Fulton, and Kasper 2005) and *Community Change Makers* (Hamilton, Parzen, and Brown 2004), we emerged with a plan that articulated a commitment to build social capital, foster strategic philanthropy, and invest in research and skill development while clearly articulating the community foundation's role in building knowledge, forging strategic connections, nurturing philanthropy, leveraging change, and strengthening community capacity.

Doing Better: How We Have Changed

At the start of our transition from a "charitable check writer" to an organization that truly embodies community, we knew that given the issues facing our community, it would make no difference to residents if a large endowment existed years from now if the community were not thriving today. We recognized that we were being called upon to act in new and different ways; and although we were not quite sure where the path would take us, we were committed to learning and "knowing better." We asked for help, and this help came in many forms. It came from visitors with experience directly relevant to a current issue or concern. It took the form of the aforementioned study tours, where we learned about how others were responding to similar challenges. It came from hired consultants who facilitated difficult conversations. And it came from people who either possessed or had access to essential resources (including but not limited to money).

What we discovered was that in order to help our community recreate its identity and tap its unrealized potential, our true work was to invest in and equip residents and the community foundation itself with the ability to learn and adopt a very different approach—one that had at its core a commitment to building adaptive skills across the community and nurturing the ability for all residents to envision and participate in a shared future. Our learning produced four key themes that continue to guide our work:

- A clearly articulated set of values that guide decision making is essential not only because values clearly define how we will do our work but also because values offer the tools to measure whether we have accomplished what we say is important. Many of our decisions are really about determining what you value most, particularly when many options seem reasonable. We can rely on our values as a strong guiding force to point us in the right direction.
- Amazing things happen when strong, trusting, and nurturing relationships are woven into the fabric of community. This requires intentional investment in providing people with both the adaptive skills necessary to navigate an increasingly complex environment and the tools to engage in civil dialogue that deals effectively with conflict and focuses attention on a shared vision of what is possible.
- Curiosity and prudent risk-taking motivates new thinking, stimulates innovation, and fosters humility. As Jeff Arnold, chief architect at Curiosity.com, notes, "curiosity is at the very heart of learning" (Arnold 2011). He talks about curiosity as what drives people to want to learn more about something and believes that once people start investigating, a desire emerges to wholly understand the topic, event, or thing more thoroughly. For Arnold, learning comes into action once people unravel the mystery of what makes them curious. For T.J. Addington, leader of ReachGlobal, "true learning takes a posture of humility. Without humility there is little growth because openness to growth is predicated on not thinking we know it all or have arrived" (Addington 2012).
- Structures (board, organization, staff, etc.) should not be static; the community foundation of the future will be nimble, resourceful, and flexible. Since the start of CPI in 2004, we have experienced significant changes in how we inform and execute our work. We are no longer just a "charitable check writer." Like our friends in Ireland, we are deeply involved in programmatic and leadership work that brings together local, regional, state, and national partners focused on creating economic opportunity and social justice in our region.

And the Learning Continues

Today, Incourage Community Foundation is an organization that promotes shared values; builds strong, trusting relationships; encourages courageous action; fosters adaptive leadership; and recognizes the necessity of genuine

humility. We function as a values-based community infrastructure organization—one that uses a variety of philanthropic tools to create the conditions for
collaboration and innovation in addition to generating actionable knowledge
that improves our effectiveness and builds the capacity of our partners.

Perhaps the most visible symbol of all that we have learned is our name
change to Incourage Community Foundation. One of the key findings that
emerged through focus groups, surveys, and conversations with residents was
that the general public did not like our original name, South Wood County
Community Foundation. Over and over again, we were told that our name and
the word "foundation" in particular felt "elitist" and "closed." These findings
prompted a much bigger engagement strategy with residents to learn more
about how we were perceived and how we could better represent our values
and our work. One of the most prevalent themes the community associated
with our organization was "if there's a challenge we need to face, get the
Foundation involved, and they'll get us involved in the solution."

Our foundation name is not *encourage* spelled wrong or *courage* spelled
long. It is a promise we made and continue to make at the foundation, to
grow stronger and face together important issues that arise in our community.
Because of the spelling, *incourage* assumes a dual meaning—one that reflects
its accurate spelling and one that reflects our values and our commitment to
our community. *Our community encourages us.* Engagement matters. We
believe in our neighbors. It is through their involvement and ideas that we
gain inspiration. *We encourage our community.* It is important to get involved.
Working together with a shared identity and purpose strengthens the community. *We act in courage together.* Authentic conversations with others lead
to courageous action.

Throughout the years, we have continued to learn, evolve, and do better.
The learning that we continue to experience clusters around three key themes.
First, we are regularly reminded about the importance of information and
the key role it plays in creating an engaged community. Second, tackling the
complex problems facing our communities requires traditional structures to
take on new activities while working with others involved in the solution. Our
work in the area of workforce development stands as an exemplar of this type
of evolution and coordinated effort. And third, communication is drastically
improved when people are reminded of the basic principles of respect and
commit to civil dialogue.

For the everyday issues facing individuals and communities, most people
have the technical skills necessary to address those challenges; yet for those
problems that require experimentation, new discoveries, or different ways
of thinking, what's needed is adaptive skills. Make an investment in learning new ways that have the capacity to ultimately change values, attitudes,

and behaviors, and people will make the adaptive leap to excel in a time of great change.

Information Matters

Through the John S. and James L. Knight Foundation's Community Information Challenge, we ventured into the changing world of media, journalism, and community information. What started as a narrowly focused project to create an online news platform in response to a reduction in local news quickly changed when we learned about the depth of our community's "digital divide." The Knight Commission Report on the Information Needs of a Community in a Democracy (The Aspen Institute 2009) provided key insights that linked the importance of information in community culture and systems change efforts. The fundamental premise on which our work is based recognizes that access, capacity, and engagement are core components of a comprehensive strategy to improve our community's information ecosystem.

We have increased *access* to information by connecting over 3,200 residents to public safety information through Nixle alerts, providing real-time community information for residents in employment transition, and establishing new computer labs for public use in two neighboring communities. We are building the *capacity* for residents to consume and produce information by offering more than 700 hours of online job application training at local libraries, delivering 13 free computer skills classes to the public, and inviting residents to test new products designed to promote opportunity. And finally, we have *engaged* the community in our information efforts. Over 80 people from all walks of life are working together to develop solutions to the digital divide and create a healthy information ecosystem, almost 30 students are volunteering to increase digital literacy, and there are three task forces involving 13 different organizations working to support efforts to help residents become informed consumers and contributors of information.

We are also working with the Massachusetts Institute of Technology's Center for Civic Media to test new approaches to fostering civic engagement through technology. *What's Up* is an experimental community system that delivers real-time employment service information traditionally found online into "offline" channels that people use every day, including an automated network of digital signs, print materials, and an all-access phone system.

New Roles, New Structures, New Partnerships

Meeting the challenges of an unemployed and underemployed workforce requires more than a single program or one-time grant money; it requires a coordinated effort among multiple public, private, and philanthropic entities prepared to think and act differently. In 2007, a national initiative announced by the National Fund for Workforce Solutions (NFWS) provided us with the vision and encouragement needed to facilitate such an effort. NFWS announced a call for proposals that would initiate what they described as a "dual customer effort" to engage employers and workers in increasing career advancement opportunities for low-wage workers. In 2008, we were selected as the first rural site to become part of the National Fund for Workforce Solutions.

Through efforts such as the Service Provider Network, a peer-learning group that brings together public, nonprofit, and faith-based organizations to share information, collaborate, and advance policies that support family-sustaining employment and business growth, and the Advanced Manufacturing Partnership, an industry-driven approach focused on achieving the highly skilled workforce required for businesses to grow and maintain a competitive edge, Workforce Central provides a forum for open, honest conversations among relevant stakeholders. This effort has become a model for rural communities across the country and for the National Fund for Workforce Solutions, and it was the first rural Social Innovation Fund subgrantee through NFWS and the Corporation for National and Community Service.

Respect and Civility Are Essential

Speak Your Peace (2012) is a civility project of Incourage Community Foundation, initiated in 2004 and continued today. Originally established by Duluth-Superior Area Community Foundation in 2003, Speak Your Peace is a citizen-led campaign to improve communication by reminding ourselves of the basic principles of respect. We believe people with something to say should have the opportunity to express themselves—and the responsibility to deliver their message with kindness and respect. Practicing civility is how you get good—and how a community gets great. At the center of this initiative are Nine Tools of Civility and one wish: for the "peace" in Speak Your Peace to be taken to heart.

Adaptive Skills Are What's Needed in Changing Times

Over 100 residents have participated in the eight-month ALI program that develops critical adaptive skills needed to support a cultural shift by identifying common interests. With a specific focus on communication, conflict resolution, change management, and trust building, this program fosters respect, civility, equity, and inclusion while teaching people to relate to each other in new and different ways. An independent evaluation of ALI (Easterling 2010) found that the vast majority of participants developed valuable new leadership skills, including facilitating a group process, gaining support for an idea, diagnosing situations, and managing conflict.

ALI participants also described how the program had allowed them to build important new relationships, gain self-confidence, and become more aware of their own strengths, limitations, and aspirations. These personal changes paid off at work, at home, and especially in settings involving community-wide conflict. Due to the tremendous success of the program, the community foundation has made a significant investment in continuing ALI. Today, in addition to the ongoing commitment to offering Advanced Leadership Institutes, we have a recently retired high school principal on staff as a community coach, along with a number of trained facilitators working to build trust and strengthen relationships in the south Wood County area.

Through community conversations, town hall meetings, community picnics, invited guests, leadership training, study tours, and strategic philanthropy, people are learning more about their neighbors, their communities, and how others have become skilled at negotiating conflict to encourage looking at the positives and letting go of the negatives. Community members benefit from the experiences and expertise of others; we are more open to learning about what's happening outside the region and its applicability to the work being done at home; and we have the motivation, determination, and the skills necessary to engage a broad group of stakeholders in changing the culture.

Our work has been instrumental in shaping a new vision for the region, shifting the culture from one of dependence with highly concentrated power to one of self-reliance with dispersed power where equity and inclusion are valued.

We are convinced that because we have learned, we know better, and we do better. We are also convinced that we will continue to learn and experiment with new approaches to community development, economic opportunity, and encouraging broad participation and civic engagement among our residents. If we have learned nothing else, we have learned that we can always do better.

Bibliography

Addington, T.J. 2012. "Humility and Learning." Leading from the Sandbox blog, January 31. http://leadingfromthesandbox.blogspot.com/2012/01/humility-and-learning.html.

Arnold, J. 2011. "Living and Learning." Discovery Communications, LLC. http://http://curiosity.discovery.com/question/curiosity-inspire-learning.

The Aspen Institute. 2009. *Informing Communities: Sustaining Democracy in the Digital Age.* A Report of the Knight Commission on the Information Needs of

Communities in a Democracy. Washington, DC: Aspen Institute. http://www.
    aspeninstitute.org/publications/informing-communities-sustaining-democracy-
    digital-age.
Bernholz, L., K. Fulton, and G. Kasper. 2005. *On the Brink of New Promise: The
    Future of U.S. Community Foundations.* New York: Monitor Group. http://www.
    monitorinstitute.com/downloads/what-we-think/new-promise/On_the_Brink_of_
    New_Promise.pdf.
Beurle, D. 2004. Speech, Community Progress Initiative (CPI) Launch. Centralia
    Center, Wisconsin Rapids, WI. April 22.
Carson, E.D. 2004. "The Road Not Yet Traveled: A Community Foundation Move-
    ment for Social Justice." Speech, Community Foundations Symposium on a Global
    Movement, Berlin, Germany, December. http://www.cfleads.org/resources/com-
    mleadership_pubs/docs/TheRoadNotYetTraveled_12.2004.pdf.
Cascadia Center For Leadership. 2004. "Cascadia's History." http://www.cascadia-
    leadership.org/history.php.
Community Progress Initiative. 2008. http://www.progressinitiative.com.
Easterling, D. 2010. Advanced Leadership Institute: Preliminary Evaluation Results.
    Presentation to the South Wood County Community. August 2.
Easterling, D., and J.L. Millesen. 2012. "Diversifying Civic Leadership: What It
    Takes to Move from 'New Faces' to Adaptive Problem Solving." *National Civic
    Review* 101, 20–26.
Future iQ Partners. 2012. "Community Progress Initiative—Wisconsin, USA." http://
    future-iq.com/projects/community-progress-initiative-wisconsin-usa/.
Hamilton, R., J. Parzen, and P. Brown. 2004. *Community Change Makers: The Lead-
    ership Roles of Community Foundations.* Chapin Hall Discussion Paper, May.
    Chicago: Chapin Hall for Children, University of Chicago. http://www.aecf.org/
    upload/publicationfiles/pb3655k866.pdf.
Incourage Community Foundation. 2012. http://www.cfswc.org.
Jones, G.O. et al. compilers. 1923. *History of Wood County, Wisconsin.* Minneapolis,
    MN: H.C. Cooper, Jr. & Co. http://digital.library.wisc.edu/1711.dl/WI.JonesHist.
League of Women Voters of Wisconsin Rapids Area. n.d. *Wisconsin Rapids Area.*
    Wisconsin Rapids, WI: League of Women Voters. http://www.scls.lib.wi.us/mcm/
    history/lwv.html.
Millesen, J.L. 2008. *Community Economic Development at Its Finest: A Case Study of
    the Community Progress Initiative.* http://www.future-iq.com/downloads/projects/
    community-progress-initiative/Case%20Study%20of%20the%20Community%20
    Progress%20Initiative.pdf.
Millesen, J.L., K. Strmiska, and M. Ahrendt. 2007. *Economic Devastation, Renewal,
    and Growth: Community Foundations As Agents of Change.* http://www.future-iq.
    com/downloads/projects/community-progress-initiative/Community%20Founda-
    tions%20As%20Catalysts%20Report.pdf.
Shunda, N. 2012. "Incourage Helps Foster Community Involvement." *Wisconsin Rap-
    ids Tribune,* October 24. http://www.wisconsinrapidstribune.com/article/20121024/
    CWS03/310240020/Incourage-helps-foster-community-involvement.
Speak Your Peace. 2012. http://speakyourpeaceswc.org.

Part V

Conclusion

21

Into the Second Century

Terry Mazany
The Chicago Community Trust

David C. Perry
University of Illinois at Chicago

We began the Second Century Project with a simple proposition: Theory building could help community foundations address the challenges facing the field. If we moved from a focus on best practices to a deeper inquiry into the underlying dynamics that shape the roles and possibilities of community foundations, might we be able to add insights helpful to individual foundations and enhance the overall vibrancy of the field? Rather than solicit case studies, we organized the Second Century Project as a seminar series with the intention of engaging colleagues in a sustained dialogue that would integrate theory and practice. Our work was made possible by the support of two key national funders, the James S. and John L. Knight Foundation and the Charles Stewart Mott Foundation, whose contributions to field-building precede this work and have proven transformative to the field's success. We mention this not only to acknowledge their funding but to highlight one of the themes within the preceding chapters. There is a natural synergy between national funders and community foundations. When the granularity of local knowledge is paired with the intellectual and financial resources of national funders, we are able to both strengthen community leadership and accelerate the pace of change in communities.

Over the past decade, commentators both inside and outside of community foundations have expressed a sense of angst over the encroachment of market-based competitors, a failing business model, and daunting challenges facing our communities that seem to outstrip our capacity to effect real and lasting change. The contribution of theory helps to ground our understanding of the macrodynamics of place and provide insights into the nature of the changes we experience. What have we learned through this inquiry?

We start with a reaffirmation of the definition of community that is not a fixed construct, but an elastic one. What is different is the impact of digital media that interacts with our physical communities to define new relationships and possibilities for connecting people with one another and the places they inhabit. At the same time, we affirm that communities are about relationships, and connecting people and places is central to the mission of community foundations. Real change in communities comes about through engagement and co-creation, whether face-to-face or in cyberspace.

Communities themselves are embedded in the larger context of fluid cities that are experiencing an accelerated pace of change driven by the forces of globalization and the concentration of greater numbers of people in urban settings. Corporate leadership has either moved out of second-tier cities or is focused globally on the metropolitan regions that are key to the world's economy. These forces drive changes at the local level that are beyond the control of individual cities and their anchor institutions, and yet, community foundations can provide leadership to respond with innovative solutions that tap the assets of people and place that ultimately define the community served.

Communities are also shaped by the evolving role of government to governance. We experience resource-strapped governments paring back funding for services once deemed vital to the well-being of our communities. The polarization of political opinion has further limited the ability of government to act. Consequently, community foundations find themselves called upon to provide leadership to address the very real and pressing needs that persist in our communities.

The acceleration of change in our world brings to the fore the tensions that exist between various interests found in increasingly heterogeneous communities. We may have a nostalgic view of simpler times, but we are now clearly forced to reckon with the pluralistic nature of our community and deal in the realm of realpolitik. It is helpful to approach our understanding of community leadership through the lens of agonistic pluralism, where we understand the competing and divergent interests represented and can strive to convene and engage these interests to arrive at locally specific solutions that will gain support. Equally important, we recognize the threat posed by the illusion of consensus that, instead, erases identity and excludes participation by an increasingly pluralistic population.

It is within this changing context that the identity of community foundations must be considered and renewed in step with this deeper understanding of community. A central thesis for this volume was the importance of anchor institutions, those nonmarket-based institutions that have as their mission the communities they serve. They are deeply rooted and their identity is gained in reciprocal relationship with the community. A characteristic of community foundations is that their roots are the donors who contribute—past, present, and future. Equally important is our legitimacy with the residents of the communities we serve and our need to be viewed as trustworthy of the mantle of stewardship of community resources placed upon us.

The mission of community foundations, however, is not limited to service to donors; it includes service to community. And herein lies a tension that is uniquely negotiated by each community foundation. While community foundations clearly provide bridging capital that connects diverse groups and interests, there is a very real potential for conflict between the interests of those with wealth who provide the financial capital, and those who experience the realities of inequality and disparity. G. Albert Ruesga brings clarity to this tension by introducing the construct of the borderland to help define the identity of a community foundation. Borderland institutions expand the examination of our role in the communities we serve and our obligation to pursue social justice in the face of those persistent challenges—namely, poverty and inequality—affecting the residents on the edges of our communities. Are community foundations simply instruments perpetuating the status quo, or do we have a responsibility to address needs in our community that may challenge the prevailing orthodoxy?

This theoretical framing becomes manifest in choices made by leaders of community foundations. Each of the preceding chapters is organized, at its core, by implied or explicit choices for leadership, be it early childhood education, building neighborhoods in Atlanta, constructing a cultural trail in Indianapolis, or courageous acts of leadership. These choices may or may not have been framed by a deeper deliberation into the context of such a choice, but all require a set of skills and the execution of roles that engage the diverse interests of community.

Finally, we come to understand that a hallmark of this era of massive change and increasing complexity is the capacity of community foundations to form networks and collaborate in response to problems that exceed the resources of any single institution. In this era of change, we see an increase in variation among community foundations as they attempt to innovate to survive, compete, and thrive. Despite the felt challenges or issues, what we see is a consistent move from transactional leadership to transformational leadership. This change is not without its risks, and the preceding chapters help to describe how various leaders think about and manage that risk. Above all, throughout the community foundation sector, we recognize a sense of optimism and aspiration, together with the courage to respond to the changes of our times in a way to sustain the role of these place-based institutions as "foundations of community" well into their second century.

About the Editors and Contributors

Emmett D. Carson (PhD) is an internationally recognized thought leader in the field of philanthropy. He focuses on issues of social justice, public accountability, and African American giving. As founding chief executive officer of Silicon Valley Community Foundation, Dr. Carson led the unprecedented merger that created one of the largest and most complex community foundations in the world. He oversees its work to help families and corporations achieve their local, national, and global philanthropic interests.

Paul Grogan has been president and chief executive officer of the Boston Foundation since 2001. He was president and chief executive officer of the Local Initiatives Support Corporation (LISC) from 1986 to 1998, and previously worked in the administrations of Boston mayors Kevin White (in office 1968–1984) and Raymond Flynn (in office 1984–1993). Grogan is an honors graduate from Williams College and coauthor (with Tony Proscio) of the acclaimed book, *Comeback Cities: A Blueprint for Urban Neighborhood Revival* (Boulder, CO: Westview, 2000).

Teri A Hansen is president and chief executive officer of Gulf Coast Community Foundation. Since 2002, she has managed the daily work of Florida's largest community foundation as it works together with its donors to transform the region through bold and proactive philanthropy.

Josie Heath has been president of the Community Foundation Serving Boulder County, Colorado, since 1995. Prior to her role with the foundation, she was the second woman elected as Boulder County commissioner. In the early 1990s, Heath served in the Clinton White House, where she helped develop the AmeriCorps program. A former candidate for the U.S. Senate from Colorado and a fellow at Harvard's Institute of Politics, she is also a member of the International Women's Forum.

Antonia Hernández joined the California Community Foundation as president and chief executive officer in 2004 and gained national recognition for her commitment to the betterment of underserved communities in Los Angeles and beyond. Established in 1915, the California Community Foundation is one of the largest and most active philanthropic organizations in Southern California, with assets of more than $1 billion. Hernández earned her BA in history at UCLA and JD at the UCLA School of Law.

Ani F. Hurwitz is vice president of communications at the New York Community Trust. Before joining the Trust in 1989, she was director of communications for the Edna McConnell Clark Foundation. Hurwitz has worked for and consulted with a number of nonprofits in the areas of health and housing and has served in several capacities in New York City government. She holds an MPA from New York University.

Henry Izumizaki is currently director of programs at the Russell Family Foundation and president of the California Consumer Protection Foundation. His past roles and affiliations include that of chief executive officer of One Nation; program executive at the San Francisco Foundation; consultant to the East Bay Community Foundation; assistant to the superintendent of Oakland Public Schools (Oakland, CA); president of TEAMS; and executive director at the Urban Strategies Council, University-Oakland Metropolitan Forum.

Nillofur Jasani is a native of India and has practiced both Islam and Christianity. She has worked in Kuwait, the United Arab Emirates (UAE), England, and Canada building cultural bridges in these faith communities. Jasani served His Highness Prince Karim, the fourth Aga Khan, as a member of the National Council of the Ismaili Muslim community in the UK and worked as communications coordinator in the UAE. Most recently, she was the program manager for One Nation.

Douglas F. Kridler is president and chief executive officer of the Columbus Foundation in central Ohio. Previously, Kridler was the president of the Columbus Association for the Performing Arts (CAPA). He oversaw the expansion of CAPA, which now owns and operates six theaters in Columbus, Ohio, the Chicago Theatre in downtown Chicago, and the legendary Shubert Theatre in New Haven, Connecticut. He is a past chair of the International Society for the Performing Arts (ISPA), an organization of leading arts professionals.

Jennifer Leonard has spent her career making the world better through nonprofit initiatives, from community organizing for the American Heart

Association in South Central Los Angeles to teaching grantsmanship world-wide to leading implementation of the first national standards for community foundations. A frequent writer and speaker on philanthropy, Leonard chaired the Community Foundations Leadership Team from 2004 to 2006 and has served as president and chief executive officer for the Rochester Area Community Foundation in upstate New York since 1993.

Paul Major has served as the president and chief executive officer of the Telluride Foundation since its inception in June 2000. He leads the foundation's multimillion-dollar development, grantmaking, capacity building, and initiative efforts. Prior to his affiliation with the Telluride Foundation, Major was director of business development for a multiresort company and spent 13 years with the U.S. Ski Team as Olympic coach and vice president of Athletics.

Terry Mazany is president and chief executive officer of the Chicago Community Trust, one of the nation's largest community foundations, that annually benefits hundreds of not-for-profit organizations in metropolitan Chicago that work to improve the quality of life for the more than 8 million residents in the region. In 2011, Mazany served as the interim chief executive officer of Chicago Public Schools, a district of more than 400,000 students and 650 schools with a budget of $6 billion.

Judith L. Millesen is an associate professor at the Voinovich School of Leadership and Public Affairs at Ohio University in Athens. She is also director of the university's MPA programs and founding director of the Regional Nonprofit Alliance, an organization dedicated to strengthening nonprofit organizations in rural Appalachia by providing online resources, affordable workshops, and hands-on help. Her research and applied work focuses on nonprofit capacity building and administration, as well as philanthropy and community change.

Eric Newton is senior advisor to the president at the John S. and James L. Knight Foundation. A writer and editor, he has managed more than $300 million in journalism and media development grants. Previously, Newton was founding managing editor of the *Newseum*, the first museum of news. Before that, he was managing editor of the California daily newspaper the *Oakland Tribune*, when it won 150 awards, including a Pulitzer Prize. His most popular books are *Crusaders, Scoundrels, Journalists: The Newseum's Most Intriguing Newspeople* (New York: Times Books, 1999) and *Capture the Moment: The Pulitzer Prize Photographs,* edited with Cyma Rubin (New York: Norton, 2001).

Mariam C. Noland is president of the Community Foundation for Southeast Michigan, Detroit, Michigan. Noland joined the foundation in 1985 as its first president. Previously, she served as vice president of the St. Paul Foundation in St. Paul, Minnesota, and program officer and secretary treasurer of the Cleveland Foundation in Cleveland, Ohio. Noland obtained her EdM from Harvard University and a BS from Case Western Reserve University.

Grant Oliphant is president and chief executive officer of the Pittsburgh Foundation, where he has established the organization as a center of community leadership. Oliphant has pushed major community initiatives to promote school reform, strengthen nonprofit organizations, support the arts, and promote better urban design. An outspoken advocate of more transparent and better philanthropy, he has served on the boards of the Center for Effective Philanthropy and Grantmakers for Effective Organizations, and he is a former chair of the Communications Network.

Brian Payne is the president and chief executive officer of the Central Indiana Community Foundation (CICF) and the Indianapolis Foundation, serving both organizations since 2000. Under his guidance, CICF has been a leader of a number of transformative community projects through its dedication to three community leadership initiatives: Family Success, College Readiness and Success, and Inspiring Places. The Indianapolis Cultural Trail—a major project of the Inspiring Places initiative—has received national acclaim.

David C. Perry is professor of urban planning and policy at the University of Illinois at Chicago. From 1999 to 2011, he was director of the Great Cities Institute (GCI) and now serves as senior research fellow at GCI. The author of 11 books and over 150 articles, chapters, and policy reports, Dr. Perry is finishing two other books, *The University as Urban Anchor Institution* (also to be published by M.E. Sharpe) and *Global Cities: Informal, Contested, and Anchored* (with Frank Gaffikin).

Alicia Philipp is president of the Community Foundation for Greater Atlanta. As one of Georgia's most influential leaders, Philipp has challenged the Community Foundation to think differently about the best ways to strengthen the larger community. Under her leadership, the foundation has served as an incubator for organizations such as the Georgia Center for Nonprofits and has created key initiatives, including the Metropolitan Atlanta Arts Fund, the Atlanta AIDS Partnership Fund, and the Neighborhood Fund.

Mark S. Pritchett (PhD) is senior vice president for community investment at Gulf Coast Community Foundation. Since 2008, he has transformed the foundation's grant and initiative strategies to emphasize systems change and public policy.

Carleen Rhodes is president and chief executive officer at Minnesota Philanthropy Partners, a network of charitable organizations—including the Saint Paul Foundation, the Minnesota Community Foundation, the F.R. Bigelow Foundation, the Mardag Foundation, GiveMN, and 1,600 other affiliates across Minnesota—that shares knowledge and services. Rhodes joined the team in 2003 with decades of experience in nonprofit management. Previously, she served as president of the Minnesota Children's Museum and as a partner in the national fundraising consulting firm Bentz Whaley Flessner.

Ronald B. Richard, president and chief executive officer of the Cleveland Foundation since 2003, has served in senior management positions in the public, private, and nonprofit sectors over a 29-year span. He has been a U.S. diplomat, a senior executive with Panasonic, and managing director and chief operating officer of In-Q-Tel, the CIA's venture capital fund. Richard holds a master's degree in international relations from the Johns Hopkins University School of Advanced International Studies.

G. Albert Ruesga is currently the president and chief executive officer of the Greater New Orleans Foundation, known for its leadership in the region after Hurricane Katrina. He earned his PhD at Massachusetts Institute of Technology and taught philosophy at Gettysburg College before entering the world of philanthropy. An accomplished writer, his articles have appeared in the *Oxford Handbook of Civil Society* and in *Social Theory and Practice*, among other publications.

Chris Rurik is a storyteller and historian who graduated from Stanford University and has special interests in philanthropy and landscape history. He is based in Denver, Colorado.

Kelly Ryan is the award-winning chief executive officer of Incourage Community Foundation. She has made economic development and civic engagement her organization's goals in order to improve the lives of residents in rural south Wood County, Wisconsin. Under nearly two decades of Ryan's leadership, Incourage has partnered with national organizations to implement initiatives such as workforce training and information-based community engagement. Ryan was recently named to the *NonProfit Times* "Power and Influence Top 50."

Lorie A. Slutsky has been the president of the New York Community Trust since 1990. She is responsible for the Trust's more than $2 billion endowment and its $150 million in grants. Slutsky began her career at the Trust in 1977 as a grantmaker, was appointed vice president for special projects, and then named executive vice president in 1987. She received her BA from Colgate University and her MA from The New School in New York City.

Tené Traylor is a senior program officer at the Community Foundation for Greater Atlanta. In this role, she oversees the Community Foundation's Neighborhood Fund and the Atlanta AIDS Fund and works to match the interest of donors with community needs. She also manages the foundation's overall community building efforts, serving as liaison for neighborhood transformation and community development.

Nancy Van Milligen joined the Community Foundation of Greater Dubuque as its first president and chief executive officer in 2003. She has grown the foundation's funds to $40 million and established it as a trailblazer in community leadership and citizen engagement. Van Milligen served on the Council on Foundations (COF) Public Policy Committee, teaches the COF Public Policy for Community Foundations course, serves as vice chairperson of the board of the Funders Network for Smart Growth, and leads the Rural Philanthropy Growth Act team.

Index